The Lost Orchard

Contemporary Issues in the Middle East
Mehran Kamrava, *Series Editor*

The Lost Orchard

The Palestinian-Arab Citrus Industry, 1850–1950

Mustafa Kabha and Nahum Karlinsky

Syracuse University Press

First Edition 2021

21   22   23   24   25   26   6   5   4   3   2   1

The book cover displays the painting *Yafa* (1979, oil on canvas)
by Palestinian artist Sliman Mansour, and it is part of the Yvette and Mazen Qupty
collection of Palestinian art and is published with permission.

∞ The paper used in this publication meets the minimum requirements
of the American National Standard for Information Sciences—Permanence
of Paper for Printed Library Materials, ANSI Z39.48-1992.

For a listing of books published and distributed by Syracuse University Press,
visit https://press.syr.edu.

ISBN: 978-0-8156-3670-0 (hardcover)
978-0-8156-3680-9 (paperback)
978-0-8156-5495-7 (e-book)

Library of Congress Cataloging-in-Publication Data

Names: Kabahā, Muṣṭafá, author. | Karlinsky, Nahum, author.
Title: The lost orchard : the Palestinian-Arab citrus industry, 1850–1950 /
Mustafa Kabha and Nahum Karlinsky.
Description: First edition. | Syracuse, New York : Syracuse University Press, 2021. | Series:
Contemporary issues in the Middle East | Includes bibliographical references and index. | Summary:
"This book portrays the unknown history of the "Lost Orchard" of pre-Nakba Palestinian-Arab society,
of the people who constituted its social fabric and of the special, amicable, bi-national and consociational
relations it established with its Zionist-Jewish counterpart"— Provided by publisher.
Identifiers: LCCN 2020050310 (print) | LCCN 2020050311 (ebook) | ISBN 9780815636700 (hardcover) |
ISBN 9780815636809 (paperback) | ISBN 9780815654957 (ebook)
Subjects: LCSH: Citrus fruit industry—Israel—Tel Aviv—History. | Fruit trade—
Israel—Tel Aviv—History. | Palestinian Arabs—Israel—Tel Aviv—Economic conditions. |
Palestinian Arabs—Israel—Tel Aviv—Social conditions. | Jewish-Arab relations—History. |
Jaffa (Tel Aviv, Israel)—History. | Jaffa (Tel Aviv, Israel)—Ethnic relations.
Classification: LCC HD9259.C53 I74 2021 (print) | LCC HD9259.C53 (ebook) |
DDC 338.1/743040899274056948—dc23
LC record available at https://lccn.loc.gov/2020050310
LC ebook record available at https://lccn.loc.gov/2020050311

Contents

Illustrations

Preface

The genesis of this book was an encounter between its two authors in the Naqab/Negev desert. The occasion was a research workshop, held at the Ben-Gurion Research Institute, Ben-Gurion University of the Negev, and organized by Professor Moshe Shemesh. The workshop brought together Arab and Jewish scholars with the objective of exploring the state of research on Palestinian-Arab and Israeli-Jewish relations, both collaborative and conflictual. At that time, toward the end of the Oslo Process and on the eve of the Second Intifada, such opportunities for contact were neither routine nor ubiquitous. When they did take place, however, they conjured up the promise of a shared future and mutual understanding. Moreover, the sense of promise and hope that had been present in the past has now been replaced by a sense of impasse. Our personal meeting and the following encounters that ensued launched our joint research project, which was also made possible by a research grant from the Israel Science Foundation.[1]

Now that we have completed the research and writing of this volume, we wish to reflect upon our professional and personal journey. Our primary scholarly objective was to use rigorous research methodologies and sources in order to present, examine, and analyze the untold story of the pre-1948 Palestinian-Arab citrus industry.

Even as we pursued the research itself with the utmost professional care and methodological rigor, the topic we chose to investigate carried deep personal significance for both of us. Kabha relates the following memories:

For me, Jaffa [the hub of the pre-1948 Palestinian-Arab citrus industry and the country's main marine port] is not simply a time-honored city where remnants of ancient buildings attest to a magnificent past. I was raised on stories of the city's splendor, glory, rich markets, beach, mosques and churches that back onto each other, narrow alleys, and new modern quarters. I grew up in the small village of Umm al-Qutuf (located in Wadi 'Ara and far from any signs of urbanization). As a child, I reveled in my father's stories of Jaffa, where he had lived in its heyday, during the years 1934–48. I was particularly enchanted by stories of the special intoxicating aroma of the citrus blossoms whose perfume would envelope Jaffa in the spring.

My father, Da'ud Ibrahim Kabha (1913–82), owned ten camels that were used to transport coal from the region of Wadi 'Ara and the al-Khattaf Mountains to the towns of Tulkarm and Jaffa. In time, he opened a coal store in Jaffa, selling coal that served as an important source of energy for heating and for use in various dining establishments and restaurants. During the long winter nights, he would tell us stories of cafés, cinemas, and the theater. He was very proud of having attended concerts by famous singers Umm Kulthum and Mohammed Abd el-Wahhab when they performed in Jaffa in the 1940s.

I first visited Jaffa with my father at the age of eight. I was very disappointed to find almost nothing of what I had imagined. My father's explanations were not convincing, and I did not find them very helpful because they were short and vague. We visited Jaffa together again eleven years later. At that time he was more open and told detailed stories that I had never heard before. I was particularly impressed by the story of his last day in Jaffa before it surrendered [to Jewish forces] in May 1948. At that time, my disappointment morphed into sorrow and pain. Whenever I visit Jaffa I am overcome by emotion and I try to reconstruct bygone sights, bygone lives, amid the lost orchards, the scent of the markets and of the fragrant citrus blossoms.

Investigating the lost orchards of Jaffa and of the other Palestinian citrus towns is no easy matter. It is, in essence, a transition from vague memories and scents to dusty archival documents as well as uprooted trees or rebranded fruits, stamped with a new identity and new owners. The once fertile lands, wells, and pools now groan as bulldozers uproot the orchards and cement trucks pour solid foundations for high-rise buildings that have changed the skyline forever.

The vivid collective memories of pre-1948 Palestinian society that informed Kabha's childhood, as well as his professional desire to reconstruct the past, differ radically from Karlinsky's experience of historical lacunae, "forgetfulness," and repressed memories.

The Zionist Israeli metanarrative grants the Israeli citrus industry in the first decades after 1948 a similar role to that awarded at present to Israel's high-tech industry. Namely, citriculture is presented as the economic power that propelled the Israeli economy forward, as it was Israel's major export industry in the first decades after the State was established. This metanarrative erroneously presents the citrus industry as a Jewish Zionist industry, mythically created ex nihilo by the hegemonic Labor Zionist movement, echoing the Zionist tenet of "making the desert bloom." The citrus industry, according to this narrative, was first established during the Ottoman rule over Palestine, expanded during the British Mandate, and reached full glory during the State of Israel's first decades of existence. Needless to say, this metanarrative does not even mention Palestinian citriculture.

Hence, when Karlinsky embarked on his previous research project, devoted to the study of the Zionist citrus industry in pre-1948 Palestine, he was surprised to discover that the metanarrative he had been taught was doubly flawed. First, he discovered that the Jewish sector of the citrus industry was not established by the Labor Movement but rather by the oft-maligned private Zionist entrepreneurs. But the second discovery was even more significant. Karlinsky's research brought him face to face with the Zionist narrative's penultimate "blind spot"—the existence of the well-established and flourishing Palestinian citrus industry that preceded the Zionist enterprise.[2]

Recognizing the existence of a repressed and/or deliberately erased Palestinian past, our initial objective was to use the historical tools at our disposal to dig up and retrieve the "lost Palestinian orchard." As our research progressed, we realized that this is but one case study of a broader phenomenon that has profound metaphorical dimensions. We became engaged in a two-pronged project that confronted and exposed the obliteration of Palestinian memory and identity on the one hand, and, on the other, also attempted to bring about the "return of the repressed" and the re-collection of the Arab histories of Palestine/Israel.

Two unexpected discoveries emerged from the primary sources uncovered. First, while there were tensions and obvious economic and national rivalries between the Arab and Jewish sectors of the citrus industry, we were surprised by the concurrent intensity and lengthy duration of the strong mutual relationships between the sectors. The pinnacle of these steadfast dialectical relationships, which began in 1900, was the establishment of an official countrywide binational organization of the industry in the first year after the outbreak of World War II. The organization lasted until April 1948, when the politics of nationalism quashed any option of binational partnership.

The second discovery relates to the fact that the relationship between Palestinian Arabs and Zionist Jews deepened and became most pronounced during the long six years of World War II. This is surprising given the fact that most scholarship related to the Mandate period is based on the assumption that by 1939 the social, political, and cultural foundations that eventually culminated with the realities of 1948 had already been set in place. Hence, more often than not scholars of the Mandate period either ignore the war years and end their research in 1939 or gloss over this period as an insignificant hiatus preceding the inevitable 1948. Our book joins a growing number of studies that challenge both that assumption and the tendency to ignore the war years.[3]

We would like to acknowledge the archives that provided foundational material for this study and to thank their staff: the Central Zionist Archives; the Israel State Archives; the Haganah Historical Archives; the Archives of Kibbutz #1; the Archives of Kibbutz #2; the Municipal Archives, Rehovot; the Izakson family and Dr. Smadar Barak for permission to use material from the Aharon Meir Mazie Archives; S. Yizhar Archives, the National Library of Israel; the National Archives, United Kingdom; and the document collections from the private archive of a Palestinian Arab orange grower family.

We wish to thank Professor Kobi Metzer for his support of this project. His suggestion that we consult the archives and protocols of Palestine's Citrus Marketing Board turned out to be an important building block for understanding the binational structure of the industry. The two anonymous readers of the book's manuscript provided constructive and helpful suggestions that improved it. We want to thank them as well.

Special thanks go to our research assistants, who provided us with much help for the purpose of this study: Mahasan Rabos, Mahmoud Mahamid, Na'ama Ben-Ze'ev, Dan Elgarnati, and Neta' Hazan. Thanks also to Mr. Zviki Peikin for his valuable assistance in processing the data of the "Census of Arab Citrus Groves" (1948–51).

Karlinsky wishes to express his appreciation and gratitude to two academic institutions that hosted him while he was away from home. At the Massachusetts Institute of Technology, the Political Science Department and MIT International Science and Technology Initiative (MISTI) provided intellectual stimuli, a welcoming environment, and access to rich library resources. Karlinsky thanks the chairs of the Political Science Department, the department's staff, and the directors of MISTI, who continued to welcome him from the first day he arrived. Special thanks are extended to David Dolev, managing director of MISTI-Israel and MISTI-Arab for his support and friendship; to Helen Ray for her invaluable assistance, friendship, and good spirits; and to Maria DiMauro, the administrative officer of MIT's Political Science Department for the friendly, welcoming, and extremely helpful support. At Boston University's Elie Wiesel Center for Jewish Studies, Professor Michael Zank, director of the Center, was so kind as to provide space and access to library resources that were crucial at the final stages of writing this book. Boston University's Center for Jewish Studies is a welcoming, inclusive, and vibrant research institute. Karlinsky thanks the staff of the Center, its faculty, and its director for their warm and friendly hospitality.

Our thanks go to the staff at Syracuse University Press, and especially to Peggy Solic, acquisitions editor at the press, for the professional and helpful manner in which they saw this book to completion. We want to thank Professor Mehran Kamrava, editor of the Contemporary Issues in the Middle East series, for his support of our study. Our special thanks and gratitude are also extended to Suzanne E. Guiod, former editor in chief at Syracuse University Press, for her belief in our project and for her steadfast support of it.

Finally, we would like to extend our thanks to Mrs. Rachel Kessel for her excellent translation of our manuscript into English.

The Lost Orchard

Introduction

Theoretical and Historiographical Considerations

During the first five decades of the twentieth century the citrus industry played a major economic, social, and cultural role in the lives of the Arabs of Ottoman—and later British Mandate—Palestine. By 1900 citrus was the main export, reaching its apex in the latter half of the 1930s, when it composed 77 percent of the total value of exports from Palestine. The citrus industry was a primary source of livelihood and sustenance for tens of thousands of Palestinian households and hundreds of villages. The industry was also the central engine that drove the development of the port city of Jaffa to becoming the second-most significant Palestinian-Arab city after Jerusalem and a hub of modernization for Palestinian-Arab society. The citrus industry was also a vehicle of social mobility within Palestinian-Arab society up until the Nakba.

When the first Zionists came to the region at the end of the nineteenth century, they already encountered a thriving and fast-growing Palestinian-Arab citrus industry. At the beginning of the twentieth century, about twenty years after their initial arrival in the country, Jewish entrepreneurs began investing in citrus as well. On the eve of World War II, the citrus industry of Palestine was almost evenly divided between the two national sectors of which it consisted, the Palestinian and the Zionist sectors. This is true both in terms of planted acreage and of volume of export. Yet in spite of the vast significance of the citrus industry of Palestine, from the waning of the Ottoman Empire until the Nakba (the Palestinian catastrophe of 1948), and its crucial impact on the lives of the Arab population of

1

the country, to date this topic has not been the subject of scholarly study. This book attempts to fill this gap.

As is well known, the research on modern Palestine, the Zionist movement, and the State of Israel is embroiled in a deep interpretational dispute. To a large extent, this dispute—or rather, disputes—is driven by contrasting worldviews regarding the nature of the Zionist movement and the State of Israel on the one hand and the essence of the Palestinian-Arab national movement on the other. In addition, these scholarly disputes are also influenced by the emotional attitude toward the land itself, by its inhabitants, and by the personal histories of those who are engaged in them. The Palestinian-Israeli conflict itself has intensified during the last twenty years and has further escalated the deterioration of Palestinian-Israeli relations. Moreover, since October 2000, conflictual positions have strongly affected the fabric of Arab-Jewish relationships inside Israel, namely within its pre-1967 internationally recognized borders. These developments have influenced scholars of Palestine/Israel and have inevitably shaped the trajectory of their research, and we are not exempt from these forces. Acknowledging the context in which our project has been conducted, we tried our best to anchor our analysis in the primary sources at hand.

Indeed, our initial goal was to research and present the untold history of the Palestinian-Arab citrus industry. However, based on the sources we uncovered, we realized that it would be impossible to disentangle the histories of the two national sectors, given the strong bilateral relationships between them. Significantly, even at times of tension and conflict, or when attempts to sever all relationships between the national sectors were made, the two sectors and their activities remained intertwined and influenced by the very existence of the other. Obviously, these bilateral relationships were evident to all during periods of close cooperation and coordinated operations between the two national sectors.

We believe that the current reality of the existence of two peoples, Palestinian-Arab and Jewish-Zionist, who reside in the same homeland, sharpened our understanding of similar phenomena during the pre-1948 era in Palestine. Moreover, it is our contention that during the British Mandate rule over Palestine (1918–48), a binational reality was created there and has been in place ever since, including of course in the newly established State of Israel during the period from 1948 to the 1967 War.

Another dimension that affected our research is the inherent inequality between Jews and Arabs that is built into the Israeli social, political, and cultural system and which also influences Israeli academia.[1] The fact that we have been cooperating for a long time now on a joint historical study is in itself a rarity. Undoubtedly, there were other scholars who preceded us in conducting joint Arab-Jewish research. However, the standard operating procedure in which historical research on Palestine/Israel is conducted in Israeli academia is to a large extent segmented and does not integrate Jewish-Zionist and Palestinian-Arab histories. These segmented historical research channels were not created by accident. Rather, they were constructed from above in order to segregate the Jewish-Zionist history from the Palestinian-Arab one.[2] We are aware of this structural inequality that is embedded in the Israeli system, and we hope that our awareness found expression in this study.

As stated above, scholarly research on the late Ottoman and British Mandate periods in Palestine is in a state of deep interpretive disagreement. But this disagreement also has the effect of generating rich and diverse theoretical and research products.

One may discern a few dominant approaches in the research on the British Mandate period. One approach emphasizes mutual encounters and cooperation that took place between the two national societies in Palestine during that period. Some studies of this trend came out as early as the 1960s and 1970s, and this approach has received new momentum in recent years. Notable among these are the breakthrough studies of Joseph Vashitz, Ilan Pappé, Lev Grinberg, and Zachary Lockman, who drew attention to Haifa's Jewish-Arab civil society, collaborations between Jewish and Arab workers in the Mandate railway system who engaged in fighting to improve their salaries and work conditions, a joint Arab-Jewish drivers' strike, and even the intersectoral solidarity that emerged during the government officials' strike in 1946. Moreover, from the turn of the twenty-first century several additional studies appeared, illuminating other dimensions of the joint life and cooperation between Arabs and

Jews during the Mandate period. Tamir Goren pointed out the extent of joint work within the Haifa Municipality, which throughout most of the Mandate period was comprised of representatives of moderate elements in the Palestinian-Arab and Jewish-Zionist societies. Deborah Bernstein too discussed areas of collaboration between Arab and Jewish workers in Haifa during the Mandate period, as well as the tendency to delineate these collaborations along national-ethnic boundaries. In her study on the liminal space between Jaffa and Tel Aviv, Bernstein pointed out an array of social and cultural partnerships among residents of that destitute area. Menachem Klein enumerated instances of friendship between prominent figures in the two national societies, while Assaf Likhovski showed that law and its institutions served as a meeting ground for cooperation and exchange of ideas, but also as a tool for constructing diverging identities. Liora Halperin, while mainly concentrating on the Jewish-Zionist community in pre-1948 Palestine (known as the Yishuv), nevertheless devoted a full chapter to encounters of Jews, and the Yishuv as an organized community, with the Arabic language and its rich cultural manifestations. Recently, Abigail Jacobson and Moshe Naor systematically and comprehensively analyzed the nature of relationships between Sephardic and Arab Jews, who saw themselves as part of the Arab cultural and social fabric, and Palestinian-Arab natives of Palestine.[3]

Nevertheless, and despite the relative increase in such studies, the dominant—and perhaps hegemonic—approach in research of the Mandate period was and still is what might be characterized as the "conflictual approach," i.e., one that emphasizes the national and religious conflict between Jews and Arabs during this period, while explicitly or implicitly arguing for the unfeasibility of Jewish-Arab coexistence. A moderate version of this approach is one that focuses exclusively on one society, many times the researchers' own, whether Arab or Jewish, with nearly complete disregard of the other. A common version, however, is one that emphasizes the points of dissension, claiming that these are irreconcilable, and tends to stress the emotional elements and violent dimension that accompany all national disputes.[4]

Another conspicuous trend in the research on British Mandate Palestine is the emphasis put in the research literature on the pre–World War II period. A major premise underlying this approach, whether implicit or explicit, assumes that the foundations of the conflict were laid as early as the first two decades of the Mandate, if not previously. According to this approach, the War of 1948 was an essential deterministic and unavoidable course. Hence, a dominant trend in Zionist and Israeli historiography portrays the period of World War II as a necessary hiatus caused by the need to deal with the Nazi enemy before the Palestinian-Zionist conflict could be renewed in force. The emphasis of this historiography is on the gathering clouds of the Holocaust overshadowing the Jewish world, the unshakable status of Amin al-Husayni as leader of the Palestinians, and how Zionist power was built up toward the inevitable confrontation. Palestinian historiography, in contrast, emphasizes the social and military decline following the Revolt of 1936–39; the deep rift between Amin al-Husayni and his followers and the considerable but delegitimized opposition to him and his confrontational policy; al-Husayni's successful attempts to disrupt any efforts at organization that did not bow to his authority; and the wide international support received by the Zionist movement throughout the years of the Mandate, particularly from Britain and Western Jewry, support that intensified following the Holocaust and left the Palestinian National Movement weak and isolated.

At the same time, here too there are noticeable exceptions to this line of argument. Several scholars did point out the changing atmosphere toward more cooperation between the two national communities once World War II broke out, which also coincided with the end of the Arab Revolt.[5] In Palestinian historiography it was one of the authors of this book, Mustafa Kabha, who spoke out against the popular Palestinian narrative. His claim, which we embrace, is that it was precisely during the war and in subsequent years that Palestinian society experienced unprecedented economic, social, and cultural growth and prosperity. Kabha perceives Amin al-Husayni as a major element who undermined these processes of enhancement and reinforcement and as the person who managed to bar Palestinian Arabs and Arab countries from reaching political achievements that could have prevented the Palestinian Nakba.[6]

However, we see no room for a further extensive review of the existing research literature. Not only have we addressed this issue in our previous studies on this period, but it is also clear that such a review would not culminate in one "correct" approach. We respect all established scholarly studies and accept that, similar to life itself, history too is unceasingly varied, interesting, and prolific. In this study, we build on many insights and previous research findings, with their different approaches and disagreements. We cite these studies where appropriate.

At the same time, we found Zachary Lockman's *relational approach*, as well as the prism of *settler colonial studies*, to be suitable general approaches for our study. Lockman stresses the fact that the two main societies that inhabited pre-1948 Palestine (as well as post-1948 Palestine/Israel) did not evolve in isolation from each other. Rather, to a large extent they were constituted and shaped by their mutual "economic, political, social, and cultural interactions," as well as "by the larger processes by which both were affected."[7] We found this approach enriching and insightful as it frees the analysis of the relationships between Arabs and Jews from deterministic perspectives and opens it up to much more fluid, dynamic, and multidirectional interpretations.

In recent years the scholarly field of settler colonial studies has gained renewed momentum. A wealth of new studies has examined variegated chronological and geographical examples of settler colonialism from the neo-Assyrians and Romans to postcolonial Latin America. Conceptually, while colonialism and settler colonialism have much in common, they also differ in fundamental characteristics. Both involve nonnative peoples who arrive in other peoples' homeland in order to subject or dominate the natives. However, colonialism tends to be temporal, and its purpose is to exploit the foreign land and its inhabitants for the benefit of the metropole. Settler colonialists, on the other hand, come to stay. Their main purpose is to establish a "new homeland" for themselves. Hence, they work to carve a separate spatial, demographic, social, and cultural space for their new homeland and its communities, distinct from the local or indigenous population. The United States, Canada, Australia, New Zealand, and South Africa are the most well-known examples of modern settler colonialism.[8]

As is well known, Zionists and the Zionist movement tried to distance themselves from practices of colonial exploitation and from accusations of using these practices. However, in contrast to religious-traditional Jewish immigrants to the Holy Land who were absorbed into the existing system, the Zionist movement's goal was to establish an "Old New [Home]land" for the Jews demographically, socially, culturally, and spatially separated from the local Arab population.[9] As shown by numerous studies of all ideological stripes and colors, in order to implement this goal, Zionists and the Zionist movement used the methods, worldviews, and languages that other European settlers used when they arrived in non-European territories; namely, of settler colonialism.[10] It should be stressed, however, that scholars of settler colonialism have shown that many times the settler project did not reach its ultimate goal. Instead, hybrid constructs came into being, in which the newcomers and the locals cooperated and shared.[11] We will use the lens of settler colonialism, and especially this last hybrid construct, in examining the relationships between the Arab and Jewish citrus industries.

The book contains five chapters. Chapters 1 and 2 are in chronological order, from the mid–nineteenth century to the Nakba, telling the story of the Palestinian citrus industry from its inception to 1948. The two chapters combine economic, social, cultural, and ideological analysis in order to examine the many layers of the Palestinian industry. We argue that these components should not be analyzed separately since they also did not operate this way. Ideological leanings, economic worldviews, one's standing in the social fabric of one's society, and one's cultural heritage all played a combined role in shaping the Palestinian industry. Based on data from the Mandate government, an extensive and detailed census of Palestinian-Arab citrus groves and of their owners-turned-refugees carried out by the State of Israel as early as 1948–50, as well as memoirs, interviews, and the contemporary press, we examine the social and economic structure of those involved in the industry. A major finding is that the industry served as a means of social and economic mobility for many Palestinians from the rural sector.

Incorporated in this are the economic activities, economic worldviews, and ideological leanings of practitioners in the Palestinian-Arab industry. A major finding here is the strong business relationships between the Arab and Jewish sectors throughout the entire period under discussion, from the late nineteenth century to 1948. In this regard, our findings support the conclusion that economic considerations and crossnational economic cooperation neutralized national conflicts to a great extent. Our study also shows that in the technological sphere as well much cooperation is evident in both directions.

Chapter 3 deals directly with interrelations between the Palestinian-Arab and the Zionist sectors.[12] It shows that these relations shifted over the years. From the late nineteenth century to the early 1930s they were characterized by constant dialectic tensions that included rivalry and attempts at sector-based separation on one hand but also business and organizational collaborations on the other. However, it was precisely after the acute conflict of 1929 that a change occurred toward stronger cooperation and mutual relations. This change reached its height during World War II with the establishment of a recognized and official binational institutional framework that included the industry's two sectors. The binational structure and relationship lasted until 1948. The chapter illuminates these relations and the binational citriculture "enclave" formed. It also shows, as mentioned above, that it was precisely during the period of World War II that a variety of unprecedented local partnerships and cooperation between Jews and Arabs emerged.

Chapter 3 also discusses the crucial role of the British in nurturing the binational structure of the country's citrus industry. From a theoretical point of view, we employ Gordon Allport's famous "Contact Hypothesis" theory. Our argument is that the years prior to World War II served as a preparatory phase for the establishment of the citrus industry's binational structure, during which some of the required parameters enumerated by Allport were met. However, the unique conditions of the war years enabled the other parameters to be fulfilled as well.

Chapter 4 deals with the Nakba. According to the 1947 Partition Plan, the large majority of Arab-Palestinian citriculture was to have been under control of the future Jewish state. At this stage the research on this crucial period lacks sufficient sources to reliably probe the views of Zionist leaders concerning the approximately 40 percent of Arab citizens slated to be included in the Jewish state. However, an examination we conducted of the "situation committee" (Va'adat ha-Matzav) files open to the public shows a clear discriminatory policy planned for the large Arab minority projected to become part of the Jewish state. This committee was established by David Ben-Gurion, the leader of the pre-1948 Zionist community in Palestine, in late 1947 in order to lay the institutional, judicial, executive, and legal foundations for the future Jewish state. Even from the meager sources open to the public it is clear that the dominant policy was to grant the projected 40 percent of Arab citizens second-rate status. In contrast, the heads of the industry's Jewish sector called upon the Zionist leadership to maintain the binational arrangement. This chapter ends with the ambiguous attitude of Jewish citrus leaders toward the Arab property and groves transferred to them after 1948. It also relates their attempts to help some of the Arab industry heads to return to their homeland and reassume control of their property.

Chapter 5 addresses the present: on the one hand, it discusses contemporary Palestinian memory of the pre-1948 Palestinian-Arab citrus industry and its "bride of the sea," the city of Jaffa. On the other, it addresses the effective endeavors conducted by Israel and by Jewish Israeli society to forget and obliterate the Arab-Palestinian citrus industry's existence. For Palestinian society, the Jaffa orange and the city of Jaffa are a symbol of the homeland that was and that will be, similar to the German *Heimat*.[13] But for Jewish Israelis the Jaffa orange is a purely Zionist and Israeli creation. This chapter analyzes contemporary "memory vectors" within Palestinian society and the memory obliteration mechanisms within post-1948 Jewish Israeli society.

We hope that despite the complexities involved in carrying out such a study, this book will contribute to the research of pre-1948 Palestine, its economy, its society, and the relationship between its two national communities.

1

The Intertwined Economic, Social, and Ideological Factors, 1850–1919

In contrast to most agricultural activities in pre-1948 Palestine, where production was aimed first and foremost at domestic consumption, citriculture was intended from the very beginning for export. Until the outbreak of World War II only a small part of the country's citrus output, 10–20 percent, was sold on the domestic market. The rest was exported to Britain and the European continent, as well as to Arab countries.[1] The citrus industry as an export enterprise began to emerge in the mid–nineteenth century. In the early 1880s, before the Zionist settlement in Palestine, it was already a well-established industry, centered around the city of Jaffa and its close environs.

Similar to the overall history of Palestine and the Palestinians, the history of the Palestinian citrus industry too was acutely affected not only by the socioeconomic circumstances of Palestinian society per se, but also by Zionist colonization and Zionism, as well as by the empires that governed Palestine—the Ottoman and the British.

As stated in the introduction to this book, we follow Zachary Lockman's conceptual framework in characterizing this reality as "relational."[2] Moreover, beginning in the early 1930s and particularly from 1939 until the end of the Mandate, the economic disparities between the two citrus sectors dwindled to a minimum. This was most evident in the basic economic unit of this industry, the citrus grove. From the late 1930s until 1948 there were only minor differences between groves in the Palestinian and Zionist sectors in terms of the technologies used, the layout of the groves, and their overall output. In many ways this basic economic unit was a hybrid entity shared by both national sectors. Moreover, the organizational structure of the countrywide industry was transformed during that period into what can be designated a binational structure.

The unique economic circumstances in Palestine, the large supply of workers ("labor" in economic terms), and the relative shortage of land and capital on one hand, and the socioeconomic profile of the industry's leadership, middle- and upper-middle-class private entrepreneurs from both sectors on the other, created conditions that facilitated the existence of these special circumstances. At the same time, it should be emphasized that these were still two different societies as regards religion, culture, residential areas, and socioeconomic composition. Moreover, the reality was also a settler-colonial one in which Zionist European settlers, who after the establishment of the British Mandate in Palestine also received the legal and practical support of the world's greatest empire at the time, strived to introduce European economic and cultural models into Palestine. At first, when the Jewish citrus industry was founded in the early 1890s, a hesitant dialectic relationship was established between the two sectors, similar in many ways to other generally hesitant and dialectic relationships established between Zionists and Arabs at those early stages. On the one hand, a clear cultural, social, and economic rivalry between the local society and the settler-colonial one came into being. At the same time, cooperation and daily contacts, mainly on a personal level, were an integral part of that reality as well. During the early years of the Mandate the competition between the two sectors of the citrus industry diminished slightly and was replaced by formal and informal institutional settings that took the path of cooperation. From the mid-1930s, and all the more so from the beginning of World War II and until 1948, close economic and social relationships were formed between the two sectors within the industry, creating to all intents a "binational bubble." This chapter and the next will discuss the intertwined factors that shaped the industry from its inception until the Nakba: the industry's social stratification and mobility, the economic worldview and ideological leanings of the sector's leadership, and the sector's economic performance.

Beginnings

Reliable solid evidence of citrus groves near Jaffa in the modern era is available from as far back as Napoleon's siege on the city in 1799, during his famous voyage to Egypt and the East. Hassan Ibrahem Sa'id's comprehensive research on Jaffa from 1799 to 1831, using material from the city Sijil of the Mahkama and the reports of European travelers, indicates that as early as the first half of the nineteenth century Jaffa was already known for the many sweet-smelling groves in its environs. Most of the groves produced oranges and only a small number of lemons. The product was sold primarily on the domestic market and to a lesser extent in Egypt, Beirut, and Turkey. The exported fruit, mainly oranges, was delivered to Alexandria and Beirut on small sailboats that embarked from the Jaffa Port. They were then sold in Egypt or loaded onto ships sailing for Constantinople (Istanbul). At the same time, some of Jaffa's oranges also began to appear on "royal tables in Western Europe," as reported by Dutchman Van de Velde in 1852, as well as in the homes of the upper classes, forming the beginning of the Jaffa orange's international reputation.[3]

Fruit originating from Jaffa had several qualities that gave it a significant advantage over its competitors, mainly Spanish Valencia oranges and Italian citrus. The Jaffa orange, or as named locally the "Shamouti,"[4] had a thick peel that provided better protection from disease and rot than other varieties. In a report he wrote in 1893 about the Jaffa oranges and their irrigation, John Dickson, the British consul in Jerusalem, stated that Jaffa's oranges remained fresh without rotting thirty to forty days from the day they were picked, and if they were packed well they remained edible even for two or three months.[5] All this, of course, in a time that preceded the technological improvements that made it possible to protect the fruit artificially. The thick peel was also easier to remove than the thinner peel of the Spanish and Italian oranges. The Shamouti was usually sweeter than the Italian and Spanish varieties and was known for its special aroma, which was another of its advantages. This combination of qualities gave the Shamouti an important relative economic edge over other varieties grown in the Mediterranean basin during the period under discussion.[6]

1. Jaffa Port—loading orange crates, 1934. Israel National Photo Collection, Zoltan Kluger.

Jaffa and its environs were a location that lent itself easily to development of the citrus industry. The light soil was well suited to growing citrus trees. More importantly, since the citrus tree needs a constant and plentiful year-round supply of water, and since Palestine has only a short rainy season, which in the period discussed was from mid-November to early March, it was necessary to find an available water source to irrigate the groves during the rest of the year.[7] A plentiful source was provided by the Jaffa region's groundwater, which at the time was very close to the surface, at a depth of merely ten to twelve meters. The water-pumping technology common at the time in the area suited these conditions. It was based on manually dug wells, which could therefore not be very deep, and on a water-pumping system called *nuriyya* that used the limited strength of an animal—camel, ox, or donkey—to operate it. This system was capable of irrigating a grove of no larger than twenty-seven dunams (about 6.7 acres). And finally, Jaffa was home to the country's main export harbor in these years. It was indeed not a well-developed port. The shallow waterbed, combined with long reef rocks that extended into the sea, prevented large ships from entering the port. Hence, these ships had to anchor in open sea while passengers and goods were ferried to and fro in small boats. Nevertheless, until the outbreak of World War I, the Jaffa Port was second in the region only to that of Beirut in the scope of its marine commercial activities.[8]

These advantages—the proximity to the port, which significantly reduced the cost of transporting the fruit from the grove to the export harbor, the availability of groundwater for irrigation, and the quality of the soil—facilitated the industry's evolvement and development in the vicinity of Jaffa. The citrus industry also required the services of auxiliary economic sectors, such as transportation, various commercial ventures, carpenters, and so on, which developed in Jaffa as a consequence as well.[9] The central economic and commercial significance of the port for Jaffa, the impressive growth of the citrus industry, as well as growing Zionist immigration, were the main factors prompting Jaffa's rapid development. By the outbreak of World War I, Jaffa was already the second largest city in Palestine after Jerusalem. Hence, toward the end of the Ottoman period, and particularly during the Mandate period, Jaffa was transformed into an economic, social, and cultural center for Palestine's Arab society, one with distinctly modern characteristics.[10] In this regard, a reciprocal relationship emerged between the city of Jaffa and its most prominent hinterland agricultural industry, the citrus industry. As agricultural economist Johann Heinrich von Thünen has shown, the closer a farm is to its main market, the city (here Jaffa's port functioned as a market), the more intensive and market oriented its product.[11] Improved means of communication and transportation shorten the travel and hauling time from a farm or factory to the market, bringing it "closer" to the city. At the same time, the city itself is transformed as well. It consequently serves not only as a market for agricultural products but also as a center for various services that attend to the needs of its hinterland. As a result, the city's economy grows and becomes more specialized and diverse, attracting more people, professions, and cultural products to the flourishing urban hub.[12] Hence, Palestine's citrus industry had an essential role in maintaining Jaffa's primary economic, social, and cultural status up until the Nakba.

The limited scope of the industry entered a phase of transformation in the mid-1870s. This was prompted by several circumstances. First of all, the markets in Britain, the leading world power at the time, showed a growing demand for fruit, including citrus fruit. A similar demand was also evident in the European mainland. Secondly, steamships with their gradually improving technology, which enhanced their commercial viability, began to arrive on the eastern coasts of the Mediterranean as well. This development shortened the time required to sail from Alexandria and Jaffa to Europe and the United Kingdom and made it possible to market Jaffa oranges in the United Kingdom and on the continent while still fresh. Finally, as a result of the continuous military weakening of the Ottoman Empire in the latter half of the nineteenth century, it was compelled to lighten its restrictions on quotas and trade with Europe, and particularly with Britain.[13]

One of the most interesting pieces of evidence for the rapid development of the citrus groves in Jaffa and the vicinity can be found in the famous Sandel map of that area, published in 1880. Theodor Sandel was a German architect and a prominent member of the messianic German Temple Society (*die Tempelgesellschaft*), which established several German colonies in Ottoman Palestine that preceded the Zionist ones. Sandel settled first in the German colony near Jaffa but later moved to the Templer colony in Jerusalem. He conducted a detailed survey of Jaffa and its surroundings and placed his findings on a colorful map that accompanied an article published by the German Society for the Exploration of Palestine and devoted to "Jaffa and its Surroundings."[14] As can be seen in the map, the green groves extended from Jaffa to the east up to the Musrara (today, Ayalon) River, as well as north of Jaffa, beyond the boundaries of where Tel Aviv would be established thirty years later.

Indeed, from the mid-1870s there was a constant rise in the export of oranges from Jaffa, and their proportion of all exports from this central port was constantly on the rise. Data meticulously gathered by Alexander

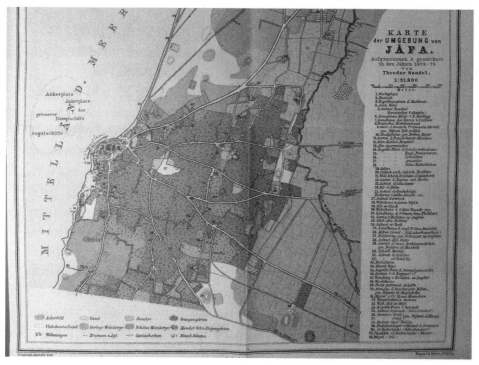

Map 1. Theodor Sandel map of Jaffa and its surroundings, 1878–79. From *Zeitschrift des Deutschen Palaestina-Vereins*, vol. 3 (1880).

Schölch (for 1856–82) and Gad Gilbar (for 1879–1913), mainly based on reports by Western consuls in Jerusalem and in Constantinople, show that from 1860 to 1882 the export of oranges from Jaffa grew more than three-fold. The planted area around Jaffa also expanded considerably. Consul Dickson reported that the planted area doubled in size from 1875 to 1893. The main incentive for the rapid growth of this industry during these years was the 50 percent hike in the price of oranges in the export markets. Hence, by the early 1880s, orange exports were the second largest of all Palestine export industries, while by the early twentieth century they had become the main export industry. On the eve of World War I (1913), orange exports constituted some 40 percent of all exports from the Port of Jaffa and from Ottoman Palestine overall.[15]

Table 1.1
Three Major Export Items, Jaffa Port, 1900–1913

Year	1	2	3	Total
1900	74,215	44,550	30,560	264,950
	(39.8%)	(16.8%)	(11.5%)	(100%)
	Oranges	Soap	Sesame	
1904	103,950	62,000	37,860	295,300
	(53.2%)	(21.0%)	(12.8%)	(100%)
	Oranges	Soap	Wines	
1906	162,000	100,000	60,000	500,000
	(32.4%)	(20.0%)	(12.0%)	(100%)
	Oranges	Soap	Sesame	
1908	168,945	141,385	54,745	556,370
	(30.4%)	(25.4%)	(9.8%)	(100%)
	Oranges	Soap	Sesame	
1910	235,605	157,959	60,925	636,145
	(37.0%)	(24.8%)	(9.6%)	(100%)
	Oranges	Soap	Wines	
1913	297,700	200,000	60,530	745,413
	(39.9%)	(26.8%)	(8.1%)	(100%)
	Oranges	Soap	Wines	

Source: Gilbar, "Growing Economic Involvement," 197.
Note: Amounts are in £ at current prices.

Citrus groves required greater investments than other agricultural products.[16] Furthermore, it took six to eight years for a grove to produce fruit in a quantity that began to provide some return on the investment. As a result, the industry was controlled at first by affluent locals, who had the means to subsist economically until their investment began to bear fruit. This investment included purchasing land for the grove, preparing the land for planting, digging a well in each grove, and acquiring an animal-run pumping device, the *nuriyya*. Investment in the grove also included growing the orange seedlings, their planting, regular maintenance and cultivation of the grove, its fertilization, and irrigation during the summer months for six to eight years until it began to produce fruit in commercial quantities, and of course also the interest on the capital invested. In 1893 Consul Dickson estimated that the required investment in an average citrus grove until its eighth year was between 48,000 and 61,000 francs. About 40 percent of this sum was used to purchase the land and to install the well.[17]

This formative period was characterized by high profitability that remained constant for the forty years from the industry's inception in the mid-1870s until World War I. Contemporary testimonies as well as our calculations show that the industry's profitability remained steady for nearly the entire period, at 10 percent return on investment. This was higher than the profits gained not only from raising subsistence crops, such as barley or wheat, but also from other agricultural crops such as olives, almonds, and grapes. Profitability was further enhanced by the high prices received for Jaffa oranges in the export markets, raising revenues for the few entrepreneurs who invested in citrus.[18]

Indeed, for the individual grower a dunam of orange grove generated much larger revenues than any other fruit-bearing grove of the same size. Taking into account that the average size of an orange grove in this period was about fifty-four dunams, while almond groves and vineyards were smaller (sometimes by at least one-third), revenues from orange groves were typically much higher than from grape or almond groves.[19] The high profitability and the considerable annual revenue were important incentives for investing in the citrus industry. Nevertheless, prospective citrus entrepreneurs also needed to come up with sufficient capital not only for the initial investment for purchasing the land and preparing it for planting, but also for covering expenses until the grove began to produce remunerative crops. These funds had the effect of setting "natural limits," as one contemporary expert put it, on the number of prospective investors. This explains the limited social strata involved in the industry during those formative years.[20]

Notably, until the end of the nineteenth century the local citrus industry was an exclusive product, controlled and owned by native Arabs. The "colonists" (as the first Zionist settlers were termed at the time by everyone, including themselves) in the Zionist "colonies" (ditto), and mainly in

Petah Tikva, only began to join the industry in about 1900.[21] Moreover, the industry's control by the local Arabs, and particularly by wealthy residents of Jaffa who owned citrus groves in its vicinity, was manifested not only in their ownership of most of the groves but also in their control of exports. Control of exports included complete control of storage and of dock work in the Jaffa Port, exclusive contracts with shipping companies that delivered the fruit to British markets, and business ties with sales agents in the United Kingdom (and particularly in the Port of Liverpool, the center of citrus imports to Britain), who ultimately sold the Jaffa oranges in British markets.

As a rule, investors in the industry were the medium to highly affluent, mostly residents of Jaffa and the surrounding villages. Some of them exchanged plots they owned for groves. Others purchased land in nearby villages and planted citrus trees. Throughout the period discussed in this book the relationship between the supply of labor, capital, and land was characterized by a large supply of labor relative to the limited supply of land, and all the more so in proportion to the supply of capital. Thus, throughout this entire period the citrus industry was a labor-intensive industry. Thousands of workers were employed in all stages of production, from preparing the land, through routine cultivation of the grove, to picking the fruit, packing it, transporting it to the port, and loading it on ships in Jaffa. Each grove had a grove manager, the *bayari*, who usually lived with his family in a house on the grove grounds and who constantly supervised the chain of production in the grove. Due to his experience the *bayari* was considered a first-rate expert on the grove and its proper operation. This included not only preparing the land but also adequately irrigating it, controlling pests and disease, cultivating the trees, and making sure that the crop generated was as plentiful as possible. Exceptionally expert and reputable *bayariya* received improved terms and were in high demand.[22] Moreover, in contrast to the prevalent image of Arab agriculture, including the Arab citrus industry, as undeveloped, "irrational," and "primitive," both at the time and among certain researchers, the data and personal testimonies show that many technological innovations were instituted in the Arab citrus industry even before the Zionist settlers joined the citriculture activities.[23]

Technological Innovations

Technological innovations in the field of agriculture are divided into two main categories: "labor-saving" innovations that lower the cost of labor per unit of output relative to the cost of land and capital and "land-saving" biological and chemical innovations that lower the cost of land per unit of output relative to the costs of labor and capital involved in producing that unit. Typical examples of labor-saving technologies are different types of machinery used in all stages of production, as well as in the irrigation system. Land-saving technology aims to increase the total output of the entire grove. This technology could include growing more productive varieties than those currently grown and, typically, using fertilization that increases productivity per unit of land.[24]

As Gilbar has shown, from 1890 to 1914 the increase in grove acreage was significantly smaller than the increase in the quantity of oranges exported. "While orchard acreage rose by about four times, the quantity of crop exported [during those years] increased by more than eight times."[25] The same trend is also evident for the years 1881–1901, before a significant quantity of oranges were exported by the budding Jewish sector. Grove land increased by about 60 percent during those years, while the quantity of oranges exported increased by about 210 percent (based on Gilbar, 200).

These figures show that, in addition to inputs of land and capital, land-saving technological innovations were employed in the Palestinian-Arab citrus industry during the last two decades of the nineteenth century as well.

One such improvement was the introduction of internal combustion motors in the irrigation system in lieu of the animals that operated the *nuriyya*. The first motors were in operation in 1898, and by 1906 more than 220 motors were already in operation in the region, the majority of them in the citrus industry (some were used to run flour mills as well). On the eve of World War I, pumps operated by internal combustion motors, which replaced the *nuriyya*, were already in use in growing numbers in both the Jewish and Arab sectors of the industry. The new technology enabled a more efficient and steady supply of water, in greater quantities than with the *nuriyya* system. It also made it possible to dig deeper wells, which supplied water from a deeper groundwater level than previously.

Table 1.2
Area of Citrus Groves, 1880, 1900, 1914 (in dunams)

	Arab sector	Jewish sector	Total
1880	7,500	—	7,500
1900	12,000	2,000	14,000
1914	23,000	10,000–12,000	33,000–35,000

Source: Gilbar, "Growing Economic Involvement," 200.

In addition, the water at these levels was more abundant than at the shallower level. The improved quantity and efficiency of the water supply led to better cultivation and to an increase in the quantity of oranges produced per dunam. The new water-supply technology also allowed growers to plant larger groves than previously, which enabled reaping the advantages of economies of scale. The fixed costs of investing in the new technology and of maintaining it were now spread over a larger number of planted trees and output units.[26]

Evidently, use of fertilizers was an important element in the increased output of a planted grove per dunam. These were mainly natural fertilizers, i.e., manure that was either reused by farmers from their own farms or purchased from other fellahin. The protocols of Pardes, the first Jewish marketing cooperative established in 1901, show the extent to which Jewish citrus growers relied on their Arab counterparts to learn the minutiae of citrus growing and marketing. In fact, these protocols also report ways of obtaining manure for fertilization from Arab fellahin, as well as Arab expertise from which they learned how to fight disease and insects that plagued the groves. These know-how methods considerably facilitated the increase in orange output per dunam.[27]

Contemporary reports by Zionist agronomists and foreign experts tell a similar story not only regarding land-saving methods but also with regard to the mechanization of large Arab-owned groves. Expectations for income flow from citriculture investments, prompted by the steady increase in demand for Palestinian citrus, encouraged some wealthy local Arab entrepreneurs to plant large groves, one hundred to even five hundred dunams each. These were planted and cultivated according to what these experts termed "European" methods. Namely, trees were planted a wider distance apart than in the common grove, which enabled use of machinery in preparing the land for planting and cultivation. More advanced irrigation systems were installed in these groves as well. The "European" method projected a larger yield per tree than the "local" method and eventually a larger output per dunam than in the "local" manner.[28]

The City of Jaffa, Its Notables, and the Citrus Industry

Since its emergence as a profitable economic branch in the late nineteenth century, the citrus industry generated far-reaching changes and transformations in the social structure of Palestinian-Arab society, in both the urban and rural sectors. This industry needed a wide variety of services and supporting industries, from caring for the legal and financial aspects of exporting the fruit, to mechanical and agronomical services, and finally manual labor. All these had an impact on the lifestyle and knowledge of those involved in the industry, whose numbers were constantly on the rise. Many of them became more active in public life and demonstrated a gradually increasing interest in different social organizations. Consequently, they sought to influence the course of life both within local communities in the various cities and villages and nationally, among Palestinian-Arab society in its entirety. Taking the city of Jaffa as an example, we shall follow the course followed by several families who attained a position of influence in various spheres as a result of their involvement in the citrus industry.

In the late Ottoman period, Jaffa became a point of attraction for migrants from the nearby rural area, from wider Palestinian circles, and even from the greater Arab region, particularly Syria and Egypt.[29] It was estimated that during the Mandate period, about half of Jaffa's residents were employed in the citrus industry and in its supporting industries and services in one way or another, whether as grove owners, grove workers, merchants, packers, tax officials, assessors, carpenters, wood suppliers for crates, manufacturers of wrapping paper, drivers, owners and managers of warehouses at the port, sailors, porters, owners of the printing houses that produced Jaffa brand labels, and other service providers.[30] In addition, as the "engine" for the development of Jaffa the citrus industry also created employment and economic opportunities for Jaffans in services and other industries that catered to the city's population as a whole.

The beginning of the citrus-picking season and its conclusion were major occasions in the life of residents of Jaffa and the environs. These two occasions were marked by popular celebrations. 'Ali al-Bawwab relates: "Information provided by the old-timers reveals that, in the early twentieth century, citrus merchants would hold a popular celebration in honor of the first citrus delivery to the port, and this celebration was called 'Zafft al-Burtuqal' (Revelry of the oranges)." Al-Bawwab also recounts that colorful fabrics would be placed on camels' backs and ringing bells fastened on their necks. The camels would be preceded by members of the Sufi tariqa,[31] "with their tambourines and bronze plates."[32]

Wedding and betrothal parties would take place around the groves' irrigation pools. The parties would last several days and nights; the groves and pools would be decorated and the best dishes served. Rawda al-Farkh al-Hudhud describes the wedding of Huda and Fahim al-Farkh, held in a grove owned by the groom's family: "The wedding took place around the largest pool in the grove. Fahim loaded the pool with apples and oranges, as well as flowers and roses. He illuminated the area surrounding the pool with colored electric bulbs. Women cooked rice-stuffed lamb throughout the wedding and fed the guests and the family. The entire family helped with the ceremony, as did all the grove workers."[33]

Jaffa's older families were the first to join the industry with all its various business, agricultural, and commercial components. In time, newly arrived families joined as well and even came to occupy a central place in the industry. Toward the end of the Ottoman period a nouveau riche class began to develop within Palestinian-Arab society from among the older families. This was particularly typical of Muslim families whose sons were employed as officials in the Ottoman bureaucracy, as well as Christian families whose sons had foreign citizenship and worked for influential European consulates throughout the Ottoman Empire. The weighty status these families had acquired by the latter part of the Ottoman period facilitated their contact with Western culture, and they learned European languages and even, quite often, embraced a Western lifestyle. Since knowledge of European languages and familiarity with European markets were an advantage for those involved in marketing the fruit, they were encouraged to adopt a European way of life, recognized as a necessary phase of modernization.

The initial capital of these families was not acquired through citriculture. Rather, many of them served as mediators between the Ottoman government and institutions and companies that carried out infrastructure projects. They were also involved in land transactions. This occupation became very lucrative due to the sharp rise in land prices, both because of modernized needs and due to the rising demand for land, which grew as a result of the increase in Jewish immigrants and Zionist settlements. Before joining the citrus industry, some of these families invested in traditional areas, such as the soap industry, and these formed the foundation of their wealth. Some of the capital accumulated was invested in time in the citrus industry. These include, for example, the Tuqan, al-Nabulsi, and al-Shak'ah families from Nablus. Members of these families, such as Haydar Tuqan, Haj Nimer al-Nabulsi, and Ahmad al-Shak'ah, who owned soap factories in Nablus, began in the 1920s to buy up land in the coastal region between Tulkarm and Netanya, on which they planted citrus groves. Haj Nimer al-Nabulsi, for example, established a large packing house on these lands that has remained almost intact to this day and is in the jurisdiction of Moshav Yanuv.[34] The profits from their expanding business activities were invested, among other things, in improving human capital and, primarily, in educating their children. The children of the new merchants were sent to schools in Cairo, Beirut, and Istanbul, and even in some European capitals, such as London and Paris. Upon their return, these students became major players in the cultural, social, and political life of Palestinian-Arab society.

Yusuf Haykal (1908–89), the last mayor of Arab Jaffa, described how the lives of those who joined the citrus industry in the final quarter of the nineteenth century were completely transformed. He paints a vivid picture of the good life enjoyed by such families in the early twentieth century. Haykal describes the large thirteen-room house built by the head of his family in the early twentieth century, in which many servants were employed. He also describes the twelve-dunam grove adjacent to the house, the well, the pool that served as a water reservoir, and the grove's irrigation system, as well as "the home of the man who managed our groves, called the *bayari*."[35] The improved social status of the Haykal family, mainly from the 1910s—several years after the family included citriculture among its businesses—raised their marriage standards. In the first decades of the twentieth century, those families that entered into marriage with the Haykals appeared to have undergone a similar process of engaging in citriculture. For example, the Hanun family from Tulkarm: Hilmi Hanun (who subsequently served as mayor of Tulkarm for many years) was a product of these marriage ties (his mother was the sister of Dr. Yusuf Haykal). Hanun himself was a major figure in the 1940s industry. Hence, we see that activity in the citrus industry redefined the social boundaries of those involved, and the potential marriage pool was a major measure of these boundaries, as evident from sociological studies.

The various historical sources and the interviews we held show that in the early twentieth century Jaffa had dozens of homes situated near the groves belonging to estate owners, in which the grove was the family's center of life and major source of subsistence. These include, for example, the estates of major citrus grower Zuhadi Abu al-Jabin, businessman 'Ali Bibi, Shaykh Muhammad Sha'ban, and many others. These groves secured a good life and a higher social status for quite a few families.[36]

In some instances the financial aspirations of these families did not remain within the country's borders, and they began to develop commercial and economic relationships in neighboring Arab countries and even invested in commercial enterprises in European countries. One example is the 'Abd al-Rahim family: the head of the family, Muhammad Fadel 'Abd al-Rahim (1880–1955), began his business career as an agent in the Jaffa Port, built up his fortune, and constructed an elaborate house in the 'Ajami neighborhood (the building currently serves as the French embassy). He was among the founders of the nationalist Muslim-Christian Society in Jaffa, but in contrast to most of Jaffa's traditional elite families, who tended to be affiliated with the Nashashibi camp, 'Abd al-Rahim was affiliated with the Husaynis and their party, the Palestinian Arab Party, and was considered the mufti's right-hand person in the city. Jamal al-Husayni,

2. King George Avenue, Jaffa (between 1940 and 1946). Matson (G. Eric and Edith) Photograph Collection, Library of Congress.

the mufti's brother and president of the party, described Muhammad as "a figure whom people were used to seeing in the sphere of national activity, and for whom they had great respect and trust in his dedication."[37]

Based on interviews we conducted and on other material, we learned that the family had several groves. One was near the family house and was called "Bayyarat al-Jabaliyya" after the adjacent neighborhood, and it covered an area of some 400 dunams. Another grove was in Ras al-'Ayn, on an area of 190 dunams, and a third was of 60 dunams. Until World War I the Arab 'Abd al-Nur family and Jewish merchants imported wood from Romania to build export crates for the oranges. Muhammad 'Abd al-Rahim broke that monopoly and began importing wood from the Balkans. After a few years he also opened up two wood factories that processed the wood and prepared crates for the export of citrus.[38]

Ahmad 'Abd al-Rahim (Muhammad's son) continued the tradition of importing wood and crates and reported the import of two million crates in 1946. He was also a member of the joint Arab-Jewish citrus grower delegation that traveled to London in 1946 on behalf of the Citrus Marketing Board (discussed in chapter 3), a delegation that consisted of three Arab and three Jewish growers. Al-Rahim's memories are confirmed by extensive archival sources on the Citrus Marketing Board and the joint delegations. He writes that on this trip an agreement was reached to equitably divide orange exports between Jews and Arabs and explains the establishment of the "'Abd al-Rahim Effendi and Partners" society by the need to counterbalance Jewish efforts at formal organization.[39]

With the flourishing of the citrus industry, and as Jaffa was transformed into the center of activities, prominent urban families (A'iyan) from the inner cities, mainly Jerusalem and Nablus, began sending representatives to settle in the Jaffa area. They did so to become an integral part of the industry and to serve as agents for members of their family who had begun to grow citrus trees on lands purchased in the inner coastal plain. An example of a Jerusalem-based A'iyan family that established a presence in Jaffa was the family of Shaykh Ragheb al-Khaldi, who bought an extensive plot of land in the Tall al-Rish area in southeast Jaffa, where he built a house and planted an orange grove. The sons of Shaykh Ragheb al-Khaldi, Ahmed Samah, Dr. Husayn Fakhri, and Dr. Hasan Shukri, were among the most conspicuous Palestinian intellectuals during the Mandate period. Another urban family attracted to Jaffa in the early twentieth century, some of whose sons became rich from the citrus industry, was the al-Shaykh 'Ali family. The head of the family, 'Abd al-Latif Hasan al-Shaykh 'Ali, came to Jaffa from Lydda in the late nineteenth century and worked as a railway construction contractor in Jaffa. Later, he bought land and planted citrus groves, and his sons were among the most prominent citrus merchants in Jaffa.[40]

One old-time Jaffa family was the Barkat family. In fact, they were two separate families who were involved in the orange industry, one Muslim and the other Christian. The Muslim family was among the most veteran in Jaffa, and some of its members assumed a prominent role in local political, social, and philanthropic efforts in addition to their activities in citriculture. The first of these was 'Abd al-Ra'uf Barkat, who served as head of the Red Crescent in Jaffa and was a member of the Citrus Control

Board. He had a magnificent house in the 'Ajami neighborhood, a seventy-dunam grove within the city of Jaffa's boundaries, and another five hundred dunams of groves in Saknat Darwish and Saknat Abu Kabir.[41]

The second was Zaki Ibrahim Barkat (1900–1971), one of the major grove owners and merchants in the industry, who for a considerable period served on various joint Arab and Jewish committees related to the industry.[42]

The third well-known member of the Barkat family was Hasan Barkat, Zaki's younger brother. He had several groves in the al-Nuzha area and in the vicinity of the al-Bassa sports field (in the present-day location of the Bloomfield Stadium). He was the only family member to remain in Jaffa after 1948 and was appointed, among others, to oversee the Muslim waqf for a short time. However, apparently due to the pressures of his new position, he was compelled to leave the country in the mid-1950s and join the rest of the family in Amman.[43]

The Christian Barkats included notable members as well, who gained their status through activities in the industry. For example, there was Salim Bishara Barkat, who was active in the Arab national societies toward the end of the Ottoman period. He was arrested for these activities and was deported to Istanbul, and only after World War I did he return to Jaffa. He grew citrus fruit and sold oranges, eventually establishing a hotel, the "Club Hotel," on a high point in the Jaffa Saknat Harish neighborhood. Barkat played an active part in the endeavors of the Palestinian National Movement to appeal to international forces and was a member of the Palestinian delegations that engaged in these activities.[44]

The al-Bitar family also had two divisions, one Muslim and the other Christian, and these were probably not related. One well-known member of the Christian division was Hana al-Bitar, a businessman who was involved, among other things, in the marble and citrus industries. He was a public figure with extensive public contacts and served as the Bolivian consul of honor in Palestine.[45]

The two brothers 'Omar and 'Abd al-Ra'uf al-Bitar from the Muslim division of the family were also well known. 'Omar was the elder brother (1878–1946) and was very active in the national sphere from the end of the Ottoman period. In 1908 he supported the Young Turks revolt. They

3. Jaffa mayor 'Omar al-Bitar (seated) and heads of Jaffa municipal departments, 1941. Israel National Photo Collection, Zoltan Kluger.

appointed him mayor of Jaffa, but once they reneged on the democratic principles of the Ottoman constitution and advocated a policy of Turkification, he turned against them and was removed from his position and deported to Anatolia. At the beginning of the Mandate period, 'Omar al-Bitar was among the founders of the Muslim-Christian societies and the Arab Executive Committee,[46] and he even served as the deputy to Musa Kathim al-Husayni, who headed this committee.[47] In 1932 he was among the founders of the Nation's Fund, and in 1934 he helped establish the Nashashibis' National Defense Party.[48] In 1941, upon the death of his brother 'Abd al-Ra'uf, who was serving at the time as mayor of Jaffa, he was appointed mayor until retiring in 1945 due to health problems. He died and was buried in Jaffa in 1946.[49]

The younger brother was 'Abd al-Ra'uf (1882–1941), a wealthy citrus grower and businessman. He was affiliated with the Nashashibi camp that opposed the mufti and was even in favor of discussions with the British and the Jews. He headed the city's chamber of commerce and was an almost regular member of the city council. In 1939 he was appointed mayor of

Jaffa after the resignation of 'Asim al-Sa'id. In late 1940, when the joint Arab and Jewish Citrus Control Board was established, 'Abd al-Ra'uf al-Bitar became the most prominent Arab member of this binational body.[50]

The family owned some four thousand dunams of land to the east of Jaffa, on the current location of the city of Bnei Brak.[51] They planted several groves on this land, the largest of which was between Salama and Abu Kabir.[52]

The Abu Khadra family was one of the oldest in Jaffa. Some of its sons resided in Haifa and others in the village of Shaykh Muwannes. Several were involved in various aspects of citriculture, primarily Hashem Abu Khadra and Sa'id Abu Khadra, who traded in citrus fruit,[53] and Khalil Abu Khadra and his two sons Isma'il and Ibrahim, who had several groves northeast of Jaffa in the western al-Auja/Yarkon basin.[54] Members of the family were very active in the public and national sphere. Rashid Ibrahim Abu Khadra (1881–1921) was the senior member of the family toward the end of the Ottoman period. He was active in the clandestine Arab national societies and was arrested by the Ottomans and deported to Anatolia. Rashid Ibrahim Abu Khadra was among the founders of the Muslim-Christian societies and a major activist.[55] His son, Rashid Hilmi Abu Khadra (1902–52), earned a master's degree in law at the University of Damascus. When in Syria, he took part in the Great Syrian Revolt and also established the Palestinian society for support of the Syrian Revolt, whose activities were centered in Jaffa. In the 1930s he operated among the young and was affiliated with the al-Istiqlal Party.[56] Sa'id Ramadan Abu Khadra (1885–1930), a graduate of the Sorbonne in Paris, was a citrus merchant who established a commercial network with French entrepreneurs and helped found the Arab Chamber of Commerce in Jaffa.[57]

The al-Bayruti family was a Christian family originating from Beirut whose members arrived in Jaffa toward the end of the Ottoman period. This family boasted two prominent citrus growers: Yusuf al-Bayruti, who owned groves in the region of Abu Kabir and on the main Jaffa-Lydda road, and Toni al-Bayruti, who had a large grove in Bayt Dajan and several buildings and properties on al-Hilwe Street in Jaffa.[58] Another member of the family was Adib Edward al-Bayruti, a well-known Jaffa lawyer during the Mandate period. He also served as deputy mayor of Jaffa, and in 1949 was a member of the Palestinian delegation to the Lausanne talks for discussions on the fate of Palestinian property. Adib al-Bayruti died and was buried in Beirut.[59]

The Tamari family was another veteran Christian family. Its members did business mainly in the wheat trade and had several shops in the old al-Dayr market.[60] In the early twentieth century, several family members also joined the citrus industry and owned groves in southeast Jaffa.[61] The most prominent of these was Wahba Tamari (1890–1970), a distinguished businessman who was involved in almost all sectors in Jaffa, including the citrus industry. The family had a large grove in northeast Jaffa and several small groves in the region of Sarafand al-'Amar (Ramle district).[62] Tamari engaged in extensive philanthropic activities and was among the founders of the Orthodox society in Jaffa, which he headed for many years, as well as of the Orthodox school in Jaffa. Wahba Tamari was also involved in journalistic affairs and was the owner and main writer of the comic newspaper *Abu Shaduf*. Politically, he was among the founders of the national bloc party Hizb al-Kutla al-Wataniyya (National Coalition) headed by 'Abdallah Salah and was one of its senior activists.[63]

The al-Darhali family was one of Jaffa's oldest families. It is probably of Turko-Circassian descent, originating from the town of Dara near the city of Adanna.[64] Parts of the family also settled in Gaza and in the village of Bayt Dajan.[65] The al-Darhali family had a strong financial standing and was involved in many business endeavors, mainly citriculture and vehicle imports.[66] An alley facing the Jaffa municipality, which housed various artisan shops, bore the family's name.[67] Prominent family members were Mas'oud 'Abd al-Hamid al-Darhali (1900–1974), Zaki Hashem al-Darhali (1917–48), and Mu'awiya Muhammad Rifat al-Darhali (b. 1927). Mas'oud al-Darhali was a well-known public figure in Jaffa, member of the city council, and deputy mayor during the time of 'Abd al-Ra'uf al-Bitar. He was among the mufti's opponents and a supporter of the Nashashibi camp.[68] Zaki al-Darhali, a graduate of the American University of Beirut, specialized in English literature. He was better known for his outstanding achievements in the soccer club, the Islamic Club of Jaffa. Zaki was the club's successful forward player and goal scorer, for which he was idolized by the youth of Palestine.[69] He was killed in a terrorist attack perpetrated by members of the Lehi (the so-called "Stern Gang") on the Saraya (the municipality building) on January 4, 1948, an attack that killed ten people and wounded about one hundred.[70] Mu'awiya al-Darhali earned a PhD in political science at the University of London and engaged mainly in journalism. He also wrote poetry and literature. After the Nakba he settled in Kuwait and then moved to Amman.[71]

The Christian Rok family had several prominent sons who were involved in the citrus industry: Iskander, Alfred, Edmond, and Alfonse. Iskander Rok had a large grove in the current-day area of metropolitan Tel Aviv, between present-day Levontin Street and Petah Tikva Road. Alfred Rok was affiliated with the Husayni camp and even served as vice president of the Palestinian Arab Party. He represented the Catholic Christians on the Higher Arab Committee on behalf of this camp.[72] Edmond Rok was among the founders of the Arab Youth Congress, an important third party in addition to the pro Husayni and Nashashibi parties.[73] He was also the Lebanese consul in Jaffa. After 1948 he left to live in exile in Amman and served for many years as the Jordanian ambassador to the Vatican.[74]

The Abu al-Jabin family claims to be descended from the Umayyad dynasty and the third Khalif, 'Uthman ben 'Affan. The family came to the city from the village of Harbiyya (today Kibbutz Karmiya) in the Gaza district. This family had branches in Safed and in the village of al-Thahiriyya in the Hebron district, as well as in the village of Harbiyya, as stated above.[75] At first the family lived in the Old City of Jaffa, and toward the end of the nineteenth century they built a large house outside the Old City, in a location that later became the nucleus of the Arshid neighborhood in the al-Manshiyah quarter, with the main street in this neighborhood named Abu al-Jabin Street for the family.[76] Amin Abu al-Jabin, a member of this family, also became the mukhtar of this neighborhood.[77]

In time, the family bought up much land around Bayt Dajan, Sarafand, and Yazur and planted citrus groves. Several members of the al-Jabin family occupied a prominent place in the industry, primarily Zuhadi Ahmad Abu al-Jabin (1889–1955), who had a large two-hundred-dunam grove in the town of Bayt Dajan. In the grove he built a palace, where he hosted important visitors to Palestine from all over the world. Zuhadi's nephew, Ruhi Abu al-Jabin, described his memories of a visit to his uncle's grove:

"On Friday, October 27, 1939, a particularly beautiful day, I arranged with my cousin Nasuh to visit the grove of my uncle Zuhadi in Bayt Dajan." Abu al-Jabin continued to describe the wealth of his uncle and his lavish lifestyle, which to a large extent stemmed from his citrus business enterprises. Zuhadi Abu al-Jabin had an expensive Packard car, writes the nephew, and a very luxurious house within the grove that was built in a strikingly modern design and adorned with a pool, a tennis court, a playground for the family's children, and stables. The stables housed two ponies that were given as a present to Zuhadi Abu al-Jabin's children by the Swedish crown prince, who had visited the grove the year before.[78]

In addition to his groves in Jaffa and Bayt Dajan, Zuhadi Abu al-Jabin had a mortgage and loan company in partnership with a British businessman, called Godwin Simons Abu al-Jabin Ltd., which also handled orange exports for Jaffa merchants. According to a common method employed in the industry, Abu al-Jabin bought the groves' future crops from the fruit merchants and grove owners for a predetermined amount paid in advance. In return, he received exclusive rights to market the future fruit of these groves in British and European markets.[79] A review of documents from a private archive, which was made available to us and includes records and lists of the company's activities, shows that Abu al-Jabin saw satisfying gains from this company.[80]

Aided by his profits, and as a major figure in Jaffa and Palestine's citrus business, Zuhadi Abu al-Jabin's public activity expanded and his status in the representative organs was enhanced. He served as a member of the Citrus Control Board (we elaborate on this organization in the following chapters) and of the municipality of the city of Jaffa for several terms. Zuhadi was affiliated with the Nashashibi opposition and was among the founders of the National Defense Party in 1934.[81] He was an active philanthropist. He established an orphanage in one of his groves, within a complex in the village of Sarafand al-'Amar (Ramle district), which housed Palestinian orphans from the center of the country and from other districts as well.[82]

Another prominent family member was 'Issa Amin Abu al-Jabin (1894–1957), an important national activist in the Manshiyah quarter and affiliated with the Nashashibi camp. Another was Khayri Abu al-Jabin (b.

1924), a journalist, educator, sportsman, official in the Office of the Censor, and secretary of the Palestinian Sports Association.[83]

The Damyani family, a veteran Christian family, had extensive ties to Europe, which granted its members status and influence among the Palestinian public in Jaffa and particularly in the citrus industry, for which these ties were crucial.[84] Some of its well-known members were Hana Damyani, Venetian council of honor to Jaffa, and Yusuf Damyani, who served as the British consul of honor in Jaffa in the first half of the nineteenth century.[85] The family had groves in various places, such as Wadi Hanin, Jamasin, Bayt Dajan, and in the area of Ard al-Mir alongside Wadi al 'Uja (the Yarkon).[86] The largest of these groves was in the village of Bayt Dajan, and it extended over seven hundred dunams and cultivated all the citrus fruits known in the country at that time.[87]

The al-Bana family was wealthy and one of the oldest in Jaffa. They owned groves in southeast Jaffa (near the village of Safriyya)[88] and around the village of Miska (Tulkarm district) in the Sharon.[89] Two of its sons—Khalil and Ibrahim—were involved in the citrus industry as well as in Jaffa's public life. Haj Khalil al-Bana was the father of Sabri al-Bana, better known as Abu Nidal.[90] Khalil al-Bana was among Jaffa's most prominent orange merchants, as well as an influential public figure within the urban strata of Jaffa and other cities.[91]

This family probably originated from the village of al-Dajaniya near Ramallah, rather than from Bayt Dajan as reported in several sources. One branch settled in Jerusalem and was, among other things, the proprietors of Maqam al-Nabi Dawoud within the al-Haram al-Sharif complex, earning them the designation al-Dawoudi al-Dajani. The head of this branch, Ahmad bin Yasin al-Dajani, graduated from al-Azhar with the rank of 'Alem (authorized Muslim cleric), and upon arriving in Jerusalem became a preacher and head imam of the al-Aqsa Mosque.[92] Another part of the family arrived in Jaffa in the late fifteenth century and founded the Jaffa branch.[93] Upon arriving in Jaffa they purchased a considerable amount of land. They were some of the first to grow citrus trees, and once this became a major export industry they were among its leaders. One of the family's first grove owners and growers was 'Abdallah Salim al-Dajani, who planted a large grove to the east of the city and another near the village of Bayt Dajan.[94] In addition, Saʿad al-Dajani planted a grove on al-Hilwe Street.[95] Members of the family sold citrus fruit and were involved in the associated wood and paper industries.[96] Due to their strong financial position, the family occupied a major role in Palestinian public life in general and in Jaffa in particular. Unlike the other veteran families, who in the national context tended to support the Nashashibi opposition, the al-Dajani family supported the Husayni camp.

Five members of the family were particularly notable for their public activity. The eldest was Mustafa Yusuf Diaʾ al-Dajani (1880–1946), who studied law and economics at the University of Istanbul. Upon his return to Jaffa he became one of the city's most important businessmen and invested in real estate and in the citrus business. He was among the founders of the Muslim-Christian Society in Jaffa and of the (Husayni) Palestinian Arab Party, and secretary of the latter's Jaffa branch. Yusuf Diʾa al-Dajani died in Jaffa in 1946 and was buried there.[97]

The second was Shaykh Ragheb Abu al-Suʿoud al-Dajani (1890–1964), a graduate of al-Azhar University. At first he served as a Sharʿi Qadi, was then certified in Jerusalem as a civil attorney, and in time became a leading expert in land transactions. He was head of the Muslim-Christian Society in Jaffa and member of the political bureau of the Husayni Palestinian Arab Party. After 1948 he left to live in exile in Ramallah, where he died in 1964.[98]

The third was Kamal Tawfiq al-Dajani (1899–1985), a graduate of al-Azhar, who engaged in literary and journalistic writing. He was one of Jaffa's major citrus merchants and was politically active in the Palestinian Arab Party and the Muslim-Christian Society. He collaborated with Musa al-ʿAlami in the Arab Development Project.[99] Subsequently, he was appointed a member of the High Arab Institution when it was founded in 1946. After the Nakba he left to live in exile in Beirut and from there moved to Cairo, where he died and was buried in 1985.[100]

Another of the al-Dajani family's notable members was Dr. Fuʾad Ismaʿil al-Dajani (1890–1940), a well-known physician and owner of the famous hospital he founded in Jaffa, which was named for him. Although born in Jerusalem, he spent most of his life in Jaffa. He was a graduate of the University of London, where he completed his residency in 1926.[101] At first he worked at the government hospital in Jaffa, but after a while he resigned and built his own hospital in the al-Nuzha neighborhood. Fu'ad's father was a citrus grower and became wealthy as a result of his business. Dr. Fu'ad used the family fortune to build the hospital, considered at the time one of the most luxurious in the region. In 1940 he contracted blood poisoning in the course of surgery, died, and was buried on the grounds of his hospital.[102]

The fifth prominent member of the family was Mustafa Hasan Abu al-Wafa al-Dajani (1890–1964), a graduate of the Sorbonne University in Paris. He was involved in education and journalism and was a member of the Higher Muslim Council and in charge of the waqf's affairs in the region of Jaffa and the center.[103]

The Haykal family originated from the Tarabin clan in the region of Be'er Sheva.[104] They migrated at first to Gaza and from there north to Jaffa.[105] The family had groves in south Jaffa in the area of Abu Kabir, Saknat Darwish, and Tall al-Rish.[106] Members of the family also traded in grain and had businesses in the city of Tulkarm and its environs. Well-known members of the family in the public sphere were educator Muhammad Haykal, who was active in the field of education toward the end of the Ottoman period, and his son Nihad Muhammad Haykal, active among the young, in the Scouts, and in sports.[107] But the most celebrated was Yusuf Mustafa Haykal (1907–89), Jaffa's last mayor, mentioned above. He began his career in journalism and then earned a law degree at the University of Montpelier in France. He went on to study political science at the Sorbonne in Paris, where he earned a PhD in law. His dissertation was about dissolution of the parliament in a democratic regime and its legal and public significance and consequences.[108] From France Haykal moved to London, where he earned another PhD in political science at the University of London. In 1937 he returned to Jaffa and published his popular book *The Palestinian Problem*. This book was written during the Revolt of 1936–39. In it, Yusuf Haykal analyzed international and Zionist documents and claimed that these two foreign forces were responsible for the creation of Palestine's crisis.[109] In that year he was a member of the Palestinian delegation to the pan-Arab Bludan Conference (1937), which opposed the British Royal Commission's recommendations to partition

Palestine and to establish a Jewish state there. As mentioned above, from 1945 to 1948 Yusuf Haykal served as mayor of Jaffa. During his time in office, Jaffa underwent major transformations in many spheres, and particularly in the realm of planning and infrastructure (establishment of modern water, sewage, and electricity systems and expansion of main streets), for which he used the services of the well-known Egyptian city planner, 'Ali al-Maliji.[110] After 1948 Haykal left to live in exile in Amman and became involved in Jordanian diplomacy. He served as the Jordanian ambassador to London and to Washington, and as Jordan's representative to the UN.[111]

The al-Hout family originated from the city of Beirut, Lebanon. Some of its members came to Jaffa and to the village of Shaykh Muwannes during the late Ottoman period. The family owned groves near Shaykh Muwannes and in the western part of the Wadi al 'Uja basin. One well-known member of the family was Khahil al-Hout, a prominent citrus grower and merchant.[112] Another was Mahmoud al-Hout (1916–98), a graduate of the American University of Beirut, a poet, journalist, and researcher who specialized in comparative literature.[113] Yet another was Shafiq Ibrahim al-Hout (1932–2012), an author, journalist, and Fatah activist, who for many years also served as the PLO representative in Lebanon.[114]

The collective profile of some of the prominent families that invested in the citrus industry, many of them from its beginnings in the last quarter of the nineteenth century, shows some common elements. First, this venture, very much like other business activities of the Arabs of Palestine up to the Nakba, was family based. The family supplied the needed capital, connections, necessary knowledge regarding this specific venture, and the required guarantees for investment in the industry, mainly through the family's extensive lands. Second, the citrus industry was an important vehicle for personal and family rise of status, as evidenced by these families' change of position and reputation in the institution of marriage. Third, these families were also important players in the local and national political arena during the years from the late Ottoman rule up to 1948. It should be stressed that these families also maintained connections with Tel Aviv and its politicians and businesspeople.[115] Fourth, the city of Jaffa, as the main seaport of Palestine, was the hub of the political, social, and business activities of these families. Finally, our records show that while a visible majority of these families supported the more moderate Nashashibi camp, the Husayni Party, as well as new and more independent political movements like the al-Istiqlal Party and the Youth Congress, also received significant support from among the citrus merchants' and growers' families.

Zionists Enter the Industry: Ideological, Social, and Economic Implications

In the early twentieth century a new factor was added to the developing and profitable industry, one that was to have a crucial effect on the industry's activity and character until 1948. This factor was, of course, the Zionist colonists in the colonies (moshavot) surrounding Jaffa, first and foremost Petah Tikva. The relationships between the Arab and Jewish sectors of the industry influenced the economic activity and social image of each sector. Each of the two sectors was affected differently by the economic structure, social stratification, and political and ideological views of the other. Even if factions within each sector, notably the Zionist Labor Movement, consciously tried to distance themselves from the other, the two sectors were nevertheless constantly influenced by each other. The very effort at separation speaks volumes about the reality of the existence of the "other" and of its importance for the construction of each sector's economic, social, and cultural structure. Although each sector had separate social, cultural, economic, and political systems, they also maintained regular mutual economic and social relationships that kept the boundaries between them flexible.

As stated, the two sectors were grounded in societies that were fundamentally separate. In this period and until the beginning of the British Mandate, two opposite trends existed in the relationship between native Arab residents and Zionist settlers. On one hand both societies, and especially the Zionist one, wished to maintain their respective separate ecological, economic, and cultural spheres. It should also be emphasized that the constantly growing Zionist community (known as the Yishuv) was the major force that strove to create a European society separate from the local one. Ideological, religious, cultural, lingual, and social differences were the foundation upon which an autonomous society of Zionist settlers was created, distinct from that of the local native population. The Zionist moshavot—Petah Tikva, Rehovot, Rishon Lezion, Nes Ziona—formed a type of concentric circle about twenty kilometers (12.4 miles) from Jaffa, thus occupying a separate geographical space from the Arab sector.

There were also economic differences, which added to the separation trajectory and state of mind. The main difference was the capital brought by Zionist settlers from their countries of origin, which was much greater than that held by their Palestinian contemporaries. The distance of the Zionist moshavot from Jaffa also provided for cheaper land. These conditions encouraged Zionist citrus growers to invest in larger groves than those around Jaffa and to leverage the economies of scale allowed by the available land and capital whenever possible.

Then again, the Zionist sector was dependent on several critical elements within the Arab sector. At first, before the Jewish citrus growers acquired knowledge and proficiency in the field, they were compelled to use local knowledge. Indeed, at the beginning citrus groves planted in the Zionist moshavot followed the model common in Jaffa and its environs. And in the years until World War I and even subsequently, most Jewish groves had an Arab *bayari* who managed work in the grove and supplied the necessary expertise for it to operate successfully.[116] A lot has been written about the fact that throughout the entire period discussed in this book, with the exception of the three years of the Arab Revolt (1936–39), most of the manual labor performed in Jewish groves, from preparation of the land, routine cultivation of the groves, and the picking and packing of the fruit, was carried out by thousands of Arab laborers who lived in villages adjacent to the moshavot. The packing of the citrus fruit also required a high level of skill and was done by groups of Arab packers who specialized in this task with almost no use of mechanization. In addition to the Arab workers, Jewish workers were also employed in the Zionist citrus industry. The hourly wages of Jewish laborers were considerably higher than those of the Arab laborers, though they performed the exact same job. The reasons for this were manifold—economic, ideological, social, and cultural—and as stated, considerable research attention has been devoted to this issue. In any case, although until World War I the supply of Jewish labor was very low and provided no more than about 10 percent of total demand for workers in the Zionist citrus industry (as shown by Israel Kolatt many years ago),[117] this fact also affected the wages of Arab workers in the Zionist sector. Thus, the wages of Arab workers in the Jewish industry were higher than those of Arab workers in the Palestinian-Arab industry for the same jobs. Consequently, throughout this entire period, the cost of producing a crate of citrus for export was lower in the Arab citrus industry than in the Zionist industry. The difference in costs was not consistent and changed according to the economic circumstances. But the difference itself was a constant element that affected the relationship between the two sectors.[118]

In addition to depending on the supply of Arab labor and expertise, until World War I Jewish citrus growers were also dependent on the Arab industry to export the fruit. Exports were controlled by a small group of Jaffa-based exporters, who had exclusive contracts with the British shipping company Prince Line to market the fruit in the United Kingdom. In this way the company and the exporters controlled the export field, and all citrus growers were compelled not only to market through them but also to agree to the commissions they charged. This necessarily created commercial relationships between the two sectors that required frequent contact throughout the export season, during the months of December to March.

Following both the national and settler-colonial state of mind, the Jewish citrus growers endeavored to establish separate marketing cooperatives that would handle their fruit exclusively. As early as 1901 leading citrus growers established the first Jewish cooperative, Pardes, in Petah Tikva. Until World War I, attempts were made to establish additional Zionist cooperatives in Petah Tikva and in other moshavot. The protocols of Pardes from these years indicate the ambivalent attitude toward the Jaffa-based Arab exporters. On one hand, they were treated with hostility due to their control of exports, accompanied by equally hostile religious and social objections to the "non-Jews." Then again, there are continuous testimonies of joint meetings and agreements between Pardes and the leading Arab exporters. This ambivalent attitude, compelled by the economic structure of the industry with its fluctuations, continued with the advent of the British Mandate of Palestine. From an economic perspective,

Pardes tried to use its organized bargaining power to reduce the commissions it paid. It also participated in an attempt, led by the head of the Jaffa city council, Shaykh Salim, to break the monopoly of Prince Line and to form contact with a rival British shipping company, Bull Line. However, the joint pressure by Prince Line, which reduced its prices, as well as by other Arab exporters and the United Kingdom's Foreign Office, which applied pressure in Constantinople in support of Prince Line's monopoly, put an end to this attempt.[119] Nonetheless, the episode well reflects the reciprocal relationship of both competition and cooperation formed between major elements in the two sectors of the citrus industry as a result of the economic circumstances.

Until the beginning of World War I, Pardes included only some of the Jewish grove owners. The others continued their commercial relationships with the Jaffa exporters. Hence, the Jewish industry depended on its Arab counterparts in areas that were important and essential for its existence. But the local Arab industry also used the support of the Jewish industry to some extent, mainly concerning technological innovations and agronomic knowledge. Until 1914 the Jewish citrus growers' major source of agronomic and technological knowledge was the agricultural experts affiliated with the Jewish Colonization Association and Baron Rothschild.[120] Contemporary sources, including the Pardes protocols, speak of a stable relationship as well as frequent consultations and mutual and constant knowledge transfer between the Jewish citrus growers and experts associated with the colonization systems established in Palestine by the Jewish Colonization Association and Baron Rothschild. This knowledge also reached the Arab citrus growers—both indirectly through laborers and *bayariya* who acquired it when working in Jewish-owned groves and then transferred it to citrus growers in their own society—and directly as evident from several examples in contemporary sources.[121]

Hence, even in this formative period each sector did not develop separately, and the mutual relations that evolved between the two sectors had the effect of slightly "bending" the social and economic boundaries between them.

Another important factor that helped facilitate this "bending" of boundaries was the market-oriented worldview shared by the leaders of the two sectors. While socialist, Marxist, and communist worldviews greatly affected the Zionist community in pre-1948 Palestine, up until 1948 the Jewish citrus industry was overwhelmingly composed of market-oriented Jewish practitioners and nonsocialist entrepreneurs. Likewise, socialist and communist ideas had only marginally penetrated Palestinian-Arab society prior to the Nakba.[122] Hence, the Palestinian "Men of Capital," as Sherene Seikaly characterized them,[123] and the Jewish citrus growers shared a common economic Weltanschauung that favored a capitalist economy over a socialist one. At the same time, most Arab and Jewish practitioners also desired to strengthen the economy of their respective communities.[124] Evidently, this ideology of economic nationalism contradicted the citrus entrepreneurs' market-oriented Weltanschauung. However, the economic structure of the industry eventually forced the two parties to reach some cooperation.

Moreover, at that initial stage of Zionist colonization both communities were still in the process of forging their respective mature national consciousness. Before World War I the Jewish-national community in Palestine had not yet formed a clear ideology of separation that would become its hallmark following the establishment of the British Mandate. During those initial years and also during the first two decades of the Mandate, the Jewish citrus growers advocated more cooperation with the native Arab society and economy than their Labor Zionists' ideological contenders. On the Arab side, the Palestinian-Arab national consciousness was still at its budding stage. The Arabs of Palestine were of course alarmed by the sudden and growing Zionist colonization and expressed their concerns on various occasions. But a noncooperation ideology, which would increasingly be dominating post–World War I Palestinian nationalism, had yet to emerge. Hence, prior to 1919 clear ideological boundaries that would subsequently need to be "bent" were only being formed.[125]

2

The Intertwined Economic, Social, and Ideological Factors, 1919–1948

On the eve of World War I, exports by Arab citrus growers were reduced from 100 percent before Jews began investing in citrus, to about 70 percent of all Palestine exports. Hence, investments in the Jewish sector of the industry were high and, as a result of the technological improvements used, productivity was considerable and growth rapid.[1]

World War I resulted in major devastation of the local industry.[2] Exports were almost completely halted to keep the ships out of danger and due to the rising price of shipping. However, there were also more significant sources of damage to the local industry. The Ottoman Army and auxiliary forces entered the country, and one year from the beginning of the war the country had become a transit station for Ottoman Army forces headed for the Suez Canal. The Ottoman Army confiscated many of the diesel engines that operated pumps in the groves, cut down trees for heating and to operate steam engines, and confiscated crops to suit its needs. All these actions led to severe harm to the industry's production, adding to the maritime shipping hardships. The situation was further aggravated by a severe locust invasion in 1915. The locusts consumed not only citrus groves but also other groves and field crops, resulting in a grave blow to local agriculture.

The "Golden Years" of Expansion and High Profitability

The years 1918–25 were mostly devoted to rehabilitation of the industry. Very few new groves were planted, and efforts were directed at rehabilitating existing ones. But these were also very profitable years. The high profitability stemmed first and foremost from the high demand for the local Shamouti in British and continental markets. The low supply versus the demand kept the Shamouti's price up in the markets for a lengthy period, and thus also its profitability. In addition, a high yield was generated by existing groves that even prior to the war had already begun to cover investments, and due to their age productivity was at its zenith. Hence, the citrus growers did not have to set aside some of their revenues to return the investment but enjoyed maximal returns. From 1925 on an accelerated trend of new planting was evident. The capital for these plantings came from two main sources. First, from the capital accumulated by the wealthiest residents in the Jaffa area, particularly during the highly profitable good years. Secondly, in 1924 a wave of Jewish immigrants began to arrive in Palestine, consisting of middle-class Jews from Eastern Europe and particularly Poland (called the "Fourth Aliya" in Zionist discourse). They brought with them capital, some of which was invested in the citrus industry. The investments of these Jews in the industry consisted, first of all, of land purchases from Arab owners. At the beginning of Zionist colonization in the late nineteenth century, land was purchased from the owners of large areas, many of whom lived outside Palestine and were considered "absentee owners," for instance the Sursuq family. However, after the British Mandate was established in Palestine, the Mandate government began to remap and record ownership of the land, particularly in the coastal plain. This area was the main focus of Zionist colonization. In this process, and probably with this goal, the recording and mapping process led to the breaking up of collective ownership of a considerable part of the lands belonging to villages in the coastal plain, villages that had previously followed the method of joint ownership of land, i.e., *musha‘*. Thus, from the latter half of the 1920s a growing number of those who sold land to Jews were fellahin from villages in the coastal plain who went through a process of "privatization" of their *musha‘* land. A number of affluent Palestinians also appear to have acquired land in this way. In quite a few cases these prominent figures had previous ownership of land in various villages, and its designation was now changed to planting groves. Moreover, the fellahin who sold their land, whether to Jews or to wealthy Palestinians, did not sell all their land, rather only part of it. Quite a few used the money received in return for the land to acquire a part in the industry. For example, Zionist sources from the early 1930s report that during this process of breaking up *musha'* land, Zarnuqa (near Rehovot) "sold 6,000 dunams to the Jews." Zarnuqa has "about 2,000 dunams of grove, some of which are already yielding fruit. . . . The same situation prevails in Sarafand al-Kharab, which sold half of its land, 5,000 dunams of 10,000, and has about 2,000 dunams of groves."[3] These reports also detailed the growth generated in the Palestinian-Arab village economy by the transition to citriculture. By selling part of their land to wealthy Arab entrepreneurs or Zionist settlers, these fellahin were able to pay off their pressing debts and to invest in small to medium-sized groves. These Zionist sources meticulously detail this change from places like Na'ana in the south to Jaljuliya and Qaqun in the Tulkarm subdistrict.[4]

Until 1932 new plantings were carried out mainly in the Jewish sector. From 1923 to 1930 Jews planted approximately 50,000 dunams of groves, multiplying the Zionist citrus area by about five. In the Arab sector only approximately 27,500 dunams were planted in those years, increasing grove land by about one and a half. Moreover, in 1918 the acreage of Arab groves was almost twice that owned by Jews—some 19,000 dunams versus some 10,000, respectively. But as of 1930 Jewish-owned groves covered a larger area than Arab-owned groves, some 60,000 dunams versus some 46,500, respectively.

Each additional wave of middle-class Jewish immigration from Germany following Hitler's ascension to power in 1933, and from other Eastern European countries, led to an even greater rise in investments in the Jewish citrus industry. During the three years of 1932–34, some 75,000 dunams of groves were added to the Jewish sector. However, from 1935 until the beginning of World War II, the planting of new groves in the Jewish sector slowed considerably. The major reason was the large increase in the supply of citrus fruit, with the groves planted in previous years beginning to bear fruit at a gradually rising pace. The considerable supply in the export markets led to a drop in prices, as well as to a sharp drop in profitability in general, and even to significant losses incurred by about one-third of citrus growers in the Zionist sector.

Table 2.1
Area of Citrus Groves, 1922–39 (selected years; in dunams)

Year	Arab sector	Jewish sector	Total
1922	19,000	10,000	29,000
1926	21,500	17,000	38,500
1930	46,500	60,000	106,500
1934	105,000	145,000	250,000
1939	150,000	155,000	305,000

Sources: Gurevich and Gerz, *Jewish Agricultural Settlement in Palestine*, table 68; Yehuda Horin, "The Citrus Industry and Its Future," *Davar*, April 18, 1945, 2; Barakat, *Observation*, 100.

A significant increase in investments in the Arab sector in new groves was only evident from 1932 onward. The delay in extensive investments in the Arab sector from 1923 to 1932 seems to have stemmed mainly from the capital required. Nonetheless, the accumulated capital from the industry's profits and the continued transfer of capital from the Jewish-settler community to the local Arab society in exchange for land sale to Jews, as well as the successful economic activity in other industries, led to investments in this profitable industry. In contrast to the Zionist sector, in the Palestinian sector new plantings did not cease after 1935.

We assume that the middle column of table 2.2 better reflects the reality in Jewish-owned groves, where Arab laborers accounted for about 60 percent of the employees. Moshe Smilansky, president of the Zionist Farmers' Federation, whose members were mainly citrus growers, was the undisputed leader of these growers. He claimed in 1937 that current annual expenditures per case in Arab citriculture were only 10 percent less than those of its Jewish counterpart. Consequently, it should be assumed that the relative proportion of Arab laborers in Jewish groves in the 1936–37 season was even higher than 60 percent. In the following years, however, due to the Arab Revolt, the proportion of Arab laborers in Jewish groves declined.

As evident from table 2.2, the harm to profitability in the Palestinian-Arab sector was not as severe as in the Jewish sector and did not result in a halt of new plantings. Table 2.2 shows that returns on investments in Jewish citriculture in 1939 ranged from 0.9 percent to about 3.4 percent,

Table 2.2
Profit and Loss per Exportable Case of Productive Grove, 1938–39
(in Palestine mils)

	Jewish-owned; Jewish labor only	Jewish-owned; Jewish and Arab labor	Arab-owned; Arab labor only
Cultivation costs	120 (LP 12.07)[a]	092 (LP 9.25)[a]	060 (LP 4.84)[a]
Cost from tree to port	170	170	102
Cost from port (FOB) to ports in the UK	200	200	200
Total operation costs	490	462	362
Price in the UK	500	500	500
Net return per case	010	038	138
Output per dunam	75 cases	75 cases	60 cases
Net return per dunam	LP 0.750 (LP 0.754)[b]	LP 2.85 (LP 2.86)[b]	LP 8.30 (LP 8.35)[b]
Investment per dunam	LP 83	LP 83	LP 50
Return on investment	0.9%	3.4%	16.6%

Sources: Nathan, Gass, and Daniel, *Palestine*, 207–12; Metzer and Kaplan, *Jewish and Arab Economies*, 39; Karlinsky, *California Dreaming*, 113–15.
[a] Cultivation costs per dunam, 1936 prices.
[b] 1936 prices.

versus about 16.6 percent in Palestinian citriculture. For most of the period between the world wars, Arab investments per one dunam of orange grove were about 40 percent lower than Jewish investments (see table 2.2).[5] The differences stemmed, first and foremost, from the lower cost of labor in the Palestinian-Arab industry. While the daily wages of an Arab laborer in the Palestinian industry ranged from 80 to 100 mils in 1939, in the Jewish industry wages were about 2.5 times higher, about 200–250 Palestine mils.[6] This difference also affected the total cost of routine grove cultivation. However, it should be emphasized again that the actual difference in wages between the two national sectors was much smaller than reflected by the two salary extremities, since Arab laborers in the Zionist industry accounted for about 60 percent of its total labor force.

Technological Innovations during the Mandate

In addition, to begin with the Zionist industry was inclined to invest more in irrigation systems, mechanization of some of the routine cultivation work, and chemical fertilization to raise output per unit of land and reduce labor costs. Instituting limited mechanization in the groves (for instance, tilling the soil with a tractor rather than with work animals) required larger spacing between trees and a reduced number of trees per land unit. But the assumption was that the slightly larger intervals compared to Arab citriculture, in addition to more fertilizing and mechanical cultivation, would increase the yield per tree and the total output per dunam. Yet, many of the Jewish immigrants who invested in the industry in these years (1920s–30s) did not have enough capital to invest in a medium-sized or large grove of twenty dunams or more. Thus, many opted to invest in the less expensive land-saving technologies in order to increase grove output. Indeed, the average output of a Jewish-owned grove on the eve of World War II was about ninety to one hundred cases per dunam, of which seventy-five to eighty were intended for export. In contrast, in the Palestinian industry, output per dunam was only about sixty exportable cases due to the lower investment in yield enhancers per land unit. Nonetheless, as shown in table 2.2, the large discrepancy between labor costs in the two sectors compensated considerably for the lower output per dunam and maintained positive profitability of Palestinian citriculture until the outbreak of World War II.

Thus, from 1932 to 1936 some 91,500 dunams of groves were added in the Arab sector. On the eve of World War II, Arab-owned groves covered some 150,000 dunams while Jewish-owned groves were only slightly more extensive, with some 155,000 dunams. A similar trajectory was evident with regard to exportable citrus. Until 1933 most citrus exports originated from the older and more productive Arab-owned groves. In 1934 the balance changed, and in the five years remaining until World War II about 60 percent of citrus fruit exports came from Jewish-owned groves.

During the Mandate period many additional technological improvements were introduced in the citriculture of both sectors. These were mainly land-saving improvements aimed at increasing output per land unit. The method of producing citrus seedlings was enhanced, and instead of growing them in the grove itself, as in pre-Mandate years, they were grown in nurseries and sold to citrus growers ready for grafting. This cut more than two years off the process of bringing a young grove to full production. Other improvements involved pest and disease control, strict irrigation procedures and timing, and above all more frequent use of manure and fertilizers. Contemporary sources indicate that these improvements were introduced in both sectors with much success. In Jewish citriculture, for which we have slightly more data, from 1913 to 1937 these improvements led to a ninefold increase in production at the fifth year from planting mark, from about five cases per dunam in 1913 to about forty-five cases in 1937. A similar trajectory was evident in the Arab sector.[7]

The most sophisticated technological methods were employed in places reached by the spreading electricity grid, for instance in the vicinity of Sarafand: i.e., electrically operated water pumps for groundwater and even for irrigating groves with underground pipes that facilitated mechanical cultivation within the grove itself. This was the "California method" used in California's well-developed citrus industry and perceived as the height of technological progress.[8]

Zionist sources from the 1930s testify to these technological improvements in a clearly concerned tone. "Sheikh Shaker (Abu Kishk) and his brothers, who sold most of the *miri* land that they owned, first paid off the oppressive large debts (about 10,000 Palestine pounds)—mortgages, etc.—and apart from that planted a 145-dunam grove near their home, with a fifteen-horsepower motor and a six-inch pump," relates a Zionist intelligence agent.[9] (*Miri* land was land owned by the ruler, but fellahin had the rights to inherit, mortgage, and even sell it.) A similar report was submitted about Shaykh Muwannes, the village on the northern bank of the al-Auja/Yarkon River. The fellahin "installed modern motors and pumps to pump water from the river . . . and all of them [did so] with modern machines and new irrigation facilities. They irrigate even the vegetable areas, which now amount to 2,000 dunams, by means of pumps and metal tubes. One hardly sees [pumping by] animal labor in the area any longer."[10] The Zionist statistician Ze'ev Smilansky, unlike his much more famous and politically moderate relative, Moshe Smilansky, watched with growing anxiety the ability of Arab citrus fellahin to skillfully and quickly adapt new technologies:

> Just a few years ago, one could find in the nearby villages wells with a beast turning the horizontal wheel. Now, all thirty-six wells in Zarnuqa are mechanized. Sarafand has groves that receive electricity. Some grove owners use the California irrigation method. Instead of planting the trees close together and in crooked rows, as in the previous method, our neighbors have begun to mark straight and widely spaced rows.[11]

With regard to picking and packing the fruit, in both sectors very limited use was made of mechanized packing carried out in central packing houses. Most of the packing remained as it had been when the industry was first established in the latter half of the nineteenth century, namely, groups of packers sat on the ground and packed hundreds and thousands of cases rapidly and skillfully, at a much lower cost than the alternative— investing in a mechanized packing house and its daily operation.

The aspirations of major entrepreneurs in both sectors to introduce capital—and technology-rich "European" or "California" models—were only partially realized. Table 2.2 well illustrates the limitations placed on these aspirations by Palestine's economic circumstances. The large supply of labor, versus the considerably low supply of land and capital in proportion to labor, dampened any attempts at implementing such plans. The groves in both sectors remained mostly small to medium sized (five to twenty dunams) and were cultivated manually. Indeed, a census of groves and grove growers held by the Citrus Control Board for 1942 shows that some 66 percent of groves in both sectors were small to medium sized. Moreover, additional censuses held by the Citrus Control Board during World War II, which reflected the composition of the industry and the areas it covered before the war (because during the six years of the war no new land was added), show that the average size of a grove in the Jewish sector was about twenty dunams and in the Arab sector was about thirty-two dunams. These data reinforce the claim that the basic unit of the countrywide industry, with its two national divisions, was a grove of approximately uniform size. It combined labor intensity with limited technological improvements, with the aim of increasing output rather than reducing use of manual labor or modernization per se.[12]

Spatial Distribution

The geographical distribution of Palestinian-Arab citriculture was affected by two major factors: availability of groundwater for irrigation of the groves and the cost of transporting the fruit from the grove to the port for export. During the entire period discussed here, the main port used was the Jaffa Port. As stated above, in the vicinity of Jaffa there was a considerable supply of groundwater fairly close to the surface. Throughout the period until World War I and in the early 1920s the fruit was transported using camel caravans, with orange crates placed on both sides of the camel's hump. Thus, proximity to the Jaffa Port was a major consideration in calculating the costs of investment in groves and an essential factor determining the concentration of Arab citriculture in the environs of Jaffa over a considerable period. Until the advent of the Palestinian planting momentum in 1932, the great majority of Palestinian-Arab-owned citrus groves were located in the Jaffa area. Another gradually evolving citrus area was the Ramle subdistrict, which like the belt of Zionist moshavot consisting of Rehovot, Rishon Lezion, and Nes Ziona, was quite close to the Jaffa Port, a distance of about twenty-two kilometers. Another citrus area was near the city of Gaza, where groundwater was fairly close to the surface and whose port served as a point of departure for the shipping of products not purchased in the domestic market. The plains near the city of Acre provided convenient land for citrus cultivation as well, and there too groundwater was accessible. However, during the Mandate period the Acre region was known for its low-quality oranges and as a location affected by intractable citrus diseases. For this reason, citrus fruit from the vicinity of Acre was sold locally.[13]

With the development of new modes of transportation in British Mandate Palestine, citrus fruit began to be transported by truck instead of camel from the latter half of the 1920s. This development concurred with the planting surge in the two sectors. Indeed, geographical distribution of the Palestinian-Arab citrus industry from the mid-1930s shows that the industry significantly expanded to areas more distant from Jaffa. The improved transportation infrastructure and the low price of land in these areas compared to the Jaffa region were major factors that affected the industry's growing dispersion in this period. Indeed, the Jaffa subdistrict maintained its primacy, with some 39 percent of the land devoted to Palestinian-Arab groves. However, the Ramle subdistrict grew to include some 27 percent of Palestinian-Arab citriculture, and the nearby Tulkarm subdistrict encompassed some 11 percent of grove acreage. Thus, the area devoted to citrus cultivation in the Ramle and Tulkarm subdistricts together almost equaled the entire Arab citrus area in the Jaffa subdistrict. Gaza, with 15 percent of the citrus land, and Acre, with 8 percent, completed the picture.

Notably, Zionist citriculture had a similar spatial distribution. Indeed, instead of the Jaffa region the initial core of Zionist citriculture was concentrated in the concentric circle of the moshavot Petah Tikva, Rehovot, and Nes Ziona, around Jaffa. But there too no real expansion was evident before the late 1920s, and most of the expansion in the 1930s was to areas in the vicinity of Arab-owned groves in the Ramle and Tulkarm subdistricts.[14]

The physical proximity of the two sectors, and the fact that Jewish citriculture grew by embracing the local Arab model, facilitated various collaborations. For example, as seen above, it was not rare for experts on both sides to consult with each other. The *bayari* was the local expert who conveyed to Zionist citriculture knowledge and expertise accumulated in the field, while the fruit of both sectors was often marketed using business cooperation and even ad hoc partnerships. Sometimes these were Arab merchants who purchased fruit from Jewish grove owners and marketed it under their own trademark. But as the 1930s proceeded, and with profits dropping constantly, both sectors were compelled to find ways to deal with the crisis. In Zionist citriculture, as a result of the higher labor costs and the sharper drop in profits, the entire system underwent reorganization and most citrus growers joined marketing cooperatives. These co-ops supervised the quality of the exported fruit and its packing, and thanks to their united bargaining power managed to force the exporters and industry suppliers to reduce their prices. Nonetheless, they also needed to increase

4. An aerial view of the Jaffa Port, 1937. Israel National Photo Collection, Zoltan Kluger.

the supply of fruit in order to maintain their bargaining power. Fruit produced by Arab citrus growers, of which a packed case at the grove gate was cheaper than the same packed case in Zionist citriculture, was one of the solutions. In addition, Arab citrus growers who marketed through the Jewish co-ops received higher returns per case in the export markets than they would have if marketing independently. This was due to the better packing and sorting by the co-ops as well as to their bargaining power.[15]

The Citrus Industry and Palestinian-Arab Social Stratification

The citrus industry produced three categories of functionaries who operated within it from the early twentieth century until 1948:

1. Grove owners (some of whom also became citrus merchants)
2. Citrus merchants (some of whom also owned groves, packing houses, and transport companies)
3. Grove managers, *bayaris*, and laborers

The most conspicuous socioeconomic upgrade was of people from the third category, called *bayariya* (i.e., grove managers). The *bayariya* found ways of benefiting from the various deals that evolved around the grove and over time accumulated capital, which they invested by buying lots and small grove plots or by becoming involved in other parts of the industry, such as fertilization, packing, and transport. Thus, people from the lower class became, in time, owners of grove plots that gradually grew in size. Some of those who originated from rural areas returned to their villages after accumulating enough capital as *bayariya*, and there they planted new groves. Stories tell of *bayariya* from villages such as Sarafand, Bayt Nabala, Dayr Tarif, Qaqun, and Umm Khaled who invested in the local citrus industry after spending a certain amount of time in the city. Some of Jaffa's grove owners began by working as *bayariya* for large citrus growers and after a while planted their own groves and joined the first category. This was true, for example, of Mustafa Abu Sayef, Isma'il 'Ashur (originally from Nablus), Muhammad Shanir, and Kamel Abu Sayef.[16]

At the same time, a special dependent relationship was often formed between the *bayariya* and the grove owners. This was a certain type of social subordination, where all members of the *bayari*'s family served the family of the grove owner, prepared their food, cleaned their house, and saw to all their needs while at the grove. Anwar Hamed described the relationship between the families of the citrus grower and *al-bayari*. He recorded the daily schedule of Ibrahim al-Bayari: "In addition to his guard duties, he had various chores. . . . One of his duties was to select the best of the grove's fruit and send it to Abu Salim's [the grove owner's] house in reed baskets."[17] Another chore was to supply food for social events that took place at the grove owner's home. According to this report, all members of the *al-bayari*'s family were in the service of the citrus grower's family when necessary and their work was not restricted to caring for the grove.

Interestingly, from a social perspective the citrus growers had to maneuver between several different and sometimes contrasting worlds. On one hand they stood on national stages and gave speeches in the spirit of the national struggle about not cooperating with the British and the Jews. But for business purposes, particularly in the citrus industry, they were not averse to collaborating with the Jews and the British, with whom they maintained strong economic and social ties.[18] For example, Anwar Hamed described such a relationship that crossed religious and national boundaries. He spoke about a weekly ritual repeated every Friday at the home of a well-known citrus grower in Jaffa. In attendance were "Abu Elias, owner of the export office," "Khawaja Ishaq," a Jew who held a prominent position in a maritime transport company, and "Major Jeffrey," a British official. These three, tells Hamed, spend the entire Friday with the *bayari*. "They begin with a morning feast, consisting of a plate of humus topped with fried meat in olive oil and pine nuts. This is accompanied, of course, by cream cheese, labaneh, and tea. After the meal they smoke a nargila together and discuss matters pertaining to their joint business, in good fluent English."[19]

Political Leanings of Figures within the Industry

As is well known, the British Mandate period witnessed the rapid rise of Palestinian nationalism and national consciousness. Practitioners in the citrus industry, from laborers to wealthy entrepreneurs, were part and parcel of this development. Based on written sources and on the interviews we held, it appears that members of the first category of veteran grove owners mostly tended to belong to the Nashashibi opposition (the Barkat, Bitar, al-Taji, al-Faruqi, and al-Darhali families). The testimonies and the data form the impression that most members of the other categories, particularly the newly rich and citrus growers of rural origin, as well as migrants from other cities, supported the Husaynis, the al-Istiqlal Party, and the Youth Congress (the 'Abd al-Rahim, al-Khaldi, Baydas, Abu Kishk, and Abu Khadra families). The major merchants involved in the citrus industry easily acquired influential positions among the Jaffa elite. These people were members of either the representative institutions (city council, chamber of commerce, and various societies) or of various national organizations and parties.

Members of the official municipal and national organs who were part of the citrus industry were affiliated mainly with the Nashashibi opposition and its allies from among the independent elements (members of the National Defense Party led by the Nashashibis). As stated, these were primarily members of the veteran Jaffa families who at the end of the Ottoman period had had ties with the Ottoman administration, and they were also embraced by the British Mandate apparatus. In some cases, the affiliation of a certain family with the traditional camps (Husayni or Nashashibi) was not consistent with the political and economic conduct of senior members of these families who went through a process of social mobility, usually rising in rank. Once the status of those who had traditionally supported the Husayni camp (some members of the Baydas family, for example) improved, their political views usually became more moderate, obscuring their former differences with supporters of the Nashashibi opposition.

From World War II to the Nakba

In its first year World War II caused a sharp drop in citrus exports, and by its second year all citrus exports ceased.[20] Commercial sailing in the Mediterranean became extremely dangerous, ships were converted for war purposes, Europe's gates were closed, and the large UK market became a war economy. Not only were plantings completely halted due to a lack of resources for the routine cultivation of groves, their irrigation, and picking of fruit, but also the quality of work in the groves diminished significantly, and many of the groves were neglected. The entire industry entered a very long period of continuous losses. Indeed, in time some of the crops were sold to Allied forces stationed in the Middle East, and others were utilized in the citrus by-product industry that rapidly developed during the war, particularly for the manufacture of juice and jams. But this was not enough to cover the losses. The government granted loans to citrus growers to cover their current expenses and deferred the repayment of these loans until the end of the war. The loans were often not enough to cover regular cultivation expenditures and some citrus growers, mainly Jewish, were compelled to sell grove equipment to pay for cultivation. The diminishing quality of cultivation, and particularly the lack of fertilizers, also led to a constant drop in crop output per dunam. Whereas in 1939 production per grove in the countrywide industry was sixty to seventy-five export cases of oranges per dunam, by 1945 it had dropped to twenty-four cases per dunam.[21]

The losses of the entire industry during World War II were estimated at about ten million Palestine pounds. However, the losses of the Jewish citrus growers appear to have been greater than those of the Arabs. Government data indicate that of about 155,000 dunams of groves in the Jewish sector in 1939, only 114,000 (73 percent) remained by the end of the war. Then again, leaders of the Jewish industry claimed that some 55,000 dunams of Jewish-owned groves were abandoned during the war and only 100,000 dunams (about 65 percent of the area cultivated in 1939) remained. Indeed, some of these lands were sold for urban usages. Nonetheless, the high labor costs in the Jewish sector and the larger investment per dunam there than in the Arab sector were crucial factors leading to neglect of the citrus work and the abandoning of tens of thousands of dunams of Jewish-owned groves. The Arab sector suffered less loss of citrus land. In 1945 there were about 122,000 dunams of Arab-owned groves. This was a drop of some 28,000 dunams (about 19 percent) compared to the approximately 150,000 dunams of groves in the Arab sector in the fall of 1939. But some 81 percent of Arab citrus lands remained cultivated, versus some 73 percent of Jewish-owned citrus lands. Arab citrus growers also requested fewer government loans during the war than Jewish growers. The lower labor costs in Arab citriculture compared to its Jewish counterpart were an important factor. But this was also aided by the general economic prosperity of Palestinian-Arab society during the war years.[22]

After the war a slow period of recovery began, due primarily to the time needed to return grove productivity to prewar levels. The slow recovery of the industry was also related to the slow recovery of the European and British economies and to the lack of raw materials for packing the fruit. In the three years from the end of World War II until the Nakba, overall citrus production gradually grew, but this process was interrupted early on by the local outbreak of war over the fate of the country.

Concurrent with the recovery process, new plantings were initiated, particularly in the Arab sector: the Arab Citriculture Census in 1948 indicates that by the eve of the Nakba the center of Arab citriculture had shifted to the Ramle subdistrict, which encompassed some 45 percent of Palestinian-Arab citrus lands. The Jaffa subdistrict encompassed some 35 percent of the lands. Some of the grove lands near Jaffa appear to have

Table 2.3

Net Return per Dunam, 1947–48 Season

	Current prices (LP)	1936 prices (LP)
40 exportable cases, at 450 mils/case	18.0	5.94
35 nonexportable cases, at 100 mils/case	03.5	1.16
Total sales per dunam	21.5	7.09
Maintenance costs per dunam	14.0	4.62
Net return per dunam	07.5	2.47

Source: Estimates provided by the Citrus Marketing Board, 1947–48, quoted in Barakat, *Observation*, 9.

Table 2.4

Distribution of Grove Land by Districts, 1948

District	Percentage
Ramle	44.9
Jaffa	34.8
Tulkarem	11.4
Gaza	5.3
Acre	3.3
Other	0.3
Total	100.0

Source: "Census of Arab Citrus Groves" (1948–51), Israel State Archives.

been converted to urban usages throughout the war and subsequently due to the development of Jaffa, Tel Aviv, and several villages in the area.[23]

Economic data on the country's citrus industry for the tumultuous years of 1945–48 are scarce. Table 2.3 presents very general data on the profit and loss of productive groves on the eve of the Nakba. The data are not comparable with the more detailed data for the years up to 1939 and even up to 1945. Nevertheless, the one item that can indeed be compared is the cost of routine cultivation and maintenance per dunam. This cost, calculated for the entire industry, is very similar to the cost of maintaining an Arab-owned grove in 1939: 4.62 Palestine pounds per dunam in 1947 versus some 4.84 Palestine pounds per dunam in 1939 (in 1936 prices; see tables). This low cost indicates the continuous lack of sufficient funding for maintaining the groves, beginning from the world war, but it also confirms information provided by other contemporary sources, namely that during and after the war there was a surge in the employment of Arab workers in the Jewish industry, with the latter constituting up to 75 percent of all employees.[24]

The Israeli Census of Pre-1948 Arab Groves

In late 1948, before the 1948 War was even over, Israel's temporary government launched a census of Arab citrus groves that had reverted to its control during the war. These groves were legally defined by Israel as "abandoned," meaning that they were owned by Palestinians who had become refugees and hence, in Israel's view, had "abandoned" their property. The census, called the "Census of Arab Citrus Groves" (1948), was conducted with a double intention: to gain information regarding claims of Palestinian grove owners demanding the return of their assets and to classify groves into those that could be immediately cultivated and those that could not. The census data present some interesting details on Palestinian-Arab citrus growing immediately preceding the war. Nevertheless, the census also had several limitations: first, it included only about 80 percent of Palestinian citrus land during the Mandate period; namely, only grove lands that had reverted to the control of the State of Israel. It did not include most of the citrus land in the Gaza district, which was relegated to Egyptian control, or groves of the Mandate Tulkarm region that were annexed to Jordan. Second, even for the land that was included in the census, the data we have is incomplete, because we were unable to procure the entire census.

One can gain some important insights regarding the Palestinian citrus industry as it stood just before the 1948 War broke out.

First, the extent of planted area in the central citrus-growing region owned by Palestinians was larger than previously known. It did not cover approximately 150,000 dunams as estimated thus far, but rather about 193,000 dunams, a third larger than previously thought. This count, as mentioned above, did not include grove land in the Gaza region and part of the Tulkarm region. Second, according to the census, 3,291 people owned groves until 1948. Moreover, about 10 percent of registered owners were partnerships, usually of family members, meaning that we can

5. The Israeli "Census of Arab Citrus Groves," 1948. Israel State Archives, file G-2/3118.

estimate that the number of owners in citrus-growing areas transferred to the control of Israel numbered about 3,600 people. These people lived in 108 locations; that is, in at least one-fifth of the 530 villages that were depopulated during the 1948 War. It can further be estimated that the citrus industry was a significant source of livelihood for these villages, and in some of them, especially those around Jaffa, Ramle, and eventually Tulkarm, it was a central source of livelihood.

The census also teaches us about the interior division of grove ownership within the Palestinian-Arab sector (see table 2.6).

The data of this census reveal that about 36 percent of all grove owners had small to medium-sized groves (between one and twenty dunams). Fifty-seven percent of all grove owners had groves that were between one

Table 2.5
Ownership by Number of Owners, Size of Grove, 1948

Size of grove (dunams)	Area of total (dunams)	Total area (%)	Number of owners	Total ownership (%)
1–9	3,654	1.9	613	18.6
10–19	9,537	4.9	617	18.7
20–39	21,498	11.1	723	22.0
40–59	19,155	9.9	382	11.6
60–79	18,493	9.6	266	8.1
80–99	18,068	9.4	202	6.1
100–199	48,165	24.9	342	10.4
≥200	54,639	28.3	146	4.5
Total	193,209	100.0	3,291	100.0

Source: "Census of Arab Citrus Groves" (1948–51), Israel State Archives.

Table 2.6
Ownership and Area by Size of Grove, 1948

Size (dunams)	Total ownership (%)	Total grove area owned (%)
1–9	18	2
10–19	18	4
20–39	21	11
40–59	12	10
60–79	8	9
80–99	6	9
100–199	10	25
≥200	4	28
Unknown	3	2
Total	100	100

Source: "Census of Arab Citrus Groves" (1948–51), Israel State Archives.

and forty dunams. These figures strengthen our previous claim, supported also by the interviews we conducted, about the creation of a middle class in Palestinian villages. This class stood above the average Palestinian farmer, who was still bound by subsistence farming, and it was created due to the citrus industry. Furthermore, according to British data from 1945 (which are arranged slightly differently than the Israel census from 1948 to 1950), only 8 percent of owners had groves smaller than six dunams.

Table 2.7
Grove Ownership in the Palestinian-Arab Sector, 1945

Grove size (dunams)	Ownership of grove lands (%)	% of all owners
0–5	0.5	8.0
6–10	1.5	10.0
11–20	5.0	19.0
21–50	16.0	28.0
51–100	24.0	20.0
≥101	53.0	15.0
Total	100.0	100.0

Source: Anglo-American Committee, Supplement to Survey of Palestine, 36.

Table 2.8
Ownership of Groves by Women, 1948

	% Total		Area (dunams)	
District	Man-Owned	Woman-Owned	Man-Owned	Woman-Owned
Ramle	97.5	2.5	76,247	1,935
Jaffa	96.9	3.1	58,222	1,888
Tulkarem	96.4	3.6	34,654	1,296
Gaza	100.0	0.0	12,698	0
Acre	98.9	1.1	5,609	65
Haifa	100.0	0.0	485	0
Hebron	92.7	7.3	102	8
Total[a]	93.7	2.7	188,017	5,192

Source: "Census of Arab Citrus Groves" (1948–51), Israel State Archives.
[a] Total does not equal 100 percent because gender of 3.6 percent of the owners could not be identified.

Since a five-dunam grove could, throughout most of this time period, provide its owners with a good annual income that would place them above the salary of a farmer working mainly for sustenance, one could estimate that the middle class in Palestinian-Arab villages, established by the citrus industry, included some 50–60 percent of grove owners. On the other hand, the British figures and the Israeli census show that about 15 percent of Arab grove owners owned about 53 percent of all Palestinian-Arab citrus lands in 1948, and according to the British data about 35 percent of them owned 77 percent of the land (the Israeli census's figures are similar: 41 percent of owners held 82 percent of all grove land). This information agrees with other sources of the time, some of which have been presented above, which demonstrate the central role that large capitalists, mainly dwelling in Jaffa, had in influencing production and marketing in the Arab citrus industry.

Finally, the Israeli census lists many partnerships (mostly among people from the same family) as owners of groves. Interestingly, the census also indicates that about 3 percent of owners were women (see table 2.8).

The Role of Ottoman and British Authorities in the Industry

As far as known from existing research, the Ottoman authorities made attempts to boost the industry, particularly through various improvements introduced in the city of Jaffa and its port. Their attitude to Zionist colonization was strongly affected by pressure applied by the major global powers on the one hand and by their wish to maintain control over their own territories and their populace on the other. As discussed above, the British government intervened with the Ottomans against the local stakeholders, Shaykh Salim and the Pardes association, in favor of the British shipping company. But as a rule it may be assumed that, ultimately, the Ottomans let the industry develop with no real interference.[25]

In the first years of British rule in Palestine, the Mandate government's policy about the industry was affected by the classical liberal perception common at the time, that the role of the government is to establish conditions facilitating activity of a market economy. Thus, so long as the industry remained profitable and aroused no political strife, the government mostly followed a policy of nonintervention with regard to the industry and its activities.[26]

Growing Palestinian resistance to Zionist colonization, as well as the wish to introduce modernized management of Mandatory Palestine's society and economy, led to a change in Mandate policy with regard to the industry as well. The change was evident from 1929 and was characterized by growing intervention of the Mandate government in the citrus industry. A major stimulus appears to have been the rampant violence in 1929, as well as the inquiry commissions established consequently and the recommendations to adapt policy concerning Palestinian agriculture and fellahin in response to the events of 1929.

In February 1931 a General Agricultural Council was established. Its main function was to provide Jews and Arabs with room and opportunity to discuss policies pertaining to domestic agricultural issues, under the supervision of Mandate officials. The council also established nine committees to discuss specific issues pertaining to each committee's field of expertise.[27]

The operations of this organ have yet to be researched. However, the most important committee established by the General Agricultural Council seems to have been the one that dealt with the citrus industry, called the Citrus Fruit Committee. It consisted of seven Arab and seven Jewish representatives, as well as two government officials, one of whom served as the head. Until April 1939 the committee held eighty-seven meetings, meaning that throughout the five months of the season—November to March—the Citrus Fruit Committee convened twice a month on average.

The fourteen members of the committee, excluding government officials, formed a typical cross section of the industry's leadership within the two national sectors. Most were residents of Jaffa and Tel Aviv and members of the Arab and Jewish middle class. There was also a representative of the official Zionist leadership, namely a representative of the workers' federation (the Histadrut). Palestinian members included both Christians and Muslims (Sa'id Baydas, Bayruti, Qutran, 'Abdul Qader Abu Rabah, 'Izzat Bey al-Taji, Fa'iq Talamas, François Gélat) who were mostly members of the Nashashibi opposition or independent, while a small number were affiliated with the Husaynis. The Zionist members were from the private "civil" and "workers" (i.e., the Labor Movement) sections of the Yishuv. Hence, members of the committee were from among the important second rank of the political and social leadership of the two national societies.

The committee dealt with various matters pertaining to the industry, and its discussions reflected the government's growing intervention, as well as that of the industry's two national leaderships, in attempts to regularize and centralize the industry's operations. For instance, the committee discussed the issue of agricultural education, primarily attempts to encourage grove owners to participate in guidance activities run by experimental agricultural stations developed by the government for this purpose. However, the committee primarily focused on trying to coordinate operations to benefit the entire industry. Such efforts included encouraging both sectors to work jointly to battle pests and diseases that emerged from time to time, funding advertising campaigns for local citrus fruit in British and continental markets, supervising the quality of the fruit's packing, recommending a uniform size for export cases, and enhancing supervision of the fruit's quality in order to maintain its reputation. These discussions usually ended in recommendations submitted to the high commissioner, who had the authority to grant them binding status.

The local press, both Hebrew and Arabic, reported on the committee's discussions, as did the local agricultural industry's newspapers, and from time to time the citrus growers and merchants expressed their opinions on the discussions and on the issues discussed. Thus, the process was not restricted to members of the committee; rather, the citrus growers were included as well.

The committee's discussions reflected a constant tension between the two national sectors as well as mutual suspicions. Beyond the national rivalry, there were also various economic interests. As stated above, from 1935 Jewish citriculture began to experience a constant and quite sharp drop in profits, while its Arab counterpart continued to receive fairly nice returns on its investments. Thus, the Jewish representatives on the committee were interested in promoting programs that promised to enhance profits by eventually reducing the supply of citrus fruit shipped to overseas markets. These programs included increasing supervision of the quality of exported fruit, advertising, and centralization of export and marketing methods. The Arab representatives, in contrast, who were not under threat of constantly decreasing profits, were interested in continuing to market large quantities of fruit, maintaining their operations and their fruit unsupervised, and keeping their control over the Arab sector's exports. Therefore, they regularly objected to imposing taxes on exports to fund advertising, or to attempts to use unified marketing methods in British and continental markets. In addition, the two industries were split internally as well. The basic rift in the Jewish industry was between members of old-time moshavot, who supported private entrepreneurship, and members of the centrally controlled socialist Labor Movement, who in time gained a gradually growing role in citrus production. But even among advocates of private entrepreneurship, there were strong rivalries and disagreements both on a personal level and with regard to the future of the industry. On one side was the strongest figure in the Jewish industry, Yitzhak Rokach, who put all his efforts into uniting not only the Jewish sector but also the entire national industry under one umbrella organization. As he saw it, this was the only way to maintain the industry's profitability. He was countered by members of the Pardes association and other old-time citrus growers who feared loss of their independence. On the Palestinian side the rivalries stemmed mainly from economic competition between industry leaders. To these traditional rivalries were added increasing demands of citrus growers in the Tulkarm and Gaza areas to be included in the industry's decision making.

Along with the mutual suspicions and tension within each sector and between the two national sectors, however, there was also a basic joint interest in protecting the entire industry. Thus, despite the disagreements and tensions, the Citrus Fruit Committee continued to convene almost monthly. The committee's minutes reflect the slow but considerable process of increasing intersector collaboration and reaching compromises in order to protect the industry's interests. The Mandate government, from its perspective, understood that it had neither the ability nor cause to force the industry to centralize production and marketing. Thus, it consistently implemented a policy of consultations and of measured advances toward this goal.[28]

The industry, which began as a private Palestinian-Arab initiative in the mid–nineteenth century and subsequently contended with colonization by Zionist European Jews who entered into competition with the local industry, went through a meaningful transformation during the Mandate period. Local conditions limited the possibility of separate economic development by each sector. They also stimulated more intensive mutual relations than those that existed between Jews and Arabs in other fields in Palestine. With the rising economic hardships of the industry beginning from the late 1930s, intersectoral cooperation burgeoned. It culminated during the years of World War II in the establishment of the only official Arab-Jewish binational organization formed before the Nakba. This unprecedented and unique development is the topic of the next chapter.

3

A Binational Enclave

In mid-January 1941, once it had become evident that the war had brought citrus exports to the United Kingdom and Europe to a halt and that the countrywide citrus industry was in danger of collapse, some two thousand Arab and Jewish citrus growers from all over the country gathered at the Alhambra hall in Jaffa for an emergency meeting.

A reporter for *Haaretz* described the gathering and stressed its uniqueness:

> Some two thousand Jews and Arabs who attended the citrus growers' meeting in Jaffa yesterday, joined in an urgent demand of the local government on four main issues, whose fulfillment in these bitter times would bring great relief to the country's major economic industry—the "backbone" or the "body" of the entire local economy, as designated by one of the speakers. . . . Side by side sat Arab farmers wearing a kufiyyeh and 'igal, city dwellers with their fez or "fayzaliya" (faysaliya), and Jews with their European attire. The large Alhambra cinema was packed and the speeches, given in Arabic and Hebrew, were interrupted by wide applause whenever concern for the citrus growers and the trees was mentioned. . . . The gathering highlighted the shared interests of tens or hundreds of thousands of local residents, both Jews and Arabs.[1]

The reporter for *Davar* used more poetic means to share the event with his readers:

> The cinema hall mentioned was unable to accommodate all the participants, Jews and Arabs from all regions of the citrus industry. The audience was colorful, sitting either in separate groups, separate rows, and some also together, fezzes and kufiyyehs, brimmed hats and uncovered heads, simple caps and shaykh's turbans, faysaliyas [a boat-shaped felt

hat worn by the most fastidious Arab nationalists, emulating the hat worn by Faysal I King of Iraq] and European women's hats, jackets and 'abayas and kiftans, rural people and city dwellers, wearing elegant and decrepit clothes. This entire spectacle was set within the dark hall with its pretension of simulating the centuries old historical building of the Arab caliph in Granada, Spain. Instead of daylight, electricity trickled in through the skylights, supposedly to remind one of the ceiling on that magnificent hall.[2]

Enthusiastic reports of the well-attended meeting at the Alhambra hall appeared not only in the Zionist press. The major Palestinian national newspaper *Filastin*, published in Jaffa, devoted considerable room to an enthused and detailed report of the meeting, its atmosphere, participants, the speeches held, and the decisions reached. "The meeting was a great success, beyond all expectations and more than any other meeting ever before held in Jaffa or in any other town or village. The success was manifested in the order, organization, and quiet that characterized it," the newspaper stated. *Filastin* also sought to emphasize the major role of the Palestinian citrus growers, and particularly the Agricultural Society of the Arab Villages (al-Jam'iyya al-'Arabiyya lilqara al-'Arabiyya), headed by Sa'id Baydas of Shaykh Muwannes, in organizing the meeting. Also mentioned extensively in the newspaper was the fact that the heads of Jewish citriculture thanked their Arab colleagues for organizing the meeting and for hosting it at the Alhambra hall.[3]

The chairman of the assemblage was 'Abd al-Ra'uf al-Bitar, mayor of Jaffa, and it was organized by a joint committee of Arab and Jewish citrus growers, the product of months of effort. Ten speakers were lined up, five from each sector. Conspicuous among the Arab speakers were Sa'id Baydas of Shaykh Muwannes, Shaykh Shaker Abu Kishk of Abu Kishk, and Shaykh Shafiq al-Khatib of Qubayba. On the Jewish side, notable speakers were Yitzhak Rokach, who spoke in both Arabic and Hebrew; Zvi Butkowsky of Hadera, president of the Farmers' Federation; and a citrus grower from Petah Tikva, Miss Elka Goodall, who gave a rousing and impressive speech. All the speeches, aside from that of Yitzhak Rokach, were simultaneously translated into Hebrew and Arabic. The assemblage elected a permanent committee of fifty-six members, twenty-eight from

6. Jaffa Alhambra cinema hall, 1937. Matson (G. Eric and Edith) Photograph Collection, Library of Congress.

each sector. In response to the demand of those present, Miss Goodall was elected to the committee as well. Other members of the committee were leading and well-known figures from both sectors of the industry. The committee appointed an executive body from within its members, the Joint Executive Committee of Arab and Jewish Growers in Palestine, which consisted of twenty-four members, twelve from each national sector.

Participants in the assemblage demanded that the government purchase the season's entire citrus crop at a price that would spare the citrus growers a loss, cancel the agricultural property tax on citrus groves, and promptly cease all foreclosures and auctions of groves whose owners were unable to pay their debts, as well as repeal the arrest warrants sent to some of them. In other words, the participants demanded that the government place the industry under its unqualified protection. The chairman of the assemblage, al-Bitar, sent a telegram to the high commissioner, Harold MacMichael, requesting that the latter meet with the joint representatives of the citrus growers.[4]

The Palestinian-Arab press was divided in its attitude to this conference. The newspapers affiliated with the Husayni camp and its allies (*al-Wihda, al-Difaʻ*) produced modest reports and focused on technical details concerning the industry's economic structure and its anticipated profits for Arab citrus growers, with almost no mention of the binational nature of the gathering.[5] In contrast, as mentioned above, *Filastin*, which was closer to the Nashashibi opposition and its allies, reported on the occurrences in detail and even stressed the need for binational cooperation.[6]

The Alhambra assemblage was unusual in its size and in the array of people who attended it, and it left a strong impression on the press and among citrus growers in both sectors. As evident from the above descriptions and from other contemporary sources, the gathering at Alhambra took place amid equitable and courteous cooperation between the two national sectors of the citrus industry. Moreover, it took many months to organize and plan the gathering, requiring frequent encounters between the representatives of the two sectors, with the aim of achieving a common goal shared by the two national sections of the countrywide industry. The joint seating arrangements of thousands of citrus growers in a single hall were also not a common sight. In addition, the equally apportioned speeches, establishment of a joint committee on an equal basis, and the fact that the speeches were simultaneously translated each into the language of the other were also a clear manifestation of principles stressed in conflict resolution and reconciliation research: recognition of the identity and culture of the other and showing respect for the other, his or her identity, and culture.[7] More than anything, the positive, enthusiastic, and colorful reports on the gathering in the contemporary press, with all its ideological and national divisions, also contributed to conveying a message of joint action and reconciliation as manifested in the assembly.

However, the Alhambra assemblage was not one of a kind, nor was it the first equal meeting of the two national sectors of Palestine's citrus industry. It was also not the last. As will be detailed below, institutional cooperation between the Palestinian-Arab citrus industry and its Zionist counterpart as collectives had begun in the early 1920s and continued until April 1948, only about a month and a half before the end of the British Mandate. Hence, this was not a one-time phenomenon, rather a reality that existed throughout most of the British rule of Palestine. One of its most important features was the gradual development from instances of mutual cooperation in various domains in the 1920s and 1930s, as well as from a joint reality of commercial collaboration (see previous chapters), to a unique binational consociational structure and reality, which emerged concurrently with the Alhambra gathering and continued uninterrupted throughout the World War II years and the three years from the end of the world war until eruption of the War of 1948.

Theoretical Framework[8]

Our approach in analyzing the processes that helped facilitate the creation of the citrus industry's binational enclave at the outbreak of World War II is informed mainly by two conceptual frameworks: Mancur Olson's theory regarding the "Logic of Collective Action" and the intergroup "contact hypothesis" formulated by the renowned social psychologist Gordon Allport.[9]

Olson showed that in an industry with multiple firms—and the citrus industry included thousands of firms—each single firm has no interest in reducing its production so that the entire industry will increase its profitability. Olson claims that such a firm will be motivated to reduce its production if the rise in prices, and hence the rise in revenue, generated by reducing the overall supply will be so high that it covers the loss incurred by diminishing production. But according to Olson, in a market with multiple firms such as the citrus industry in the period discussed here, the marginal revenue of a firm derived from reducing its production would be significantly lower than the reduction in this firm's marginal cost of production. This situation becomes even more acute when the industry encompasses different-sized firms. Large firms will benefit from the reduction of overall production more than small and medium-sized firms, which will receive only a small part of the profit derived from this reduction because their part in the overall industry is smaller. Hence, only a severe economic crisis that affects an entire industry will push most firms to take part in a joint action of reducing their output for the benefit of the collective.[10]

In his comprehensive, sophisticated, and well-documented study *The Nature of Prejudice*, Allport proposed five parameters or conditions that he considered essential for facilitating the reduction of a group's prejudice toward other groups and in enabling more accommodating relationships between the groups. It should be emphasized that Allport was well aware of the possible reversal of reductions in a group's prejudices. Allport's approach still stands at the center of many studies about and practical policies for building trust and cooperation between groups. A recent meta-analysis of 515 studies that examined relationships between intergroup contact and prejudice confirmed the validity of Allport's approach.[11]

Allport postulated that groups may reach mutual accommodation if the following conditions are fulfilled: (1) the groups have common goals; (2) the groups work together to achieve their common goals, which leads to intergroup cooperation; (3) the groups that work together to achieve the common goals enjoy equal status (the equal status is limited to the specific groups that work together—it does not necessarily include the larger societies from which the small groups originate); (4) the groups are supported by authorities, laws, or customs; (5) there is personal interaction between members of the groups.[12]

Our claim is that from the late nineteenth century until the outbreak of World War II a dialectic relationship of competition and cooperation between the Arab and Jewish citrus industries took place. Along the way, some of Allport's conditions were fulfilled. However, only upon the outbreak of the war were all these conditions met. This, accompanied by the severe economic crisis that plagued Palestine during the first few years of the war, facilitated the establishment of the country's binational citrus enclave. The following section details this process.

Notably, the citrus binational setting in which the two national sectors operated from 1940 to 1948 was generated independently of binational ideologies proposed at the time by various political and ideological individuals and organizations. Moreover, the latter proposals were never realized in practice, while the institutionalized citriculture industry, with its tens of thousands of members, constituted a living example of an active, dynamic, and effective binational system.[13]

Until the Outbreak of World War II

As shown in previous chapters of this book, expert information was exchanged between the two national sectors on the level of individual citrus groves. Jewish citrus growers learned cultivation, picking, packing, and management methods from Arab citrus growers and employed Arab experts as *bayaris* who served as professional managers of the groves. Arab citrus growers consulted with Jewish Colonization Association agronomists and Zionist agronomists on various horticultural issues.

Moreover, joint encounters between Jewish and Arab laborers occurred constantly during the long hours and days of working together in the groves. During the period examined here the Labor Movement, as well as much of previous and current Zionist and Israeli research on this period, emphasized efforts to encourage use of "Hebrew labor," particularly in the Zionist citrus industry. In contrast, pre-1948 Palestinian leadership and the British stressed the fact that efforts to promote Hebrew labor were also, and primarily, aimed at removing Arab laborers from the Zionist labor market.[14] In this regard, the "struggle for Hebrew labor" was an important factor that did not contribute to the reduction of prejudice. Nevertheless, a few contemporary testimonies indicate that throughout the entire period discussed here the groves were also a site in which Jewish-Zionist and Palestinian-Arab laborers worked, rested, and learned from each other. While the attempts to bifurcate the citrus labor market into two separate national components were well documented and much discussed, the friendly day-to-day encounters between Arabs and Jews were only rarely documented. In some cases these relationships, following the distinction coined by Rafi Nets-Zehngut, could be defined as "passive reconciliation." Other testimonies point to real friendships between Jewish and Arab workers.[15]

Joint Exhibitions

At the beginning of the British Mandate period, the government attempted to encourage collaborations between the industry's two sectors. In a joint meeting of citrus growers from the two sectors (represented on the Palestinian side by 'Omar al-Bitar and 'Abdullah al-Dajani), headed by a British official, a decision was made to organize joint agricultural exhibitions in the summer months and joint citrus exhibitions in the winter months. Indeed, in 1926, 1927, and 1929, joint Jewish-Arab citrus exhibitions were held in mid-February. In the summer of 1926, a joint agricultural exhibition was also held, displaying a variety of agricultural crops. The citrus exhibitions were organized by representatives of the Mandatory government who headed the organizing committees, representatives of the municipalities of Jaffa and Tel Aviv, and representatives of the Arab and Jewish citrus growers and their associations. (The agricultural exhibitions as well were organized by a committee headed by a government representative, together with Arab and Jewish representatives as well as representatives of the German settlers.) Notably, several prominent Palestinian leaders from the Husayni camp, such as Alfred Rok, also took part in organizing the citrus exhibitions. The exhibitions themselves were attended by hundreds of citrus growers from both sectors, and they included prize-winning competitions related to the industry—for instance, for the most attractive packaging and booth. Rok participated in all three exhibitions and won several prizes, as reported in the contemporary press.

Nonetheless, although the organization and running of three joint exhibitions in consecutive years attests to a reality of constant and public

7. Program from the Jaffa Orange Show, 1927. Courtesy of Kedem Auction House Ltd.

collaboration, they also served as a focus for and manifestation of national tensions between the two sectors. The Hebrew press proudly stressed the achievements of Jewish citrus growers and their various associations, particularly the Pardes cooperative, while minimizing any mention of Palestinian growers. At the same time, although the newspaper *Filastin* was in favor of the exhibitions, it also clearly articulated the national conflict that they reflected. Its reporters criticized the Mandate government and the organizing committee for choosing to hold the exhibitions in Tel Aviv at the local fairgrounds (at that time in the southern part of the city), although advertised as the "Jaffa Orange Show." The newspaper's reporters also contended that the exhibitions' choice of location and use of the English language in some of them was an insult to national honor. In addition, it voiced strong criticism of the organizing committee and the Mandate administration for the small number of representatives from among the "nationalists" (*watani*, i.e., Arab Palestinians) as compared to the Jewish representatives: "Indeed, the citrus fruit is 'nationalist,' neither Jewish nor Zionist," claimed the paper. *Filastin* was sharply critical of the "nationalist" Arab Palestinians who made no effort to send a sufficiently respectable delegation to the exhibitions and was indignant at the meager place allocated to the industry's "native born" (i.e., native Palestinians). Nonetheless, coverage of the 1929 exhibition, which took place in February, before the violent conflagration in the fall of that year, was more positive. *Filastin* praised the Jewish presenters, who this time added signs and explanations in Arabic.[16]

Joint and Separate Institutions

This state of affairs—of collaboration on one hand and consideration for the interests of the national movement with which the citrus growers were affiliated on the other—was characteristic to a large degree of the atmosphere within both sectors in the 1930s. Each sector's inward focus was countered by processes that drew the two national citriculture sectors toward each other. The great planting momentum from 1925 onward not only attracted to the industry new investors, both Arab and Jewish, and significantly expanded its geographical distribution, but also transformed Jewish citriculture into the larger of the two sectors. This changed the balance of power within the industry. The violent events of 1929 and the various committees formed as a result convinced some of the Jewish citrus growers that the Zionist sector must unite under one organizational umbrella. At the initiative of Shmuel Tolkowsky, a Zionist citrus grower and activist from among the nonlabor ("civic") faction of the Zionist community, as well as other citrus merchants and growers from that faction—such as Yitzhak Rokach, Zalman Jacobson, and Lazar (Elazar) Rabinovitz—the Jaffa Citrus Exchange was established in 1929. Its main goal was to form a Zionist marketing cartel that would include all Jewish citrus growers. However, due to the conflicting interests and ideological rivalry between the "civic" and "labor" factions within the Yishuv and the fact that the industry's normal course and profitability were not affected by the events of 1929, the Exchange had no real power within the Zionist sector. Nonetheless, it continued to exist and thus reflected the sector's inclination to converge internally.

On the Palestinian-Arab side, the industry's major players, mainly merchants and exporters, joined forces to form the "National Chamber of Commerce, Jaffa." This action was taken as early as 1922, following the violent incidents of 1921, when the Jaffa-based merchants decided to leave the joint Jewish-Arab chamber of commerce that had operated until that time.[17]

Furthermore, and as emphasized in previous chapters of this book, beginning from the mid-1930s the overall profitability of the countrywide industry steadily declined. The declining profitability led to a drawn-out crisis in the Zionist sector, which compelled Jewish citrus growers to form marketing cooperatives. As mentioned previously, in order to maintain profitability levels, the Zionist cooperatives formed business partnerships with many of the Palestinian-Arab citrus growers. As a result, the economic crisis experienced by Zionist citriculture from the mid-1930s had the effect of increasing intersectoral collaboration over the above-mentioned tendency to cooperate exclusively with their own national sector.

Still, after the 1929 events the government continued its efforts to form joint agricultural consultation and education bodies for the two national sectors. As pointed out in the previous chapter, these were headed by the General Agricultural Council established in February 1931 with an equal representation of Jews and Arabs and headed by a senior British official. As discussed in the previous chapter, one of the major entities established by the council was the Citrus Fruit Committee. This committee met some of Allport's conditions. It was authorized by the Mandate government and supported by it. And it was a sphere of intergroup cooperation and personal interaction between members of the committee. But as shown in the previous chapter, Arab and Jewish members of the committee had significant disagreements regarding the common goals of the committee. While the Jewish members argued for more supervision and central control of the country's industry, Arab members, driven mainly by economic considerations related to the Arab sector, objected to these measures. As for equal status, it seems that before the beginning of World War II the Jewish members of the committee enjoyed a slightly better standing with the Mandate authorities than the Arab members. This was mainly due to three factors: (1) the general terms of the Mandate, which had not yet been radically changed by the White Paper of 1939 that called for the establishment of an independent Arab state in Palestine, (2) the 1936–39 Arab Revolt, and (3) the objection of the Arab members to the centralization of the industry, a trend supported by the Mandate government.

Concurrent with the Citrus Fruit Committee, Arab and Jewish citrus growers also established ad-hoc committees for joint efforts. For instance, in February 1932 citrus growers from both sectors elected a joint six-member committee that operated independently of the Citrus Fruit Committee to combat plans to impose taxes on citrus fruit, both in Palestine and in British ports. One prominent name among the Palestinian members of the committee was that of Muhammad 'Abd al-Rahim, a notable Palestinian citrus grower and a known supporter of Amin al-Husayni. In March 1932 members of the committee sent a telegram to the daily newspapers in London. The telegram, sent on behalf of both national sectors of the industry, was signed by the Arab and Jewish members. In their announcement, the signatories demanded that the British government refrain from taxing citrus fruit imported from Palestine to Britain. The Jewish Telegraphic Agency, which reported about the telegram, emphasized that the committee had been established to manage the joint interests of the industry's two sectors. Thus, it is evident that the leaders of the Arab and

Jewish citriculture industry were not concerned with appearing in public as an Arab-Jewish entity acting for the common interests of both sectors.[18] Obviously, these protests reflected specific economic interests of citrus growers and merchants from both national sectors.

In this state of interrelated tension and collaboration, the local government occupied an important role. As we have seen, the government operated as early as the mid-1920s to stimulate cooperation, even if limited, between the two sectors in the form of joint citrus and agricultural exhibitions. Establishing the Citrus Fruit Committee in 1931 was an even more important step in this direction. Another step toward potentially uniting the countrywide industry was taken by the government in 1935. Through the General Agricultural Council, the government established a special investigative committee comprised of equal numbers of Jews and Arabs as well as a British official—the chief horticultural officer—and headed by Harry Viteles, the manager of the Central Bank for Co-operative Institutions. The official purpose of the committee was to inspect the transportation conditions of the citrus fruit from the grove until loaded on ships in the ports of Jaffa and Haifa. But in practice, the main issue with which it contended was assessing attitudes within the industry toward the possibility of founding a "Shipping Board" similar to that used in South Africa. The proposed shipping board, based as stated on the South African model, was to manage and supervise all citrus exports from the country. This would include setting dates for transporting the packaged fruit from the groves and determining the specific regions from which it would be transported, through supervising packed crates of fruit at the export ports, to setting schedules for the ships and their destinations in British and European markets. This model sharply contrasted with the existing state of affairs, where coordination between the exporters was minimal and informal aside from the invisible hand of the market. This had been the dominant system since the industry began its operations, and so long as profitability did not decline it was accepted by the parties involved, despite repeated complaints of its shortcomings.

The proposal to establish a shipping board in the citrus industry met with wide resistance from all sectors. Paradoxically, the long-term advantage of unifying the industry's activities was self-evident. This, particularly in light of the constant drop in profitability and of the wide-held assumption that this trend would continue due to the anticipated increase in the amount of exportable fruit as a result of considerable planting in previous years. If so, how can the sweeping resistance to establishing a shipping board be explained, as its precise purpose was to try and regulate all activity in the industry in order to prevent fatal harm or even complete collapse? In other words, resistance to establishing a shipping board appeared to clash with the interests of all citrus growers as well as with those of the entire industry. Indeed, the analysis offered by Mancur Olson can be used to explain the attitude of the citrus growers.

In our case, these were the large Jewish cooperatives, and particularly the Pardes cooperative and the Jaffa Orange Syndicate, as well as the large Palestinian merchants, particularly the group led by Muhammad ʿAbdul Rahim and that led by Alfred Rok. Some of these had reason to reduce production and thus raise the price they would receive on the export markets. In the state of the industry in late 1935, however, these large groups competed against each other, both within each sector and with groups in the other sector, and therefore had little incentive to work together to achieve common economic goals. In addition, about one-quarter of all sales in the industry were not controlled by any of the large groups. Therefore, in late 1935 when the Viteles committee held its discussions, only a small number of citrus growers had an interest in reducing their production. This explains why general opinion in the industry objected to establishing a shipping board.[19]

The government could not compel the industry to establish a shipping board. The very existence of the committee, however, as well as its discussions and the proposal to establish a central shipping board, had a unifying effect on the countrywide industry. First of all, the joint work that took place within the committee for several months during the spring and summer of 1935 involved hearing the testimonies of industry leaders from both sectors and discussions aimed at reaching joint conclusions. This was a learning process that involved working together as well as generating compromise formats. Secondly, the government's threat to establish a shipping board had the effect of uniting citrus growers from both sectors against the outside "threat." Leaders of both sectors acted together and committed to coordinating export dates and amounts of fruit exported, with the aim of circumventing plans for a shipping board. This voluntary coordination was also the main recommendation of the Viteles report submitted in January 1936.[20]

The outbreak of the Arab Revolt in the spring of 1936 blocked execution of the Viteles committee's recommendations. For a period of about two years, even the Citrus Fruit Committee reduced its meetings. The revolt did not halt citrus exports and did not prevent the rise in overall output as a result of extensive plantings. The increased supply of Jaffa oranges further lowered prices, and many of the citrus growers, particularly the Jewish growers, incurred losses. Increasing proposals were made for unification of the entire industry or only of its Jewish sector. Nevertheless, even the Jewish sector, whose profitability had begun to drop prior to 1936 and continued to diminish annually, did not reach a state of internal unity. The various particularistic interests within this sector overcame long-term business considerations advocating unification of the Jewish sector.[21]

Initial Steps toward Unification of the Countrywide Industry

The government, understanding the centrality and significance of the citrus industry for the country's economy, began actions to unite it in spring 1938, amid the Arab Revolt, without consulting with leaders of the countrywide industry. Recently appointed high commissioner Harold MacMichael asked the Colonial Office to send him detailed reports by countries in the British Empire on their administrative systems for export-focused agricultural industries. The search was on for an administrative and organizational model that could be emulated in Palestine, with necessary adjustments.

Another central element that was to play a crucial role in the citrus industry in the next few years was the appointment of Geoffrey Walsh as economic adviser to the high commissioner, a newly devised position. The official occupying this position was to be in charge of all economic activity of the Mandate government. When he arrived in Palestine in 1938, Walsh was already a veteran of twenty-five years in the British Colonial Service and had served in Africa in various economic capacities. Contemporary sources indicate that Walsh was a very intelligent person who believed in his course of action and was determined to achieve it even at the price of tough confrontations. He appeared to enjoy MacMichael's full trust and support. During World War II Walsh also occupied the role of food controller, a position that was part of Palestine's War Supply Board and was responsible for food supplies for Palestine's residents. In October 1945 Walsh was appointed a member of the Executive Council of the Mandate administration (the de facto cabinet of the Mandate). Walsh was the most senior British official killed in the Zionist terrorist bombing of the King David Hotel on July 22, 1946.[22]

Walsh was the living spirit and force behind the accelerated efforts to establish a countrywide administrative agency to manage the entire citrus industry. The three main models on which the government based its format for organizing the citrus industry in Palestine were the South African ordinance on marketing fruit, a similar ordinance in New Zealand, and the Federated Malay States rubber control ordinance. These ordinances provided Walsh and the government with an initial administrative framework. In contrast to the other countries, however, the unique reality in Palestine involved two national industries that had to be accommodated under one roof. This was in addition to the rifts within each sector, which had to be overcome as well, as stated above. During 1938–39 and until World War II broke out, the Citrus Fruit Committee held several meetings on this matter but reached no agreement. In addition, the Arab Revolt had a limiting effect on plans to unite the countrywide industry, as it created an atmosphere that prevented constant and open collaboration between the two sectors. Profitability continued to drop as well. However, too many of the citrus growers—both Arabs and Jews—were not yet incurring losses and thus had no stake in subjecting themselves to an external agency. When the war broke out in September 1939 this situation was radically transformed.[23]

Palestinian-Zionist Binational Enclave

Contemporary sources indicate that surprisingly, once the war erupted, the tensions and violence rampant among local Jews and Arabs in the three years of the Arab Revolt abruptly and considerably lessened. Contacts between Jews and Arabs were promptly reinstated, members of the two nationalities resumed their mutual visits and business in each other's residential areas, joint sports and cultural encounters were held, and the tensions and animosity appear to have largely dissipated. Instances of social, economic, and cultural cooperation were particularly evident in shared urban spheres of Jewish and Arab daily life in Haifa, Jerusalem, and Jaffa–Tel Aviv. Arabs and Jews met unabashedly in the markets, on the Tel Aviv promenade, in Jaffa and its markets, and at joint cultural events such as gatherings of the Rotary Club with its Jewish and Arab members.[24]

Specifically, for example, Arab and Jewish journalists held a friendly encounter at the Palatine café in Tel Aviv. One of the editors of *Filastin*, Akram Khaldi, called upon the "seventh power," i.e., the press, "to guide the public in this holy land towards internal unity." His words were translated into Hebrew by Muhammad 'Atiya of *al-Difa'*, while those of the Jewish speakers were translated into Arabic by one of the Jewish journalists. *Haaretz* published a series of articles titled "From the Life of Our Neighbors" by Palestinian-Arab writers, and an Arab-Jewish club, the Civil Club, was established in early 1941, with over fifty members, including 'Abd Ra'uf al-Bitar, mayor of Jaffa, and Me'ir Amzaleg, Jewish member of the Jaffa municipality. The club was located, as *al-Difa'* and *Davar* informed their readers, "in the Rafiq Jabbor building on the Jaffa-Jerusalem road, near al-Hilwani's café." At the same time, mayors of the large cities (Jerusalem, Tel Aviv, Jaffa, and Haifa) held official public meetings to coordinate management of the wartime economy, efforts that required them to meet regularly and also to appear together before the government.[25]

Indeed, even researchers who adhere to the conflictual approach admitted that most of World War II was characterized by a drop in animosity and violence between the two national societies in Palestine. Several reasons seem to have contributed to the special circumstances that facilitated intersectoral cooperation and reduced tensions during World War II. As a result of the long years of revolt and internal terrorism, as well as the military quelling of the revolt by the British army, a considerable part of the Arab public was worn out by the struggle, with its human and material price, and chose to distance themselves from military solutions for the time being. At the same time the unprecedented achievement of the revolt in the form of the White Paper of 1939, although formally rejected under pressure applied by Amin al-Husayni, created the feeling and understanding that Palestinian independence was possible. In contrast, the Zionist movement was at a loss, faced as it was with the choice between fighting the White Paper that promised to cancel the Mandate and establish a Palestinian state within ten years (albeit, with some Arab-Jewish power-sharing arrangement), and joining the Allies in their efforts against the Nazis and the Axis forces. Finally, the external threat—first and foremost the economic threat but also the military threat—to the very existence of the current social and economic system was the last unifying impetus that helped forge this atmosphere and the newly formed cooperative environment. As evident from sociological and social psychology research, external threats create internal cohesiveness in endangered societies. The economic flourishing of the country beginning from 1941, as a result of the huge rise in demand for industrial, textile, entertainment, and cultural products, as well as agricultural products for the Allied forces stationed in the Eastern Mediterranean and in Palestine itself, generated extremely conducive conditions for continued cooperation between the two local nationalities. New plants opened in a variety of industries, production in agriculture and in the service industries grew constantly, and experts and blue-collar workers from both sectors were employed in the economic industries of the two national societies.[26]

In a book published in early 1948 that discussed the "development of the Palestinian economy," David Horowitz, director of the Jewish Agency's Economic Department at the time under discussion and later the first governor of the Bank of Israel, devoted an extensive chapter to the local economy during World War II. To a certain degree under constraint, Horowitz showed that during the British Mandate the Arab middle class experienced a clear process of growth. "An Arab middle class is gradually emerging," wrote Horowitz. "The number of merchants, industry owners, officials, and free practitioners is increasing, and their weight in Arab society is growing. The number of Arab officials in government services is also on the rise." Horowitz's contemporary insights concerning the spheres of growth in the Palestinian economy during the Mandate period, especially with regard to the growing weight of services and manufacture relative to agriculture, were further corroborated by the findings and updated analyses presented by Jacob Metzer in his book on Palestine's economy during the British Mandate.

Of special relevance to us is Horowitz's discussion, as stated, on the domestic economy during World War II. With regard to the Arab economy, Horowitz says: "Deep and far-reaching transformations were evident in the Arab economy during the war. *The disparity between the Arab and Jewish sectors diminished considerably, and it is now possible to note a certain similarity between the Arab economic sector and the structure of the Jewish economy*" [emphasis added].[27]

Hence, the economic processes that took place until the outbreak of the war in 1939 and the transition of the entire local economy to a wartime economy—including capital formation, sales to locally and regionally stationed Allied armies, the growth of new industries manufacturing products for the army, and full employment—helped create the necessary conditions and circumstances that led to an improved relationship between the two national societies in the country.

Establishment of the Citrus Control and Citrus Marketing Boards

Indeed, the factors that facilitated the special atmosphere of Arab-Jewish cooperation by the outbreak of World War II did not bypass the citrus industry. But in contrast to other instances of cooperation and joint activity, from encounters between mayors to friendly soccer games, the citrus industry served as the grounds for a completely different, unprecedented, and unparalleled structure throughout the Mandate period. These were not temporary or even ongoing incidents of collaboration, rather a cohesive binational system.

The outbreak of the war led to immediate widespread comprehension of the threat to continued free marketing of the fruit to Britain and Europe, as well as to the continued demand for citrus fruit on a similar level to that before September 1939. The common danger served to draw together those who had previously felt estranged. Toward the end of 1939 Walsh was already prepared with a draft of a unified system, binational and egalitarian, for administration of the industry. Similar to the models he had before him from other countries under the British imperial umbrella, Walsh too suggested a central establishment that would supervise and organize all stages of citrus marketing, from the grove to loading the fruit on ships in local ports of departure. The proposed entity was called the Citrus Control Board (CCB), and it was defined as a corporate body capable of filing court cases as well as serving as a defendant. Its members would be select representatives of the industry's various sectors, with an equal number of representatives from each national sector as well as representatives from subsectors within each national sector. Thus, both Muslims and Christians were represented from among the Palestinian sector, and in the Zionist sector room was allocated for the large cooperatives, citrus growers not included in the cooperatives, and the citrus industry belonging to the Labor Movement. Members of the CCB from among the citrus growers were designated "producer members." At the same time, the CCB would also incorporate British "official members" who were to head the board.

Typologically, the proposed system resembled the power-sharing arrangement established in Northern Ireland following the Good Friday Agreement in 1998. In both cases, the format was basically compatible with the power-sharing model proposed by Arend Lijphart for countries or societies that are deeply and essentially divided on a national or ethnic basis, a model called consociationalism. Lijphart's theory stirred a wide and many times fierce debate between consociationalists and their critics. In addition, the specific conditions and organizational principles of consociationalism have also been passionately debated. However, in the last analysis Lijphart sees two fundamental components to a consociational agreement: a power-sharing system and group autonomy. Lijphart's model, however, based as it is on real examples from different countries, assumes that the consent reached by conflicted parties in a deeply divided society requires only internal consent. Researchers of the Good Friday Agreement in Northern Ireland added to Lijphart's model the important insight whereby external forces beyond the divided society have an important role in reaching the consociational agreement. They showed that not only US involvement in achieving the agreement, but also primarily the active role and representation given to the British and Irish governments in its process of implementation, were extremely important factors that facilitated both the achievement and successful implementation of the agreement.[28]

Top-Down Process

Indeed, in our case a third party, i.e., the British, had an important role in creating the binational institutional structure of the citrus industry. The British regime urged its formation and, during the time that it operated, constituted a most significant influence that encouraged its maintenance. Nonetheless, in the context of British Mandatory Palestine's deeply divided society, it would have been impossible to force tens of thousands of citrus growers, as well as other components of the industry, to reach a consociational agreement. This would have generated wide resistance, undermining the agreement. In addition, at the time—and in fact throughout the entire Mandate period—the British did not have the political power to enforce such an agreement. Indeed, the two failed British attempts to establish a shared Arab and Jewish Legislative Council attest to the limits of their political power in enforcing shared institutions. Accordingly, this was an agreement reached by mutual consent of the three elements involved in the industry.

In December 1939 the General Agricultural Council established a subcommittee to examine the possibility of founding a Citrus Control Board.[29] The committee was headed by Walsh himself and its members were equally composed of Arab and Jewish representatives. The committee heard many dozens of witnesses from the entire citrus industry, who flocked to voice their opinion concerning the proposed system. The main role of the committee was clearly not to form a completely new organizational structure for the industry, as this had already been devised by Walsh in the previous year and a half. Rather, it appears to have been charged with making the industry's different sectors feel part of the process of creating a unified organizational structure and thus receiving their support, even if their specific proposals were not accepted.

A look at the testimonies of the various witnesses—Husayni supporters such as Muhammad 'Abd al-Rahim and Ibrahim Banna, as well as renowned supporters of the opposition, such as Sa'id Baydas, François Gélat, 'Ali al-Mustaqim, Shukri al-Taji, Ra'uf al-Bitar, and various figures from the different parts of the Zionist sector—shows that they attempted, first of all, to convince the committee that the proposed system should uphold their specific interests. The testimonies also indicate that although at first, in early 1940, there was still considerable resistance to establishing the CCB, as the months passed this resistance weakened significantly. In this context it is notable that, due to the war, prices of shipping by sea had risen considerably and despite the significant yield of some seventeen million crates, only about half had been exported due to the rising prices of shipping, the gargantuan customs fees in the destination countries and particularly in Britain, and the declining demand.

Bottom-Up Process

Concurrent with the top-down process of establishing the CCB, initiated as stated by the government, another binational process also took place, one initiated from below by the industry's two national sectors. In addition to the general factors mentioned above, the bottom-up process of unification was also stimulated by the government's policy toward the industry. The high commissioner declared that, in contrast to other local industries, the government would not provide the citrus industry with assistance. This declaration led major figures in the industry to join forces in an action that would compel the Mandate government to retract the declaration and support the industry. On the Palestinian side these included Sa'id Baydas, Shukri al-Taji, Rushdi a-Shawwa (mayor of Gaza), Shaykh Shaker Abu-Kishk of Abu-Kishk, Radi Nabulsi of Nablus, 'Afif Haj Ibrahim of Tulkarm, and Shaykh Shafiq al-Khatib of Qubayba, while notable figures on the Zionist side were Zvi Butkowsky, chairman of the Farmers' Federation, and Yitzhak Rokach, the industry's major figure in the Jewish sector. This joint active Arab-Jewish cooperation received prominent coverage on the front pages of the contemporary press.[30] The organizers decided to hold a mass joint protest gathering that would subsequently convey the message of the entire industry to the high commissioner.

The first gathering was held in Petah Tikva on January 16, 1940. The Hadar cinema in Petah Tikva was packed with some six hundred citrus growers from all over the country. One hundred of these were Arab growers. Similar to the above descriptions of the assemblage at the Alhambra cinema hall in Jaffa (which took place exactly one year after the Petah Tikva gathering), here too the Hebrew press made a special effort to emphasize the uniqueness of the gathering as a one-of-a-kind occurrence, describing its colorfulness and atmosphere of friendship and collaboration. The speakers stressed the shared interests of those involved in the industry versus the danger of its collapse. Their words were translated simultaneously, and at the end of the assemblage Avraham Shapira, a popular figure well-received by both sides, held a feast in honor of the Arab guests.

The decisions reached at the Petah Tikva conference reflected the assumption and hope that with the government's assistance it would be possible to continue exporting the fruit in reduced quantities. The resolutions therefore focused on posing demands to the government to reduce customs in the United Kingdom, lower the local property tax, and award guarantees for bank loans that would enable the continued routine cultivation of the groves. In addition, a joint delegation was formed to bring the message of the citrus growers before the high commissioner. The delegation indeed met with Harold MacMichael about ten days after the Petah Tikva gathering. This meeting with MacMichael was also attended by Walsh, as well as by the government treasurer, indicating the significance that the government ascribed to the industry.

Contemporary sources confirm the logical conclusion that MacMichael's declaration about withholding government assistance to this important industry was not innocent. Indeed, most of the sources we have before us prove without a doubt that the high commissioner and Walsh, his economic adviser, acted purposely to aggravate the crisis in the citrus industry. They predicted correctly that as long as the industry was not in a state of severe crisis where, according to Olson's theory, individual citrus growers would accept that the industry's unification and reduced sales would be more beneficial for them than the loss incurred by such unification, establishment of the CCB would not be possible. Thus, the discussions of the General Agricultural Council's subcommittee and the testimonies it collected had another goal as well. They were motivated not only by the desire to have citrus growers feel part of the decision-making process, but also by the wish to draw the process out until the end of the export season. In this way, the crisis would be aggravated and losses would accumulate due to the growing discrepancy between the quantity of exportable fruit and actual exports.[31]

The sources we consulted do not explicitly indicate that the citrus growers, both Arabs and Zionists, were aware of this intention of the Mandate government. But they do show that the industry's leaders well understood the urgency of creating order and organization in the industry. Thus, it may be assumed that industry leaders implicitly supported this cool-headed course initiated by the government.

At the same time the government's steps, and particularly the high commissioner's declaration that no support would be granted to the citrus industry, led all those involved to suspect the government's intentions. In this way, distrust of the government and its intentions united the two sectors. This distrust did not disappear in the subsequent war years and thus continued to unify Arabs and Jews in the industry. Concomitantly, the mistrust created constant suspicion of the government, damaged the industry's regular activities during the war years, and as we shall see below, also led to crises between the government and the industry's two national sectors.

It is tempting to analyze the intensive collaboration between the two sectors during these years in quasi-Marxist terms.[32] Such analysis is also compatible with the image of Jewish and Arab citrus growers as wealthy people whose interests in terms of their position in the country's class structure surpassed their ethnic and national consciousness, an image that was common in the years up to 1948 and that has trickled into subsequent research as well. There is no denying, as proven earlier in this book and by the research in general, that common economic interests have the power to bend social and national boundaries and to increase their flexibility. However, it has also been proven that the most important separating line within the countrywide industry in general was cultural-religious-national affiliation. Moreover, segmentation of the number of grove owners in the industry by the area they owned shows that the industry itself, countrywide and within its two sectors, was mainly composed of small to medium-sized grove ownership. In other words, each sector was segmented along class-based lines, in which the very wealthy were at the top while the owners of small to medium-sized groves were at the bottom.

Indeed, a document prepared by the CCB in 1941, containing data as of 1936 on citrus groves and growers by their national affiliation, shows that in the Jewish sector some 48 percent of grove owners had a small grove of one to ten dunams. These were not poor people, but they cannot be included among the local middle class or among the wealthy citrus merchants or growers. Any drop in profitability might have left them impoverished. In the Arab sector, some 32 percent of all grove owners (1,278 out of 3,997) owned a grove of one to ten dunams. In the entire countrywide industry, some 42 percent of grove owners had a small grove. If we include in the calculation groves of up to twenty dunams, some 75 percent of owners in the Jewish sector had small to medium-sized groves (one to twenty dunams) in 1936, while in the Arab sector the rate was about 57 percent of all grove owners. The proportion of small and medium-sized groves among the entire countrywide industry was about 68 percent.[33] A class-based interpretation would require that wealthy Jewish and Arab citrus owners form a separate organization from their small to medium-sized counterparts. However, the fault lines of the Petah Tikva and Alhambra gatherings, as well as of the CCB, were national and not class based.

The wide attendance of the Petah Tikva gathering in January 1940, and the even wider attendance of the assemblage at the Alhambra hall in Jaffa one year later, consisting as it did of about two thousand citrus growers, show that the joint actions received the sweeping support of all local citrus growers, despite the different social classes within each national sector.

The Petah Tikva assemblage resulted in several achievements for the industry. The delegation that met with the high commissioner some ten days after the assemblage, and subsequent conversations with senior government officials, had the effect of reducing the agricultural tax on groves from 400 Palestine mils to 150 Palestine mils. Moreover, and in particular, these efforts led to government guarantees for bank loans given to citrus growers for the purpose of regular cultivation of the groves. In the summer and fall of 1940, however, the crisis worsened. Exports came to an almost complete halt when Italy joined the Axis forces in June 1940. At the same time, the process of establishing an organization that would manage the industry and see to the needs of all citrus growers had not yet been completed.

This situation led to a second emergency assemblage of Arab and Jewish citrus growers. The assemblage was held in late September 1940 at the palace of Sa'id Baydas in the village of Shaykh Muwannes. The citrus-picking season was about to begin, and export options had been dramatically reduced. From the time of the first assemblage in Petah Tikva in January 1940 to the second assembly in Shaykh Muwannes in September of that year, a regular joint Arab-Jewish committee had also been founded to represent the industry before the authorities. For the first time the Labor Movement, the leading Zionist organization in the country that wielded extensive hegemonic authority and influence, was also represented on the joint committee. The committee included Sa'id Baydas, Shukri al-Taji, and François Gélat on the Arab side and Yitzhak Rokach, Moshe Smilansky, and Yehuda Horin (manager of the Labor-owned company Yachin) on the Zionist side. A reporter for *Davar*, the newspaper of Mapai, attended the meeting and reported enthusiastically:

> [The assemblage, which took place in the "palace" of the Baydas home, was attended by] some two hundred representatives of forty Hebrew colonies and Arab villages, as well as a delegation from the [Zionist] workers' farms, together with the regional officers Kuperman and 'Abd al-Raziq and the representative of the Registrar of [Cooperative] Societies, Mr. Nayton, some ten Hebrew and Arab journalists—a magnificent many colored array of people from East and West, some in a keffiyeh and some in a fez, some in a hat and some in a cap. . . . Before the discussion began the guests were offered glasses of natural preserved citrus juice and cups of coffee.[34]

Attendants of the assemblage demanded that the government establish an organ to take care of the growers' debts accumulated to date and prevent foreclosure of property to cover the debts. But most of all they demanded that the government subsidize the industry: that it arrange for ships for export purposes and commit to purchasing a minimum amount of fruit so that the growers would be left with a reasonable sum with which to prepare the groves for the next season.[35] This conference was extensively reported in the contemporary Arab press, beginning with preliminary announcements that called for considerable participation in order to pressure the Mandate government to take action to solve the "stifling crisis," as described in *Filastin*.[36] Subsequently, the event was widely covered, with most newspapers declaring it a success that could save the approaching orange season.[37]

At the same time, preparations were completed for establishing the CCB. In April 1940 the General Agricultural Council approved its subcommittee's report, and in May the high commissioner's Executive Council approved the recommendation to establish the CCB. A draft of the proposed board's ordinance was published in the *Palestine Gazette* in July and a final version was published in October 1940. The worsening crisis in the citrus industry toward the end of the 1939–40 season in spring 1940, and the understanding—even among those who several months earlier had objected to establishing the CCB—that the industry's fate depends on its organizational unification, led to a change of mind. Now debates began within each national sector to determine who would represent them in the new organization.

As we have seen, the Zionist sector experienced alternate processes of disintegration and unification in the years preceding World War II. These ended at the beginning of the war with the creation of two major categories. The private citrus growers, constituting the "civil" faction, were headed by Yitzhak Rokach, and most of the cooperatives, comprised of private citrus growers, followed his lead. The second faction belonging to the Labor Movement was headed by Yehuda Horin, manager of the Yachin marketing company, and Israel Traub, manager of Tnuva. Moreover, some of the Jewish citrus growers were affiliated with neither of the two main categories and were designated "independents."

As previously mentioned, Palestinian-Arab citriculture did not experience similar dissolution and unification processes prior to World War II. Palestinian-Arab citriculture was split along three main axes. First of all, geographically. The center of the industry, both physically and particularly with regard to the leadership, was situated in Jaffa and the region. The two main secondary centers were the Tulkarm/Nablus region and Gaza.

The second split was between Muslims and Christians. Industry leaders and the British government ensured that the Palestinian Christian minority would be duly represented at all times. The third split was between supporters of Mufti al-Husayni and of his opposition.

According to CCB ordinance, the major organizations in each sector were to submit to the government names of candidates who would serve as members of the board. But the final decision would be up to the government. The Jewish sector managed to draw up an agreed-upon list, except for the independent representative. But Yitzhak Rokach was bitterly resentful, as evident from his journal, that the Labor Movement did not recommend him as a member of the CCB although the "civil" faction did list representatives of the Labor Movement.[38] In the Arab sector the number of players and splits was, as stated, larger than in the Zionist sector. Nonetheless, the main division was between the Husaynis and their opponents, since in terms of geographical-economic distribution Jaffa and its environs was clearly dominant. The group of Husayni supporters was headed by Muhammad 'Abdul Rahim, together with Alfred Rok and Zaki Barakat. In the mid-1930s this group controlled some 40 percent of the fruit exported by the Arab sector. The other group was that of the opposition, which gathered around the National Chamber of Commerce in Jaffa and its head, 'Abd Ra'uf al-Bitar, mayor of Jaffa. However, the major figure in the Arab industry was, as stated earlier in this chapter, Sa'id Baydas.

Notably, not only supporters of the opposition were proposed to the government as members of the CCB. The names of 'Abdul Rahim, Rok, and Zaki Barakat were also submitted by their supporters. With regard to the geographical split, at this stage of establishing the CCB none of those elected were from areas outside Jaffa. Only after the war ended, in late 1945, was Hilmi Hanun of Tulkarm appointed a member of the CCB. In contrast, various members of the al-Shawwa family of Gaza, proposed from time to time as appointees to the board, were never included. The distance from the Arab industry's center of activities and from the offices of the CCB, also located in Jaffa, appears to have been a decisive consideration in preventing a representative from Gaza as a member of the board.[39]

The sources we have before us show that the government did not consider appointing any Husayni supporters to the CCB. Not just the Mandate government's animosity toward Amin al-Husayni appears to have played a part here. The dissenting views of Muhammad ʿAbdul Rahim and his supporters when discussions of establishing the CCB were first held proved to their disadvantage.

The first meeting of the CCB was held on December 23, 1940, at the Ministry of Agriculture's offices in Jaffa. Participants included three official members: Geoffrey Walsh (chairman), Arthur F. Nayton (registrar of cooperative societies), and Frank Reginald Mason (director of the Department of Agriculture and Fisheries), and four producer members from each sector: Raʾuf al-Bitar (mayor of Jaffa), Saʿid Baydas, ʿAbdel Raʾuf Barakat, and François Gélat (Christian representative). All were from Jaffa, longtime supporters of cooperation with the Mandate authorities and with Jewish citrus growers, and longtime supporters of the opposition. On the Jewish side the members were Yitzhak Rokach (representing the private Jewish cooperatives), Moshe Smilansky (leader of the Zionist Farmers' Federation), Yehuda Horin (Labor Movement representative), and Emile Visser (representing the independent Jewish growers).

The acting manager of the CCB was A. C. Shill, chief horticultural officer. He did not hold voting powers, but the nature of his position gave him some influence. The CCB had two secretaries, one from each national sector, who handled the daily work of the board. These were Nicolas Gélat and Shmuel Tolkowsky. They received the title of "joint secretaries."

As evident, the board comprised eight "producer members" and only three "official members." Nevertheless Walsh, as chairman of the CCB, had of course a great deal of power to determine the board's agenda and whether a certain decision would be accepted or rejected. Moreover, the fact that very senior figures in the Mandate's economic apparatus—Walsh, as senior economic adviser to the high commissioner; Nayton, the registrar of cooperative societies; and Mason, the director (i.e., secretary) of the Department of Agriculture—were "official members" of the board indicates its significance as perceived by the Mandate government. However, the "official members" could not force decisions by majority vote. Indeed, throughout the period until 1948 and particularly in the formative years at the beginning of the world war, the opinion of the "producer members" was very often opposed to the policy that Walsh attempted to dictate, and he was compelled to retract his proposals. Moreover, although the disagreements between the two national sectors represented on the board did not and could not be dispelled, a tradition was set from the very beginning—and was not breached—whereby no representatives of either sector would join forces with the "official members" against the other. This tradition was preserved thanks to Walsh's wisdom in recognizing that preserving the unity of the industry was in the government's basic interests. The alternative was continuous disorder and severe harm to the entire local economy, of which the industry was a basic foundation. Thus, Walsh—and the board's subsequent chairmen—avoided enforcing a policy of "divide and rule." This tradition was also maintained since the "producer members" understood that in order to preserve the industry's power they must remain united against Walsh and the government. As a result of these circumstances and of the continuous crisis in the industry, it took a very short time from the establishment of the CCB for it to begin reaching consensus-based decisions.

According to its ordinance, the CCB was in charge of registering the groves and also responsible for fruit production processes, supervising the quality of the fruit marketed, transporting the fruit from the grove to the port, and shipping the fruit. However, the regulations concerning the industry's most important economic aspect—the process of marketing the fruit in the local market and its export overseas—were vague.[40] Hence, parallel to the CCB the government established another entity, the Citrus Marketing Board (CMB), which was responsible for controlling all aspects of marketing the citrus fruit. The announcement of the CMB's establishment came as a surprise and was only made in late December 1940, when the CCB's final composition and establishment was declared. The sources we have before us are not clear on whether Walsh had planned to establish the CMB to begin with, or whether during the lengthy process of founding the CCB (about eighteen months, from summer 1939 to December 1940) he concluded that a separate entity was necessary to achieve better control of the industry. In any case, leaders of the citrus industry and the citrus growers themselves voiced no objection to establishment of the CMB.

Where the CCB was defined as operating within the regular legal framework of the British Mandate, i.e., it was a corporate body that could

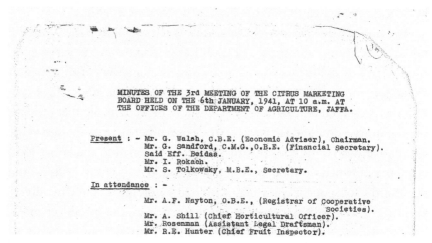

8. Minutes from the third meeting of the Citrus Marketing Board, 1941. Israel State Archives.

file court cases and serve as a defendant, the CMB was founded under the Mandate Defense Regulations. Hence, it required no public process or consultation with the two national sectors of Palestine's citrus industry. Moreover, the decisions of the CMB were not subjected to the regular legal process, as their validity stemmed from the Defense Regulations and hence from the CMB's definition in the Defense Regulations as a "competent authority." The CMB's decisions had more significance and force than the CCB's; therefore, the CMB was the more senior of the two complementary boards founded in December 1940.

The CMB consisted of only four people: two senior government representatives—Walsh as chairman and G. Sandford, the financial secretary—and two representatives of the citrus growers, Baydas and Rokach. For several years Shmuel Tolkowsky served as secretary of the CMB, along with his duties as secretary of the CCB. After some time Nicolas Gélat, the other CCB secretary, joined Tolkowsky as well. The composition of the CMB indicates its significance. It also demonstrates Walsh's efforts to create a power-sharing structure in which no one side had an advantage, neither the government over the citrus growers, the citrus growers over the government, or any national sector over another. The industry's policy and activities were determined in practice by the CMB, while in most cases the CCB followed this policy. Nonetheless, the fact that the two senior representatives of the citrus industry, Baydas and Rokach, were members of the CCB as well and that Walsh headed both boards created a de facto union between them.

The CMB shaped the industry's binational nature, formed during World War II, considerably more than the CCB. According to available sources, Baydas and Rokach held innumerable unofficial meetings to coordinate the industry's policy on various topics, and they quite naturally included in these consultations colleagues from the CCB and the industry's entire leadership, and in certain cases even all its members. In addition, they were appointed time and again to official subcommittees of both the CCB and the CMB to investigate different issues. As representatives of the industry they often traveled to neighboring Egypt, Lebanon, and Syria (after the latter two were liberated from Vichy rule in July 1941) to check out the option of marketing locally produced fruit in these countries. Moreover, Baydas and Rokach were considered the very epitome of the industry's binational character. Even after the CMB was expanded in January 1945 to include two additional members, François Gélat and Yehuda Horin (previously members of the CCB), Baydas and Rokach remained the two main figures on the board and in the industry.

W. F. Crawford, who served as chairman of the CMB from December 1945 to May 1946, commented on the role played by Baydas and Rokach:

> The present Board is ruled to a great extent by Rokach and Baydas, who are both strong personalities, represent very important interests, and have been in the Board from the start. The other two members of the Board are by themselves far more reasonable and open-minded, but generally collapse before the first two.[41]

Notwithstanding the establishment of the CCB and CMB, the industry's two national sectors remained extremely wary of the government's intentions with regard to the citrus industry. Hence the bottom-up binational efforts, which had begun with the assemblage in Petah Tikva in early 1940 and continued with the assemblages in Shaykh Muwannes in September 1940, remained in force. Thus, in mid-January 1941, about three weeks after the CCB and CMB were founded, the largest binational gathering was held at the Alhambra hall in Jaffa, described at the beginning of this chapter. The joint Arab-Jewish organization established at the Alhambra conference, designated the Joint Executive Committee of Arab and Jewish Growers in Palestine, continued to exist throughout World War II and subsequently. It was headed by Shukri al-Taji, and its members included organizers of the previous meetings, with the most prominent being Shaykhs Shaker Abu-Kishk and Shafiq al-Khatib. Also notable was Zaki Barakat, who was affiliated at first with Muhammad 'Abd al-Rahim but at this time displayed open support of the Joint Executive Committee. In addition to the Arab representatives, representatives of the Zionist Farmers' Federation also took a most active part in the activities of the Joint Committee. Moreover, many times the "producer members" of the CCB, among them Baydas and Rokach, also participated in the committee's meetings. The minutes of the CMB and CCB show that the committee's existence angered Walsh, as did the fact that members of the boards actively participated in meetings of the Joint Committee and the pressure it put to bear on the government, but to no avail.

It seems, therefore, that by early 1941 the three parameters of Allport's "contact hypothesis," which had not been met previously, were now fulfilled. These were establishing common goals for the two sectors of the industry, creating a mechanism for intergroup cooperation in order to achieve these goals, and equal status for the representatives of the two sectors within the established mechanism. Undoubtedly the economic, social, and political conditions created in British Mandate Palestine during World War II facilitated the fulfillment of Allport's parameters. Concurrently, the severe economic crisis that befell the country's citrus industry forced the majority of citrus growers to join the collective action of unifying Palestine's citrus industry.

Thus, in the spring of 1941 the binational setting of Palestine's citrus industry was already in place. It was fully accepted by its respective constituencies and by Palestine's two national communities and enjoyed their approval and legitimization. The CCB and CMB met at least twice a month during the citrus marketing season and regularly, although less frequently, in between seasons. The protocols of these two boards, as well as routine reports in Zionist and Palestinian newspapers on the industry in general and on the meetings, decisions, and activities of the boards in particular, attest to the fact that this binational reality was comprehended by all as a natural feature of World War II Palestine.

The following discussion addresses a few noteworthy matters that occupied the attention of the industry throughout this period.

Walsh and the Citrus Growers: Appreciation Tempered by Suspicion

What lay behind the wariness, or even hostility, expressed by citrus growers of both sectors toward Walsh? Incongruously, the hostility was accompanied by a great deal of appreciation and respect toward the government in general and Walsh in particular. Citrus growers from both sectors recognized that the government had saved the citrus industry from collapse. They admitted the importance of establishing the CMB and CCB, the property tax reductions that the government had granted the industry, and the guarantees it had given the banks as backing for loans granted to the growers. During the war the citrus growers received additional loans, supplementing those given in the summer of 1940 and mentioned above. In the absence of regular income from exports, these loans enabled the citrus growers to continue cultivating their groves in order to facilitate production in future years. Since in this industry the grove itself normally served as collateral, and since during the war the groves had lost some of their value due to the almost complete halt of exports, the Mandate government continued (with the approval of the Colonial Office in London) to grant the banks guarantees for loans given to the growers.

As stated above, the economic flourishing of Palestine during World War II also generated a certain respite for the citrus industry. Some of the produce was purchased by the army, and the by-product industry that manufactured citrus juice and jams used another part. For instance, in the 1942–43 season the fruit yield was some five million crates (or two hundred thousand tons of fruit). About one-quarter of the produce (some fifty thousand tons) was purchased by the by-product industry; about 15 percent (thirty thousand tons) by the army; a similar proportion of the entire crop was marketed to neighboring countries (Transjordan, Egypt, and mainly Syria); and the rest, some 45 percent (about eighty-five thousand tons), was consumed locally.[42]

But together with this appreciation, the entire industry shared the well-based notion that Walsh, with the support of the high commissioner and the Colonial Office, sought to use the crisis period to generate a structural change in the countrywide industry. Even before the war broke out, at the beginning of the industry's financial crisis, it was already clear to everyone, including the Colonial Office in London and the government in Palestine, that the area allocated for growing citrus in Palestine was excessive relative to the demand for Jaffa oranges. Prior to the war, the assumption was that free market forces would generate a balance between demand and supply and would have the effect of diminishing the amount of land devoted to citrus growing to fit current demand. The outbreak of the war changed the economic regime in Europe and Palestine to one dominated by control and centralization.

From the beginning, when granting collaterals for the first round of loans in the summer of 1940 and on a regular basis throughout the war and subsequently, the Colonial Office openly declared that loans would only be given for a total of 170,000 dunams of groves. This although citrus groves covered an overall area of about 300,000 dunams, divided almost equally between the two national sectors. Walsh and the Colonial Office anticipated that in the first years after the war (the end of which was not yet in sight) the demand for citrus fruit would be low and the prices accordingly. Therefore, it was essential to reduce the amount of citrus land. According to the estimates, the owners of about one-fourth of the overall citrus land (some 75,000 dunams) did not apply for loans at all. Some, particularly owners of large groves, had sufficient capital and chose not to apply. Their cultivation of the groves was also on a higher standard than others', and they took advantage of their large citrus areas by employing economies of scale in the routine cultivation and picking and packing processes. Others, particularly in the Arab sector, preferred not to take loans because, as we have seen, the cost of labor in Arab citriculture was considerably lower than in Jewish citriculture and therefore their profitability was less affected than that of the Jewish sector. Arab citrus growers whose groves were planted near the large Jaffa–Tel Aviv urban region, which was the main local market, benefited more than others from this advantage. Their transportation costs to this market were lower than those of groves located in more remote locations, and their profitability appears to have suffered much less than that of others.

Thus, the total area for which loans could be requested was about 225,000 dunams. But only for some three-quarters of it (170,000 dunams) were funds allocated for loans. In order to grant the loans, the CCB and the government created a scoring method for the groves according to their state of cultivation and management. The Mandate government did not conceal its intention to grant loans only to high-scoring groves. There was a certain economic logic to this. Poorly cultivated groves had a lower chance of recovering and resuming a state of profitability after the war, and granting loans to their owners was riskier than granting loans to other growers. Large groves, whose cultivation per land unit was cheaper than that of medium-sized and small groves, were also on a higher priority level for loans. The bottom line was that owners of small and medium-sized groves whose land was located further from the center of the country were affected more than others. Since about 48 percent of Jewish grove owners had groves on areas of one to ten dunams, Zionist citriculture was most severely affected by the government's loan policy. Indeed, during the 1941–42 season some 41 percent of all those who submitted a request for loans were Arabs and some 59 percent were Jews.[43]

In any case, the loans offered per dunam of grove would not cover the cost of its routine cultivation. (This remained true as a rule although the precise amount changed from year to year.) In other words, even after receiving the loans, single growers had less funds than necessary to properly cultivate their groves. This resulted in a constant decline in the quality of grove cultivation and a continuous drop in yield per dunam of productive grove. Thus, whereas before the war the average yield was some eighty exportable crates per dunam, by the 1942–43 season it had dropped to some twenty-five crates of exportable fruit per dunam, a decline of about 70 percent.

Walsh, who was also in charge of food provisions during the war, attempted to encourage small citrus growers to dig up their groves and use the land to produce food for the local populace. He also advocated planting vegetables between the rows of citrus trees in order to increase the supply of vegetables during the war. Indeed, many Jewish citrus growers who could not cope with their losses pulled up the groves or sold the land for urban development. The government's loan policy achieved its original goal. About one-fourth of all prewar citrus land (eighty thousand dunams) was dug up or abandoned with no hope of recovery. More land was lost in the Jewish sector than in the Arab sector, about one-third versus 20 percent, respectively.[44]

Where the Mandate government and Walsh perceived the policy of reducing the amount of citrus land as economically logical and beneficial in the long term, this policy posed a real and immediate threat to the very existence of those working in the industry and of its leadership as well as to their economic viability. Thus, it is no wonder that the industry's two sectors were distrustful of Walsh.

Disposal Permit Fee

The first two seasons experienced during the world war were challenging. The crops were bountiful (some seventeen million crates and twelve million crates in the 1939–40 and 1940–41 seasons, respectively), while sales were reduced mainly to the local market, which had a maximum consuming capacity of some two million crates. The by-product industry was only at its initial stages, as were sales to the army. Production surpluses were large and losses high. From its initiation the CMB formed a plan to assist the industry: the "disposal permit fee." In order to deliver fruit from the groves to the city-based markets, a permit was required. The mandatory fee for the permit, called the "disposal permit fee," raised the price of fruit for consumers and increased overall proceeds. All fees were deposited in an account run by the CCB, which was intended for the entire industry. At the end of the season, each grove owner received about 150 Palestine mils per dunam from this joint fund.

The plan met with many difficulties as it required constant surveillance of the roads and markets. Limited government personnel were available for surveillance purposes. Moreover, as in any financial supervisory regime, a great deal of smuggling went on. Many citrus growers avoided using vehicles to deliver the fruit, opting for dirt roads to smuggle the fruit to the markets. Nonetheless, this plan had its advantages for the industry. In addition to a certain rise in overall proceeds, the plan made it possible to provide aid to all citrus growers, including those whose groves were not in good shape or were further from the city centers.

After the disposal permit fee plan had been operating for about two years, however, during the 1940–41 and 1941–42 seasons, Walsh and the financial secretary concluded that it was doing more harm than good. In addition to the financial costs and the personnel required to supervise its implementation, the plan had the effect of slowing down the diminishing of planted land. This was a result of the fees redistributed to all citrus growers, which facilitated continued cultivation of the groves, albeit minimally. Moreover, the fee raised the price of citrus (mainly oranges) on the markets and was an incentive for citrus growers to bury their surplus fruit. Reducing the supply of fruit was good for the citrus growers because it raised the prices, but it also hampered Walsh's attempts to ensure a supply of food. He would have preferred to flood the markets with surplus citrus fruit, bringing prices down. In this way, the citrus fruit could serve as a cheap alternative for other types of food that were scarcer and more expensive. Walsh and the other government officials were aided by the gradual decline in production. The 1941–42 season yielded some nine million crates, with only about five million crates in the 1942–43 season. As we have seen, this was the equivalent of the local demand with the addition of sales to the army, the by-product industry, and neighboring countries.

Despite protests by industry leaders, bitter arguments between government representatives and industry representatives in the CCB and CMB, as well as protest gatherings of the Joint Committee and protest telegrams sent by the committee to the high commissioner, the government canceled the disposal permit fee plan unilaterally for the 1942–43 season. The resentment toward Walsh was considerable and only added to the industry's previous wariness.

Linking

To lessen the criticism aimed at him, but more to reach the goal of reorganizing the industry and maintaining control of the amount of fruit offered on the local market and its price, Walsh came up with two new proposals. First, he made a commitment to purchase the surplus fruit left over from regular sales. From the industry's perspective, this was a commitment that would guarantee sales revenues. As for Walsh's role as food controller, this would give him the ability to control the amount of food on the market and its price. The second proposal was to create a controllable marketing and export system. The system was called linking, and it would require each citrus grower to be associated, or "linked," with a certain trader. This, in contrast to the free market system customary before the war, which involved no control of the number of exporters and the quality of their business. Now, twelve recognized traders were determined in each sector. They were required to sign contracts with single citrus growers or with cooperatives of citrus growers in their national sector. In addition, they had to sign export contracts with the CMB rather than directly with sales agents of companies in British and continental markets, as before 1939. The CMB was to manage the export of the fruit and its marketing on the local market. All sales of fruit were now put into the hands of twelve individuals in each sector. This proposal was made in the context of a renewed rise in revenues with the increase in demand for citrus by the by-product industry, army sales, limited exports to neighboring countries, and also the rise in local consumption. These had been translated into more investments in routine grove cultivation, with a forecast for a further increase in the supply of citrus in coming years. From the government's perspective, and in the industry's long-term general interest, there was need for a plan to control production and marketing processes.

The Jewish citrus growers did not find it particularly hard to agree on their twelve recognized traders. As explained above, in the Jewish sector processes of disintegration and reorganization had begun even before the war, and these reached a climax when it broke out. The thousands of Jewish growers were now already affiliated with a large organization that served as their "trader." The situation in the Arab sector was different. Reorganization processes in this sector had only begun at the war's outbreak. At first, there was a far greater number of owners and individual exporters than in the Jewish sector. These were split, as we have seen, into different stakeholders and geographical regions. And as stated above, those who gained the most from establishment of the CCB were citrus growers affiliated with the opposition to Amin al-Husayni. The animosity between Husayni's supporters and the opposition was considerable and remained so during the war as well, although this only became evident in 1943–44. As a result, the Palestinian-Arab sector did not manage to reach an accepted list of recognized traders.

In the meantime, in his role as the person in charge of food supplies rather than as chairman of the CMB and CCB, Walsh postponed purchase of the citrus fruit surplus to the season's end. Consequently, the industry remained in a state of uncertainty throughout the 1942–43 season concerning the fate of the crops. Thus, the tensions and hostility between Walsh and representatives of the industry escalated from the beginning of the season in November–December 1942 until April 1943. The Joint Committee held open gatherings against Walsh, which received extensive coverage in the press and were attended by "producer members" of the CCB. The CCB and CMB also held charged debates between representatives of the industry on one hand and representatives of the government, with Walsh at their head, on the other.

The situation became further aggravated in the 1943–44 season. An accepted list of traders could not be attained. Here too, as with regard to the boards' establishment, Mancur Olson's insight concerning the logic of collective action, which in our case focuses on creating an agreed marketing system, comes in handy. Since the Arab sector was deeply split, composed of hundreds of exporters, they had no interest in relinquishing their independence so long as this would not mean incurring losses. Only if the marginal cost of joining a centralized system would be lower than the revenue received as a result of such action, would it be worthwhile for single Arab exporters to take part in the industry's process of centralization.

Therefore, Walsh prevented organized export to the British market, which had begun to accept imports once the war finally turned in favor of the Allies. In addition, processes involving purchasing wood for manufacturing crates were also delayed. But above all, Walsh refused to purchase the surplus fruit as he had promised. The relationship between Walsh and the rest of the industry reached an impasse. In April 1944 Walsh was compelled to resign. The CCB welcomed his "wise decision to devote most of his energy to his responsibilities as food controller."[45]

In their summaries of the 1943–44 season, Rokach and other leaders of the industry vehemently claimed that this had been the industry's worst season.[46] Walsh, however, managed to achieve his goal. His replacement, R. H. R. Church, the district commissioner of Lydda district who was appointed interim chair of the boards, managed to receive an acceptable list of traders from both sectors, thus initiating the centralized export of citrus fruit through the CMB.

The industry's binational configuration, formed and enhanced during the war to a large degree as a result of the struggle against a common rival, proved its strength and durability in the three years from 1945 to the Nakba. Then again, the work of the boards' "official members" entered a period of crisis from the time of Walsh's resignation. Chairmen were replaced and positions split. Finally, on May 7, 1946, Walsh was reappointed chairman of the boards. But he was killed about a month and a half later, on June 22, 1946, in the Zionist terrorist attack on the King David Hotel in Jerusalem.

Conclusion

Several components may be said to have facilitated formation of the binational citrus industry enclave that existed from 1939 to 1948. First, the many years of collaboration, both within the groves and in lengthy membership of joint committees, created some of the conditions suggested by Allport: familiarity between the leaders and individuals of both sectors in the groves themselves and in the industry's management and ongoing government support for such cooperation. Second, the common economic interests as a result of the economic crisis that befell the industry during the war years led individual practitioners to the understanding that cooperation is more profitable than other alternatives. Third, the unprecedented social and political conditions that were created in Palestine during the war, which facilitated variegated joint activities of Arabs and Jews, enabled the fulfillment of Allport's other parameters: common goals, intergroup cooperation in achieving these goals, and equal status for members of both sectors of the industry. Fourth, it appears that Walsh's aggressive personality, as well as the general policy of the high commissioner and the Colonial Office aimed at reducing the number of practitioners in the industry and its geographical area, served to create a common rival for the industry's two sectors, against which they joined forces. Fifth, the model designed with the purpose of consolidating the industry's binational format was typologically similar, in many ways, to that implemented many years later in Northern Ireland. In other words, aside from the understanding that the sides have reached a dead end, where victory is possible for neither, an external actor occupies a central role in the process of creating the binational structure and in its continuity. Finally, the intensive successive cooperation between the two sectors and between their leaderships created what the study of conflict resolution designates conditions of pooling sovereignty.[47] In this way, the industry's two national sectors formed a relationship of trust, affinity, and common interests.

4

Nakba

That which is self-obvious merits repeated emphasis. The binational phenomenon of the citrus industry was generated by members of two societies that were both separate and rival. As stressed at the beginning of this book, these two societies were separated geographically, culturally, socially, religiously, and to a large degree economically as well. They also held separate national aspirations to the same parcel of land. Once World War II ended, the winds of national rivalry gained increasing strength as the Zionist leadership led the Yishuv into an open revolt against the Mandate and for an independent state for the Jews in Eretz-Yisrael/Filastin.

Evidence of this new phase, which had the obvious effect of entangling the Arab population as well, can be found in the diary of a major figure in Zionist citriculture, Yitzhak Rokach. In March 1941 Yitzhak Rokach, his wife Hilda, and his mother-in-law Mrs. Gesundheit, were at the Tiberias hot springs. They had come for a reception held for editorial board members of Arab newspapers. Rokach states that he was glad to meet the attendees: "The guests included, aside from the newspaper editors, also my friends 'Abd al-Rahman Bay Taji and 'Omar 'Afandi Bitar. Both were glad to see me and we spent a pleasant hour together." Afterward, relates Rokach in his diary, there was a reception. He himself opened the reception and addressed the guests in Arabic. He was followed by "the Jewish mayor of T. [Tiberias], Dihan, who read aloud a prepared speech, and then his assistant from the al-Husayni family—who spoke excellently, followed by two of the journalists." Hence, Rokach's description is compatible with the testimonies we offered in the previous chapter concerning the friendships between the heads of the citrus industry. 'Omar al-Bitar, the mayor of Jaffa, was one of these, and 'Abd al-Rahman al-Taji too was one of the heads of Palestinian citriculture. Also notable are the friendships and collaboration between Jews and Arabs in the city of Tiberias, evident from Rokach's description, which are well known and do not require any further proof.

But the divisive forces are evident from Rokach's diary as well. At the event Rokach also met Aryeh Shenkar, chairman of the Yishuv's Industrialists Union. Rokach noted in his diary that, after they spoke about various topics,

> the conversation came around to the future of Palestine after the war. Here is what he said to us word for word—as spoken to me and to Hilda [Rokach's wife] and Mrs. Gesundheit [her mother]: "In my opinion"— said Mr. Shenkar in all sincerity—"we Jews will have no future in Palestine unless we get rid of the Arabs," and he added in Yiddish: "*Man muz zey areyn warfen in yam*" [One must have them thrown into the sea]. When I said to him: "Indeed? And why do we complain that Hitler did this to the Jews?" he answered: "The Arabs have many countries: Syria, Egypt, Iraq, etc. etc., they should go there and leave Palestine for us." We were amazed to hear a respected and important man utter words that I would not have accepted from an 18 year old Chauvinist! [Chauvinist: a member of the right-wing Revisionist movement.][1]

Rokach's diary includes no further testimonies of the radical type expressed by Aryeh Shenkar, the first president of the Zionist Industrialists Union in the Land of Israel. In his diary, however, he relates that with the end of the world war the conflict in Palestine with regard to the countrywide citrus industry became more prominent. Rokach repeatedly mentions the impact of the national circles and the national leadership of each side on binational activities. In one incident in early 1946, when the Zionist uprising against British rule was at its height, Rokach relates that after a meeting at the government offices in Jerusalem he met with Moshe Shertok (later Sharet), "the political secretary of the Jewish Agency." The topic of their conversation was whether Jewish representatives on the CMB and CCB should initiate a counterboycott against the Arab boycott of Jewish citrus exports to Arab countries. Shertok's instruction was to avoid a boycott. In another incident Rokach relates that six months earlier, in the summer of 1945, the Arab CCB representatives felt obliged to consult with all the Palestinian political factions (the Arab representatives were associated with six such factions) and receive their consent to continue cooperating with the Jewish-Zionist sector.[2]

The conflict intruded on the regular activities of the industry after World War II primarily with regard to organization of citrus exports. As mentioned in the previous chapter, from the 1944–45 season until 1948 exports were organized following the "linking marketing scheme." Nonetheless, the industry was still in dire straits. It had not yet resumed a free market course, while the debt to the government resulting from bank loans guaranteed during the war years continued to grow. It was necessary to sign collective agreements with British and continental governments. The Mandate government applied pressure to form a joint delegation representing the Arab and Jewish citrus industries, which would travel to European countries and Britain, negotiate with the governments, and sign export contracts on behalf of the countrywide industry. The Palestinians, taken by surprise by the Zionist uprising and feeling vulnerable, strongly objected to any joint delegation. However, the Arab citrus growers themselves and the heads of the Arab industry understood that continued joint organized activity was still essential. After consulting with the various Palestinian factions, and in light of the tough situation in the industry, approval of the joint delegations was finally granted. Three such delegations embarked in the summers of 1945, 1946, and 1947. Hence, despite the external political pressures the binational configuration formed during the war proved durable.[3]

Conflicting Visions for Palestine's Future

At the beginning of the Zionist uprising against British rule in October 1945, the attacks against main traffic arteries and particularly against the railroad system, and the terror attacks against the civilian population as part of the resistance, had only a partial effect on the regular activities of the citrus industry. At the same time, the uprising aggravated intersector tensions within the industry. Thus, the limited war declared by the Zionist movement against the British, which lasted from the fall of 1945 until late 1947, cast a constant shadow over the future of the land and of the industry.

However, the United Nations Partition Plan of November 1947 (UN Resolution 181) and the interethnic war that broke out the next day between the Palestinian Arabs and Zionist Jews changed everything. The entire country entered a state of uncertainty. In light of the situation, and because Arab residents had the option, not open to most members of the Jewish community, of leaving the country for neighboring countries until things calmed down, some of the Arab industry leaders decided to relinquish their membership on the citrus boards.

The retirement letter written by Nicolas Gélat, longtime secretary of the CCB and CMB, reveals the significance of the joint history of cooperation between the sectors, as well as the trust formed among members of the boards and their staff as long as these existed:

> I happen to be, in my capacity as member of the Palestine General Agricultural Council, one of the promoters of the establishment of the Palestine Citrus Control Board and a member of the Sub-Committee appointed by that Council to work out the statutes of the then proposed Citrus Control Board.
>
> I take pride . . . [in] the success of this Board . . . There has always been prevailing among them all a sense of and a spirit of family, without which the Board could not have deserved the esteem and confidence which it enjoyed among the Public and the Government Departments.[4]

While some Arab leaders of the industry left the country, the majority who remained were concerned about the future of the industry following the expected British departure. According to the 1947 UN partition resolution several Jewish communities were to have remained within the Arab state (mainly the settlements of Gush Etzion and the Jewish settlements in the Western Galilee, including the city of Naharia), with a population totaling approximately 1 percent that of the proposed Arab state. On the other hand, the proposed Jewish state was supposed to have included approximately 55 percent Jews and 45 percent Arabs, some of them residents of cities such as Haifa, Safed, and Tiberias, as well as residents of hundreds of villages. While the Arab state was supposed to have encompassed a very small Jewish minority, the future Jewish state was in fact to have been a binational state.

The official position of the hegemonic Palestinian leadership was that the partition resolution was not legally acceptable as it impinged upon the legitimate national rights of the native Palestinian people to all of Palestine. The leadership, headed by Amin al-Husayni, also saw Zionism as a European colonial movement attempting to take control of all Palestine. Hence, the struggle against Zionism was perceived as an overall fight for national liberation.

The Zionist view was more complex. The Zionists saw themselves as returning to their historical homeland, but they also realized that the land was inhabited by another nation that saw Palestine (which for Jews is Eretz Yisrael, the Land of Israel) as its homeland. Another related factor was the lengthy Jewish history as a diasporic minority under the patronage of non-Jewish societies and regimes. Thus, a major aspect of the Zionist rhetoric and thought was the demand that the future Jewish state's attitude to its minorities must in no way replicate the attitude toward the Jews during their years of exile. Author Amos Oz, in his autobiographical novel *A Tale of Love and Darkness*, summarized this well as voiced by his aunt, Aunt Sonia:

> We thought that soon, in a few years, the Jews would be the majority here, and as soon as that happened, we'd show the whole world how to treat a minority—our own minority, the Arabs. We, who had always been an oppressed minority, would treat our Arab minority justly, fairly, generously, we would share our homeland with them, share everything with them.[5]

In December 1947 Ben-Gurion established a committee, which he headed, called the "Emergency Committee [Va'adat ha-Matzav]," with the purpose of preparing detailed plans of how the future Jewish state would be administered. The Emergency Committee was divided into five subcommittees that dealt with the future administrative structure of the Jewish state, its legal system, the future of Jerusalem, economic issues, and future government ministries. As far as is known, based on the publicly accessible archival material of the Emergency Committee, no subcommittee discussed the Arab residents of the prospective Jewish state. The little research on the Emergency Committee, including that focusing on the law and legal system whose foundations were laid by the relevant subcommittee, devoted almost no attention to the place of the Arab population in the future Jewish state.[6] Nevertheless, it is only logical that the leadership of the Zionist movement gave much thought and time to this issue. At present we have only a small number of testimonies, on which we will base our analysis.

It is evident from the files of the Emergency Committee and its subcommittees that are open to researchers, that in the few cases where Arab residents of the prospective Jewish state were explicitly mentioned, they were perceived as a financial burden and as a minority that could not be trusted. For example, in a memorandum prepared by Dr. Yehoshua Greenbaum in early February 1948 on "the employment of Arabs in the Ministry of Commerce, Industry, and Transportation," he recommended that the employment of Arabs in this ministry be avoided as much as possible. He contended that although the future Jewish state was obliged to provide equal rights to all its citizens, the question of loyalty to the state superseded the principle of equality. He brought examples from post–World War I Czechoslovakia and from the British Mandatory rule, and argued that as a matter of principle it would be wrong for members of an ethnic, racial, or religious minority to receive equal opportunities in occupying government positions, even if their skills transcended those of other candidates. He also recommended that "all the key positions in the ministry be held by Jewish officials, even those that pertain to the Arab sector."

A report submitted in December 1947 by Dr. Esther Pines from the Economic Research Institute of the Jewish Agency concerning the necessary investments in education, health care, and social services for the Arab population in the Jewish state claimed that these would constitute an economic burden. Her specific recommendations are still classified. However, the title of her report speaks volumes regarding the future Israeli government's policy toward its prospective Arab population: "The Financial Burden Involved in the Maintenance of Educational, Social and Health Services for the Non-Jewish Population of the Jewish State."[7]

Other testimonies that have come to our attention show that even before the Emergency Committee was established, the Arab section of the Haganah's Information Service (SHAI) discussed plans to transfer Arabs from the future Jewish state. Ezra Danin, a major figure in the Arab section of SHAI, who recruited many agents from among the Palestinians and was an enthusiastic advocate of Palestine's ethnic cleansing of Arabs, presented this position openly in his autobiography. Moreover, in a private letter he wrote to author S. Yizhar in April 1947, Danin presented his position on this matter, which may be taken as the position of his entire section. The letter was prompted by Yizhar's work on a memorial book in honor of Yehiam Weitz, a member of the Haganah who was killed in July 1946 in an operation to blow up the railroad bridge near the village of al-Zib. Weitz and Yizhar were close cousins. Danin's letter to S. Yizhar indicates that Weitz and Danin had collaborated on the issue of ethnic cleansing of the Arabs from a future Jewish state:

> There are two dreams that [Weitz] had and that we often discussed: a. Developing the Middle East by transporting Arabs from here to there and thus expanding our hold on the land; b. Seeking new means of struggle to enable our nation to live a respectful life amidst the terrible pressures to which we are being subjected . . .
>
> These issues are very interesting, albeit in our current life circumstances and considering the rampant hypocrisy of our world, where everything is permitted only to the strong—they cannot be discussed, and all the more so written about, at length.[8]

In the actual memorial book for his cousin Yehiam Weitz, Yizhar included a letter that Weitz had written on this topic to his father, Joseph Weitz, who had taken decisive steps to realize the transfer concept. The letter is from January 1945:

> And finally, such a plan [the Jewish State] will never materialize without a comprehensive transfer of the Arabs from Palestine. Even if their development shall be expedited, this shall not happen for many generations. The problem is that there shall be no transfer. I know that you are a big advocate of the transfer, and I too agree with you on this matter,

however there is nothing to be done, as no indication of such a transfer is evident.[9]

The position of the Jewish and Arab citrus growers was completely at odds with these radical stances. Indeed, the situation of the Arab citrus growers was much worse than that of their Jewish colleagues. This, since according to the Partition Plan some 85 percent of the local citrus land, including the large majority of Arab-owned groves, were to have been included within the borders of the Jewish State. But so long as the military conflict between Palestinian Arabs and the Yishuv did not take a turn for the worse, the two sides continued to formulate joint plans in preparation for the 1948–49 export season. This despite the opposition voiced by the Palestinian leadership, which forbade any collaboration with the Zionists.

The deteriorating military situation and the growing animosity between the two societies compelled the CMB and CCB to split their joint offices in January 1948. Beginning from their establishment and until the end of January 1948 the offices of the boards were located at Bayt Hinnawi in Jaffa, near the headquarters of the British secret police, the CID. In February 1948 the Jewish members of the boards moved to offices in Tel Aviv, and contact was maintained mainly by telephone or through messengers.

The binational configuration of the industry and its operation in this form, entailing as it did equal administration of the sectors, appeared to Arab and Jewish citrus growers the most simple and straightforward way of continuing its activities after the departure of the British. Consequently, it also encompassed a practical vision with the purpose of enabling binational existence in the future Jewish state. This was expressed by Yitzhak Rokach in his speech to Jewish farmers in February 1948. He called upon the leaders of the Zionist community and future leaders of the proposed Jewish state to declare that the industry's legal and organizational structure would be maintained and that the legal rights of the Arab members and their position would be assured:

Our leaders should declare their intention of maintaining the [Marketing] Board in its present legal status and organization, with no fundamental changes. From hints dropped by the leaders of the Arab citrus growers, it is apparent that they are concerned about their future status in the Jewish state. It is therefore necessary to ensure the rights of the Arab growers and exporters on the [Marketing] Board and assure them of their secure position.[10]

As we know, the binational position publicly advocated by Rokach as early as February 1948 was not accepted.[11] Toward April 1948 the boards ceased to operate, although they were not officially dissolved, and their assets were divided between the two sectors. Most leaders of the Arab industry left their place of residence for locations deemed safer for them and their families.

The worsening conflict increased each community's sense of identification with their initial group of affiliation.[12] On May 7, 1948, Rokach visited Haifa, which had been occupied by Haganah forces. He wrote in his diary:

> I visited occupied Haifa this week and I liked what I saw. The entire port is Jewish . . . I passed the Burj, the Hamra, the train station, and lots of other places in which Jews had not set foot for months . . .
>
> Abba Hushi—the city's governor for the foreseeable future—was in the hospital with a broken leg. I visited him and I saw him running the city from his hospital room. He is furious that the Arabs were not treated fairly in known instances—for example, care was not always taken with the mosques, or the Arabs' merchandise was taken without payment.[13]

At the end of the war, most of the citrus lands owned by Arabs were transferred to Jewish hands. Most of the Arab industry's leadership and thousands of citrus growers became refugees. Rokach, Horin, and their friends, however, tried to convince the Israeli government to bring some of the industry's leaders back to the country and even to return their property.

In January 1950, five industry leaders from the newly founded State of Israel sent a letter to the minister of foreign affairs, Moshe Sharet. In their letter the five authors, members of both the Labor Movement and the Zionist "civil sector," requested that "four Arabs who are former members of the country's Citrus Board, as well as the widow of the late mayor of

Jaffa, along with their families" be permitted to return to their homes and reclaim their property.[14] In his response, Sharet explained that he realized that their application was limited to a "very small number of persons who were of the more moderate among Palestine's Arabs, and had personally attested to their moderate views by collaborating with their Jewish counterparts in a joint central institution."

The letter written by Rokach, Horin, and the others to Moshe Sharet was an irregular act at a time when many people and organizations—including citrus growers and citrus companies—were fighting to appropriate Palestinian property in what had become Israel. The minister's response was of course negative, unequivocally articulating the government's policy of blocking the right of return, undertaken already during the 1948 War:

> However, allowing these people to enter would certainly create an opening for similar demands by many others. It would most definitely rekindle in the refugee camps the hopes of returning to the land, and would undermine the attitude of accepting the verdict to settle in other countries—an attitude which it is extremely important for us to spread and strengthen.

Sharet ended with a clear insinuation concerning Palestinian property that had been transferred to Jewish citrus growers: "I myself would like to know whether it is not clear to you as well, that the return of citrus growers means the return of groves, and whether you truly believe that abandoned Arab groves should be returned to their former owners."[15]

The letter's authors did not give up and wrote to Sharet once more. It appears that the shared domain formed by citrus growers throughout the years that preceded the Nakba had created the necessary conditions for this unusual act by Rokach et al. At the same time, our sources show that the success of industry leaders in returning the property of those Arab growers who had helped create the mutual Zionist-Palestinian space was extremely limited. Moreover, sources show that former Palestinian groves were subsequently handled by companies run by Rokach, Horin, and the others, though the precise scope of this phenomenon is as of yet unclear.

הקריה, ז' באדר התש"י
24 בפברואר 1950
מס' 157/50
ח/ק/2154/31116

לכבוד
ח'ה צ. איזקסון, י. חורין, י. טוקסלי, ג. מכנס וי. רוקח,
תל - אביב.

א.נ.

קבלתי את מכתבכם מ-23 בינואר ש"ז בו אתם מבקשים מתן
רשות כניסה לארץ לארבעה ערבים שהיו לשעבר חברים במועצת ההדרים
הארץ-ישראלית ולאלמנת ראש עירית יפו המנוח, הם ומשפחותיהם.

למען הסדר עלי להעיר, כי הרשות שאליה יש לפנות בבקשת
רשיונות כניסה לארץ היא משרד העליה ולא משרד החוץ. אולם אני
מבין כי פניתם אלי משום אפיית המדיני המובהק של בעית מתן
רשיונות הכניסה במקרה המיוחד הזה ולכן הנני מלמד היתר לעצמי
להחזיר לכם תשובה ישירה על פניותכם.

ודאי לא נעלם מכם, כי הדבר אשר אתם מבקשים עומד בסתירה
גמורה למדיניותה המוצהרת של הממשלה בשאלת החזרת הפליטים הערבים,
אשר היא שוקדת לקיימה בכל ההקפדה האפשרית, בהשענה על אישור
הכנסת למדיניות זו ועל תמיכת דעת הצבור בה.

במשך הזמן נעשו נסיונות מרובים, הן מצד המעונינים
עצמם והן ע"י ועדת הפיוס, להביא את ממשלת ישראל לידי הסכמה
לנהוג דין יוצא מן הכלל לגבי הפרדסנים שבקרב הפליטים, לא רק
על מנת להחזירם לארץ לאלתר מתוך העדפה זכותם על כוח המוני
הפליטים מדלת העם, אלא על מנת להחזיר להם את פרדסיהם. הממשלה
התנגדה לחלוטין למתן זכות בכורה כזו לקבוצה מיוחסת והתנגדותה
בעינה עומדת.

איננו סבורים שאם יש לנהוג לפנים משורת הדין לגבי איזו
קבוצה, הרי הדבר מגיע דוקא לבעלי היכולת שבקרב הפליטים, בשעה
שהמוניהם נשארים מופקרים למחסור. יתר על כן, דוקא החזרתם של
פרדסנים כרוכה בבעיה חמורה, באשר חזירתם מוכרחת לעורר מיד את
שאלת החזרת רכושם ועלולה לפתוח פתח לתביעות משפטיות הרות סיבוכים
קשים.

2/...

- 2 -

אני מבין היטב, כי אתם מייחדים את בקשתכם למספר מצומצם
בתכלית של אישים שהיו מהמתונים בקרב ערביי ארץ-ישראל ונתנו עדות
ממשית למתינותם בשתפם פעולה משך שנים עם חבריהם היהודים במוסד
מרכזי משותף. אולם היתר כניסתם של אלה אי אפשר שלא ישמש פתחון-
פה לתביעה דומה מצד רבים אחרים. הוא מוכרח ללבות מחדש במחנות
הפליטים את התקוה לחזור לארץ ולערער את הלך הרוח של התפשרות עם
גזירת ההשתקעות בארצות אחרות, אשר כה חשוב לנו להפיצו ולחזקו.

ועל הכל, גם חזירתה של קבוצה קטנה זו תעורר מיד את בעיית
רכושם הנטוש של החוזרים ותיצור סבך אשר יקשה מאד להתירו.

מכל הטעמים האלה הנני נאלץ להשיב את פניכם.

כשלעצמי הייתי מעוניין לדעת אם לא ברור גם לכם, כי החזרת
פרדסנים פירושה החזרת פרדסים, ואם באמת אתם סבורים כי דינם של
פרדסים ערבים נטושים להיות מוחזרים לבעליהם הקודמים.

בכבוד רב,

מ. שרת
שר החוץ

At the same time, there is no doubt that an overwhelming majority of groves owned by Palestinian Arabs until 1948 did not return to their original owners. Our sources also show that a significant number of Arabs holding Israeli citizenship, defined as "present absentees" and who had become refugees in their own country ("interior refugees"), were not permitted to reclaim their possessions and groves.[16]

5

Memory and Forgetfulness

The Lost Palestinian-Arab Groves

The history of the pre-Nakba Palestinian citrus industry and its relations with its Zionist counterpart, presented in the previous chapters of this book, is shrouded in obscurity. This obscurity is no coincidence. Palestinian-Arab society on one hand and Jewish-Israeli society on the other have displayed different approaches toward the unique past of this industry and the central role it played in the economy, society, culture, and relationship of the two communities prior to 1948. Accordingly, the two societies also constructed different memories and histories of the industry. In post-Nakba Palestinian-Arab society, the Jaffa orange and the city of Jaffa have a major cultural and symbolic role in preserving the memory of the city, its inhabitants, and pre-1948 Palestinian-Arab society in general. As scholars of collective memory have convincingly shown, the active and continuous act of remembering the past is part and parcel of the effort to construct collective memory and identity for the contemporaneous national imagined community.[1] Hence, the ongoing effort to bring to life the pre-1948 Jaffa orange and the city of Jaffa, "the bride of the sea," should be regarded as an integral part of (re)constructing Palestinian national identity. Jewish-Israeli society, in contrast, took various steps to repress this past and any memory of it in its own efforts to construct a collective identity and memory devoid of the presence of Palestinian-Arab society.[2]

As we know, the Nakba was and has remained a constitutive continuous source of trauma for the Palestinian-Arab people. In another sense, the Nakba was traumatic for Jewish-Israeli society as well. The role played by hundreds of Israeli soldiers in generating the Palestinian catastrophe, and the fact that major parts of Israeli society subsequently reaped the material benefits of this catastrophe, contrasted sharply with Zionist and Israeli self-consciousness. The latter depicts the Jewish people as a constant victim of the circumstances of its history and stresses the commitment of Zionism and of Israel to refrain from becoming the victimizer: to uphold universal humanitarian Western values as well as the recognition of every nation's right to self-determination in its historical homeland. In contrast, their extensive role in creating the Palestinian catastrophe, particularly after the first ceasefire of the 1948 War, and their significant and active part in the expropriation of "abandoned" Palestinian property after 1948, strongly contrasted with their former set of values and led to a deep cognitive dissonance within Israeli society.[3]

About half the citrus land included within the borders of the State of Israel in 1949 had been previously owned by Palestinians turned refugees, and their property was declared "abandoned." At the same time, the newly established State of Israel absorbed hundreds of thousands of Jews, Holocaust survivors from Europe and new arrivals from Arab-speaking and Muslim countries (Mizrahim). It was necessary to integrate them in the emerging Israeli collective, in that defined as the "civil religion" of the Israeli era of Statism (Mamlachtiyut). The manner in which Israeli collective memory was structured with regard to the citrus industry and its history might, therefore, serve as a suitable prism for viewing the structuring of the entire pre-1948 past by the young state.

Our reconstruction of the methods used by Palestinian society to remember, and by Israeli society to forget, the pre-Nakba Palestinian citrus industry is based on the insights formed and developed by scholars of collective memory. The study of collective memory deals mainly with how societies construct and disseminate their own particular memories. In most of these studies, forgetting is regarded as the necessary outcome of remembering, which is always partial.[4] Based on several major studies, and particularly on the main insights of the field's founder, Maurice Halbwachs, we too postulate that the creation and preservation of collective memory is socially constructed.[5] However, in contrast to Halbwachs's

famous assertion that memory and historical writings are two different and opposing ways of reconstructing the past, scholars of collective
memory have long demonstrated that the boundaries between scholarly
historical writings and the many types and ways of remembering the
past are much more fluid than he had contended.[6] Henry Rousso, in his
groundbreaking study of the ways in which France tried to remember,
and to forget, its Vichy years, termed these memory mechanisms "vectors of memory."[7] Olick, Vinitzky-Seroussi, and Levy, who summarized
the state of the field of collective memory, concluded that memory is
instilled and preserved in many ways that include the various techniques
and institutions through which it is conveyed: mass media, political
circumstances, private and public social settings, cultural institutions,
commemoration, and so on.[8] Finally, scholars of history and memory,
including scholars of Palestinian history and memory, emphasized the
importance that should be ascribed to nonscholarly works in the construction of national consciousness. These include "memory books" of
destroyed villages; oral history accounts; various memory maps of towns,
villages, and even bus routes; photography; architecture; oral testimonies; art; virtual communities; and much more.[9] Thus, we see the various
ways in which Palestinians remember the pre-1948 citrus industry and its
hub, the city of Jaffa, as an integral part of remembering their nationhood
while also creating it.

The decision of what to remember necessarily involves the decision
of what can be remembered less. Yet, there appears to be an important
difference between the choice not to emphasize a certain route or past
and the conscious and active attempt to obliterate a memory or even
to erase the past or parts of it. Henry Rousso discussed the collective
mental need to repress the past and the social and institutional mechanisms that help instill required consciousness and repress undesirable
history. Eviatar Zerubavel, in his eye-opening study on silence and
denial in everyday life, and Uri Ram in his fundamental study on institutional mechanisms of forgetting and of obliterating memory, uncovered the processes used by society to forget rather than to remember.[10]
Our reconstruction of how Israeli society attempted to repress or erase

all memory of the Palestinian citrus industry is based to a large degree on these studies.

Jaffa's Citrus and Palestinian Collective Memory

In the novel *Al-Safina* (*The Ship*) by renowned Palestinian author Jabra Ibrahim Jabra, the narrator remarks: "All Palestinians are poets by nature, perhaps they do not all write poetry, but they are poets, because they have known two important things: the beauty of nature and the momentous catastrophe. Anyone who has experienced these two things together will unquestionably become a poet."[11]

The Palestinian people and all their communities in the homeland and in the Diaspora have several symbols that are emblematic of their life in the past and present. Notably, the meaning of these symbols and their usage were completely transformed after 1948, the year of the Nakba, with its radical transfiguration of Palestinian life and its meaning. This transformation resulted primarily from the changed circumstances, where instead of a people residing on their land and in their homeland, one that was in a process of realizing national aspirations, they became mostly a people of refugees controlled by different sovereign entities. As shown by Barry Schwartz, who studied Abraham Lincoln in American memory, although Lincoln was perceived differently in each era following changes in society and culture, this memory also contains an element of continuity. Hence, it is possible to say that despite the changes in its symbols, Palestinian collective memory retains a dimension of continuity rooted in the time when the Palestinian people were living on its land.[12]

Palestinian literary critic Faysal Darraj contends that the symbols of Palestinian national consciousness derive from three sources: the stolen homeland, which is the homeland of the sad orange; the olives and grapes of Hebron; and the exile. The diversity of the symbols reflects revulsion at the dismal present.[13] Symbols adopted from Palestinian life and from local nature were used before the Nakba as well. Oranges, olives, grapes, hyssop, oaks, and carobs are some of the many symbols used both locally and nationally. After 1948 the local dimension of the symbols and of their use gradually diminished due to the remoteness of Palestine and of life in the land, and use of the national dimension increased and contributed significantly to the structuring of Palestinian collective memory.

Previous scholars have already analyzed the place to which certain *lieux de mémoire* were elevated to become major symbols for Palestinian collective identity. Carol Bardenstein, Susan Slyomovics, Gannit Ankori, Mark LeVine, Salim Tamari, Nur Masalha, and others have shown that memory books for destroyed Palestinian villages, photography of pre-1948 Palestine, images of the prickly-pear cactus, the *sabir* (sabra), olive trees, fellahin toiling on their land, oral history, the "Jaffa orange," the city of Jaffa itself, and other *lieux de mémoire* are central components of past and contemporary Palestinian collective memory.[14]

The prominent Palestinian artist Sliman Mansour plays an important role in this endeavor to construct identity. Since the 1970s, Mansour has been creating numerous paintings of monumental Palestinian women who wear traditional dresses adorned with indigenous Fellahi embroidery. The women's features often deliberately reference Canaanite art, linking them with the ancient inhabitants of the region. Indeed, these figures become allegories of Palestine, harking back to its historical and prehistorical past, but also alluding to the present and future of the homeland. In the painting reproduced on the cover of this book, *Yaffa*, the female personification of Palestine is inextricably linked with ripe oranges, the citrus groves of Yaffa (Jaffa), and the Palestinian fellahin who are an inseparable part of the land and its fruit. The painting evokes the distant past through a visual reference to Assyrian art, thus expressing the deep bond between Palestinians and the land for millennia. Mansour's paintings deliberately preserve the memory and celebrate "the lost Palestinian orchard," the pre-1948 Palestinian citrus industry. However, by transforming the past into iconic and beautiful images of rootedness and fruitful promise, the paintings also perform an act of resistance. They articulate a refusal to forget the past and a model for present-day acts of resilience and *sumud*, the steadfast rootedness of Palestinians in the land.[15]

Our own analysis is informed by these studies as we focus mainly on the various manifestations of the citrus industry in Palestinian culture.

Jaffa and the Oranges: Symbolism Combined with Sadness and Longing

Yasmin Badwan, whose grandfather had previously owned a grove in the Jaffa region, wrote on Facebook that even if she herself has never enjoyed the taste of Jaffa oranges, "those who tasted them before me said that they taste like heaven." She continues to relate that her grandfather left a small wooden sign near his grove that says, "Badwan's Grove." The sign is still there, says Yasmin Badwan at the conclusion of her Facebook post, "guarding over what we have there until such time as we can return."[16] Her words well reflect the association formed by those who write about Jaffa, between the citrus of the city and its environs, the Nakba, refugee status, and the dream of return.

Of all Palestinian towns destroyed and severely damaged as a result of the War and the Nakba of 1948, the city of Jaffa most symbolizes the Palestinian splendor, pride, and glory gravely wounded in this catastrophe.

10. Jaffa and environs, between 1898 and 1914. Matson (G. Eric and Edith) Photograph Collection, Library of Congress.

Jaffa with its buildings, port, cultural life, and mainly its groves, is an important source of Palestinian nostalgia and longing for the homeland, regardless of where each individual resided before being displaced. The longing, nostalgia, and structuring of collective memory using Jaffa's oranges as a formative tool, have been expressed in many realms, such as poetry, prose, cinema, and even in public spheres in the form of signs, names, and commercial advertising.

Poetry

The city of Jaffa has a strong presence in the lyrical imagery of Arab poets in general and of Palestinian poets in particular, since it was one of Palestine's important urban centers that served as a platform for the revival, renewal, and instilling of modern values as early as the late Ottoman period. It was a source of inspiration for poets prior to 1948, as well as a symbol of the loss of a homeland, displacement of a people, and destruction of its revival after 1948. Poets have used many images and names for Jaffa: "bride of Palestine," "bride of the sea," "bride of the coast," "city of flowers," "beautiful Jaffa" (*Yafa al-jamila*), "city of fragrance" (*madinat al-ra'iha al-zakiyya*), "lost heaven" (*al-firdws al-mafqud*), and "land of the sad oranges" (*ard al-burtuqal al-hazin*).

Almost every renowned poet among the Palestinian poets and in the Arab world wrote at least one poem in Jaffa's honor, both before and after the Nakba. Before the Nakba, Jaffa was a symbol of the glory, romance, and spiritual uplifting that poets depicted as a colorful mosaic of burgeoning groves, orange blossoms with their strong perfume, the magnificent beach, brilliant weddings, a glamorous life, and celebrations that lasted until the early hours. For example, in 1947 Palestinian poet Hasan al-Buhiri of Haifa (1919–98) wrote:

> What are you asking about?
> Are you asking about the orange blossom?
> About the secret of its enchanting flowers?[17]

Another example is the poem written by celebrated Iraqi poet Muhammad Mahdi al-Jawahiri (1900–1997), entitled "Yafa al-jamila" (Beautiful Jaffa). The poem was written in 1941 in honor of al-Jawahiri's visit to

Jaffa, and it was first recited by him at the Arab Club in Jaffa. Jawahiri told his listeners that he was "enchanted by Jaffa." In the poem he likened the orange groves that encircled Jaffa to a belt that encircles a person's waist, while "Palestine" is portrayed in the poem as "the good mother and its daughters the towns."[18]

After 1948 oranges became a symbol of steadfast perseverance, *sumud*, and of Palestinian reluctance to part with the land. At the same time, Jaffa was also described as a symbol of destruction and loss, a city of death, a "necropolis." The transition of Jaffa and its image in Palestinian memory was well described by poet Rashed Husayn (1936–77):

> Jaffa the city from which I nursed the milk of oranges . . . was a city
>   that exported oranges.
> One day it was destroyed and transformed into a city that
> exports refugees.[19]

In another poem titled "Baqin fi Yafa" (Still in Jaffa) (referring to the oranges), Rashed Husayn describes a large ship coming to uproot the city of Jaffa and to displace its oranges, as previously experienced by the city's residents, but the remaining oranges refuse to leave. They are extremely happy to have held on to the land and refuse the ship's signals to join the displacing voyage.[20] Husayn stresses the ignorance of the "other" regarding the essence of the Palestinian emotional and symbolic attitude to the oranges. Through the orange metaphor Husayn depicts the catastrophe, the displacement, and the transformation into a nation dispersed throughout the world.[21]

In a poem entitled "laji' 'arabi" (The Refugee Arabs), written by famed Iraqi poet 'Abd al-Wahhab al-Bayati (1926–99) after seeing an advertisement for "Jaffa Oranges" posted by Israelis in a European city, he wrote: "Who has seen Jaffa in a small notice in a foreign country / The defaced name of Jaffa on a box of lemons / Oh, he who is knocking on the door? / The refugees died / And 'Jaffa' is an ad for lemons."[22]

The poet Mu'in Bseiso (1926–84) found lost Jaffa, like Jonah (Yunus), within a whale that roams the seas, waiting for the moment when it can discharge the city back onto its shores.[23] One might identify in this allegory a gentle criticism of the Palestinians of Jaffa, who like the prophet Jonah, temporarily lost their faith in God and in their homeland and abandoned their city. Now, after they have repented, they are waiting for God to bring about their return.

While poet Mahmoud Darwish (1941–2008) also used other Palestinian images and symbols in his poetry, over the years he devoted considerable attention to oranges. The recurring motif of the orange received special significance in his work particularly after he and the other best-known Palestinian poet, Samih al-Qassem (1939–2012), were designated "the two parts of the Palestinian orange." Author Muhammad 'Ali Taha gave them this appellation following the correspondence between Darwish and al-Qassem, published simultaneously in the Haifa-based newspaper *al-Ittihad* and the Palestinian newspaper *al-Yawm al-Saba'* printed in Paris. This correspondence subsequently appeared in a book called *Kitab al-Ras'il* (The Book of Letters).[24]

Mahmoud Darwish mentioned the oranges in sixty-seven of his poems, published in his many poetry collections throughout his lengthy creative career. In the first poetry collection, published in 1964 under the title *Awraq al-Zaytun* (The Leaves of the Olive Tree), he mentioned oranges in two places. In the poem "Ruba'iyyat" (Quartets) he says: "Through the holes in the wall of the detention center I saw the eyes of the oranges."[25] In this image Darwish attempted to depict the oranges as emblematic of the prisoner's hope and of his wish to be released from his shackles. The prisoner seems to symbolize the entire Palestinian people as well.

Secondly, in a poem titled "Lorca" (for the renowned Spanish poet), Darwish states that all the pain and disasters born of the Nakba cannot erase the main feature of the orange tree, the intoxicating perfume it exudes. He says there: "And the orange blossom still spreads a perfumed fragrance," i.e., spreads hope despite all that happened in the Nakba.[26]

In the poetry collection published in 1966 with the title *'Asheq min Filastin* (A Lover from Palestine) and a poem of the same title, the lover emphasizes his love for the oranges but also declares his hatred for the new status of the Jaffa port: "I write in my diary / I love the oranges and hate the port."[27]

In the poem "al-sajeen wa al-qamar" (The Prisoner and the Moon), Darwish portrays the "steadfast perseverance" of the orange fragrance, which arouses the anger of the authorities and leads to a spree of arrests against those who sing this song and use it as a means of protest and struggle.[28]

In a poetry collection published in 1970, titled *al-'Asafir Tamut fi al-Jalil* (The Birds Dead in the Galilee), and in a poem titled "matar na'im fi khareef ba'eed" (Light Rain in a Distant Fall), he likens the setting sun to a grove and himself to a "stolen orange."[29] And in the poetry collection *La Ta'tazer 'Amma Fa'alat* (Do Not Be Sorry for What You Have Done), Darwish links the constant yearning for the land to the fragrance of the orange, which guides and directs the immigrants and the migrating birds.[30]

The poet Ziyad Mahamid (b. 1959), inspired by the Ten Commandments, wrote a poem titled "al-wasaya al-'ashr" (The Ten Commandments). It begins "In Jaffa God created the orange . . ." and ends with these lines: "See, I am your orange / . . . And even if my blood shall be extracted from me / I shall remain within you / For you / In the land of the oranges."[31]

Prose

Most of the writers who mention Jaffa describe an eternal triangle comprised of Jaffa, the sea, and the oranges. This triangle encompasses a mixture of emotions: what Svetlana Boym terms a "reflective nostalgia" for past good times and for the visions, scents, and sense of uplifting at the sight of the homeland, combined with the pain of the catastrophe, loss, and dispersal, as well as hope that the past will be reinstated, what Boym calls a "restorative nostalgia."[32] On a reflective nostalgic level, Jaffa-based author Mahmoud Sayef al-Din al-'Irani (1914–74) described this triangle: "Jaffa, the bride at the feet of whom the waves of the Mediterranean have always expressed their yearning love, morning and night. These waves will never be deterred. . . . Facing the sea with the orange gardens at its back, the city is in the middle, taking pleasure in a grace awarded none other."[33]

The intellectual Hisham Sharabi (1929–2005), originally from Jaffa, described the effect of the orange blossom's fragrance and of the sea's beauty on the cultural and intellectual behavioral patterns of Jaffa's inhabitants before the Nakba. "This is what the generation uprooted from Jaffa in 1948 remembers," wrote Sharabi, "the intoxicating fragrance, the blue sky, and the raging sea."[34]

Author, playwright, and journalist Ghassan Kanafani (1936–72) gave one of his story collections the title *Ard al-Burtuqal al-Hazin* (Land of the Sad Oranges). Literary critic Faysal Darraj says that Kanafani's choice of this title makes two statements that will always remain interconnected: "The land of oranges" is Palestine, while "the land of the sad orange" is Palestine that was taken by others.[35] Darwish added another dimension to this image, in the form of the olive. For his second poetry collection, Darwish chose the title *Awraq al-Zaytun* (The Leaves of the Olive Tree), replacing the orange with the sacred fruit that residents of the Galilee like and admire— the olive. These two authors shaped Palestine's symbolism through its bitter fate: olives as a symbol of something that passes from the owner to the hands of strangers and oranges as a symbol shared by sad refugees.[36]

The oranges reminded Kanafani of the day his family left Acre and traveled north. On the way they saw an Arab farmer sitting by the road with a basket of oranges. They stopped their truck to buy some oranges from him. Everyone wept, Kanafani tells us, and men burst out crying like miserable children. Kanafani writes: "Your father's eyes contained the sparkle of all the orange trees he had left behind for the Jews. He saw them all before him and they were evident in his uncontrollable sobs, standing before the officer at the border police checkpoint. When we reached Sidon in the afternoon, we became refugees."[37]

Author Jabra Ibrahim Jabra too used a childhood memory to indicate the threefold destruction of Jaffa, the sea, and the oranges. In his novel *al-Safina*, mentioned above, the author links the calamity and the dispersal of the Palestinian people with the sight of a box of oranges that had spilled into the sea, its contents bobbing on Jaffa's blue waters: "Many years ago, when I was a young child, the monks took us for a trip to Jaffa. On the port we boarded a ship loaded with orange crates. There was a pleasant smell, the scent of the sea mixing with the scent of oranges. One of the orange crates had fallen from the crane and burst open alongside one of the ships. The fruit scattered right and left on the blue foam. To this day I have not forgotten the sight of the cursing porters. But I enjoyed watching the orange spheres floating in and out, right and left, dancing."[38]

The historical novel *Yafa Tuʿid Qahwat al-Sabah* (Jaffa Prepares the Morning Coffee) by Anwar Hamed (b. 1956) incorporates actual oral testimonies. In this novel about British Mandate Jaffa, the author makes frequent use of oranges as a recurring element and describes how the development of the citrus industry affected Palestinian social life and social stratification. Thus, in exile as well they planted several orange trees in their new gardens and hung on their walls historical photographs depicting groves, citrus trees, and cypress trees used to fence in the groves. This is evident, for example, in the character of the literary critic who roams Amman in search of original residents of British Mandate Jaffa who can tell him about the city. At first, he visits the home of Dr. Fuad, a well-known physician from Jaffa. Dr. Fuad's grandson takes the narrator into his grandfather's room. On the walls he sees photographs of horses, groves, cypress trees, and family gatherings on the beach. A photograph of a spacious house draws his attention. There is a wide garden in front of the house that includes several orange trees and three giant cypresses.[39]

The narrator also visits the home of Bahiya, Dr. Fuad's first sweetheart, who came from a lower-class family. She was the daughter of a citrus worker, the *bayari*, who worked in the groves that belonged to Dr. Fuad's family. The narrator describes his visit to Bahiya's home in the town of al-Shuna in northern Jordan, accompanied by Baha, Fuad's grandson. A typical Jaffan garden was recreated in front of the house. It had three orange trees, a lemon tree, and a fig tree. Beside them was a small area planted with vegetables: tomatoes, cucumbers, and green peppers.[40]

Bahiya's room too was designed with Jaffa's sights and sea in mind: "When I entered, I found myself in a room like none I had ever seen. The curtains on the windows were authentic fishermen's nets, the walls were painted blue, and they were decorated with drawings of fishermen's boats and white ships."[41]

Writer Tawfiq Fayyad (b. 1938), in his novel *Wadi al-Hawarath*, chooses to describe the orange trees as witnesses to events in the village of al-Haram (Sidna 'Ali) in 1948. In this novel a clear comparison is drawn between 'Aisha, a brave woman who lost her husband in the battles for the village and remained a national activist at the Deheyshe refugee camp where she arrived after her displacement, and the orange tree.

He describes the day the village fell: "'Aisha looked at the mosque courtyard, where the people had gathered. The fighting men also began to arrive there, bringing the dead with them. The blood of the fallen mixed with the tears of the oranges and the raindrops."[42] One of the fallen was the child Husayn, 'Aisha's son, who was killed when playing on one of the orange trees. Fayyad describes 'Aisha's son as "the eternal bridegroom on the orange tree in the village of al-Haram."[43] Hence, oranges are a source of nostalgia for the lost land and homeland and also a source of longing for the return and a symbol of the continued romantic relationship with the homeland.

Oranges and Citrus in Routine Journalistic Reports

Palestinian groves, and particularly those of Jaffa, were a central element in the publications of the Palestinian press from its establishment to the present. Whereas before the Nakba the presses' descriptions included a combination of symbolic and national elements,[44] after 1948 the issue remained primarily symbolic, encompassing dynamic memories of loss of the Palestinian homeland and of the national dream.

In a report on the demolishment of the Nablus homes of Palestinians who acted against Israeli settlers, journalist Bassam Abu al-Rub described the two trees, an orange tree and an olive tree, growing at the entrance to Karem al-Masri's demolished home, as symbolizing Palestinian identity and Palestinian endurance. The trees remained tall and erect despite the destruction of the house, its ceilings and walls. Abu al-Rub titled his article "I, the Bullets, the Oranges, and Memory."

> Yesterday, on Saturday, the Israeli occupation forces blew up the homes of detainees Karem al-Masri, Yehia al-Haj, and Samir Kusa, accused of murdering settlers east of Nablus early last October. At first light . . . residents of Nablus began to arrive at the demolished homes . . . All the destruction and the strong blasts could not uproot the orange tree and it remained strongly rooted in the earth, just like the people who live there.[45]

Collective Memory in Cyberspace

In addition to the various modes presented above of remembering the pre-1948 Palestinian citrus industry and its two major symbols, the oranges and the city of Jaffa, in recent years the internet has become a central space for constructing and maintaining Palestinian collective memory, including the lost pre-1948 citrus industry. Among these sites Palestineremembered.com holds a prominent place. Established in 1999, the site initially functioned as an online memory book for the hundreds of Palestinian villages that were depopulated during 1948 and subsequently. To a large extent, it initially relied on Walid Khalidi's famous book, *All That Remains*, which provided specific information on many of the depopulated Palestinian villages.[46] At present, however, this site has been engaging in new and much more active directions of collective identity construction. Thus, in addition to the list of depopulated villages, specific web pages dedicated to Palestinian towns have been added. Hence, besides demographic information, information about land ownership, and a short history of each place and its individual fate during the Nakba, Palestineremembered.com also contains images of the places and their maps. As Sophia Chloe Stamatopoulou-Robbins has convincingly shown, the original virtual memory book developed rather quickly from a virtual *lieu de mémoire* (which also includes a dynamic and constantly growing Palestinian archive) to an active memory community, a *milieu de mémoire*, that engages in active storytelling about its own community, and finally into a virtual Palestinian homeland.[47] Consequently, each village or town has its own dedicated web page in the collective Palestineremembered.com website that features, in addition to the above-mentioned data, an oral history subsite; links to Facebook, Wikipedia, Google Maps, and other external websites that contain information about the village or town; articles dedicated to the place and its history; contact information of "members" whose personal histories are connected to the place; and the option for viewers to post their comments.

The citrus industry, Jaffa and its port, and the "Jaffa" orange brand are an integral part of this multifaceted memory community in cyberspace. This is most evident in web pages dedicated to villages that were engaged in citrus growing and in the web page dedicated to Jaffa itself. A large part of the more than nine hundred pictures of the city that were uploaded to the city's website are of and connected to the citrus industry: the port, extensive citrus groves around Jaffa and its vicinity, irrigation machinery, picking and packing of oranges, and so forth. Indeed, the Facebook entry for the Bayt Dajan virtual community calling for the annual gathering of Bayt Dajanians in the Diaspora has as its symbol the bright orange from the homeland.[48]

Finally, it seems that recently Palestineremembered.com has adopted a policy of catering to a potential Israeli-Jewish audience. The site now links most of the individual place sites to Hebrew Google Translate to enable Hebrew-language readers to comprehend the information provided in it. In addition, some pictures intentionally show peaceful coexistence and even joint business ownership of Arabs and Jews before the Nakba. For example, the web page for al-Shaykh Muwannes contains several pictures of Samir Baydas from al-Shaykh Muwannes and his business partner, Ephrayim Baruch, in front of their jointly owned café. The Hawaii Café was established in 1947 on the northern bank of the al-Auja/Yarkon River as a joint venture of seven veteran Jewish soldiers of the British army and Samir Baydas, who owned the land on which the café was built.[49] The al-Shaykh Muwannes web page proudly displays several pictures of the two partners.[50] In the same vein, the web page for Abu-Kishk shows Shaykh Abu-Kishk standing in front of his vast citrus groves with the head (mukhtar) of the Zionist colony (moshava) of Petah-Tikva.[51]

Palestinian Arabs have been constructing a memory of the lost pre-1948 citrus industry and its main symbols, the city of Jaffa and its healthy and bright oranges, as anchors for both reflective and restorative nostalgia. In a way, these serve similar purposes of internalizing the concept of a Palestinian imagined community as the images and concept of the Heimat in constructing a German national identity.[52] Despite the fact that Palestinian memory and history are presented from various, sometimes conflicting angles,[53] it seems that the trauma of the Nakba and the symbols of the lost homeland have created what Yael Zerubavel termed a "master commemorative narrative." Namely, they created "a basic 'story line' that is culturally constructed and provides the group members with a general notion of their shared past."[54] While we did not detect a conscious attempt to forcefully erase the memory of the Jewish citrus growers, the emphasis on the Palestinian memory of pre-1948 Palestine in this context sidelined the memory of the Jewish-Zionist "other."

The Citrus Industry in Jewish-Israeli Consciousness

In contrast, the construction of the Jewish-Israeli "master commemorative narrative" included an attempt, and a successful one at that, to forcefully and consciously forget the Palestinian groves.

Obliterating Memory

In the two first decades after the State of Israel was established, the citrus industry was an important foundation of the state's economy and a significant element in the Jewish-Zionist population's self-consciousness. Inhaling the intoxicating scent of the citrus blossoms in the spring, excitedly awaiting the first crop of clementines and oranges in the fall, and "recruiting" schoolchildren to help pick the citrus fruit were all part of the conception that this was an industry based on the fundamental values of Zionism: return to the land, its cultivation by "Hebrew" labor only, and utilization of its fruit. To a certain degree, this self-conception continued the construction of Zionist ideology in prestate years. Then too, efforts were made to direct Jewish-Zionist consciousness inward. "Official bearers" of the collective identity helped emphasize the distinction of the Zionist settlement and its uniqueness. At the same time, a significant difference was also evident between the pre-1948 and postwar period. Before 1948 Palestinian society constituted a majority of Palestine's population, and therefore its presence could not be completely eliminated from Zionist consciousness. Moreover, as shown in previous chapters of this book, it was precisely the countrywide citrus industry that was an important point of encounter between the two national communities living in the country at that time. As shown above, the Arab citrus industry that preceded the Jewish-Zionist industry was a source of imitation, study, competition, and cooperation. Jaffa owed its economic, social, and cultural development to the centrality of the citrus industry in the local economy, while Tel Aviv significantly benefited from Jaffa's central economic place in the country. Above all, from 1930 and even more so from the beginning of World War II and until April 1948, the country's industry was directed and managed by unique joint organizations of Arab and Jewish citrus growers. Friendships were formed between leaders of the industry, as well as between Palestinian employees and their Zionist employers.

Nevertheless, in an extremely short time (only a decade from the end of the War of 1948), the very existence of the flourishing Palestinian-Arab citrus industry was eradicated almost completely from Jewish-Israeli collective consciousness and memory, as were the strong relations between the Jewish and Arab industries before the Nakba. What mechanisms facilitated this rapid process of forgetting the pre-1948 local Palestinian-Arab citrus industry, which encompassed hundreds of villages and tens of thousands of families?

Demographic and Physical Forgetfulness[55]

The first factor involved is the dual demographic change. The Nakba resulted in the exile of most Palestinians, some 700,000 people who until 1948 had lived in what subsequently became the State of Israel (within the so-called "Green Line"). This was matched by considerable Jewish immigration to Israel of Holocaust survivors, as well as immigrants and refugees from European, Arab, and Islamic countries. In two and a half years, from May 1948 to late 1951, the population of Israel doubled from approximately 650,000 Jews in pre-1948 to 1,370,000. In 1951, only about 167,000 (12 percent) of Israel's total population of 1,370,000 were Palestinian Arabs who had remained within the Green Line. In other words, already in the first two and a half years after the Nakba almost half the population had no memories or personal direct knowledge of life in the country before their arrival. Moreover, from 1948 to 1967 Jewish immigration to Israel totaled 1,275,000, while in 1967 the entire population numbered 2,776,000. If we deduct from this the 393,000 Arab citizens living in Israel in 1967 and the Jewish population living in the country before 1948, this means that by the eve of the 1967 War approximately two-thirds of the population had no memories or direct knowledge of pre-Nakba reality.[56] Thus, much of the information or memory that this population subsequently acquired about the prior history of the country was necessarily provided by Israel's cultural construction mechanisms.

Secondly, from 1948 to 1966 Israel's Arab population was under military administration, which among other things strictly limited any Arab-Jewish contact. Hence, for most of the Jewish population, particularly in rural areas, Arab citizens of Israel were physically and symbolically invisible.[57]

Third, in steps well documented by Benny Morris, Arnon Golan, Aharon Shai, and other scholars, during the initial stages of the war in 1948 and even more so after the UN acceptance of Resolution 194 dealing with the Palestinian right of return, the Israeli government acted systematically to demolish the hundreds of Palestinian villages remaining within the Green Line.[58] This "physical forgetting," as defined by Uri Ram, removed from view hundreds of Palestinian villages, leaving only scant remnants. For the hundreds of thousands newly arrived in Israel, most having experienced various degrees of trauma—from the terrible experiences of the Holocaust, to harassment and persecution in some Arab-speaking and Muslim countries of origin, to the regular challenges and traumas of immigration—the main concern was to rehabilitate their life. To a large degree remains of Palestinian villages became, therefore, an integral part of the new place they had reached.[59]

Collective symbolic forgetfulness is a psychological defense mechanism used by hegemonic institutions and cultural agents to create a symbolic and ethical tapestry aimed at relegating threatening circumstances to the subconscious, but mainly at repressing acts committed by society that are incompatible with that society's ethical system. Hence, these threatening circumstances and acts created a collective dissonance that demanded resolution.[60] Uri Ram contends that giving Hebrew names to Palestinian-Arab villages, towns, and streets occupied during the 1948 War was an act of *symbolic forgetting.*[61]

One may add other examples of Israeli symbolic forgetting to Ram's list. A prominent example is the Israeli concept and legal definition of "abandoned" Palestinian property. Thus, legislation regarding the status of Palestinian refugees and their property also created a symbolic tapestry of obliteration and repression. The definition of this property as "abandoned" obfuscated the reality of the takeover, irreconcilable as it was with the ethics of Zionism and of the newly established state, which could not come to terms with such an inner conflict.

How much of pre-1948 Palestinian-Arab grove land was defined as "abandoned" by the newly established Israeli state? By the eve of World

War II, the grove lands were almost equally divided between the two national sectors, with each having about 150,000 dunams. However, and as discussed in previous chapters of this book, suspension of export activities during the war affected the ability to continue cultivating the groves and many were deserted, particularly in the Jewish-Zionist sector. Moreover, quite a few groves near cities were uprooted and their zoning specifications redefined in the service of urban development. In the three years of 1945–48 the industry experienced a certain recovery and some of the groves were restored. One way or another, according to our data, by the end of the fighting in 1948 the territory under Jewish control included about 100,000 dunams of groves owned by Jews and some 132,000 dunams owned by Arabs. Some 15,000 dunams of groves that were owned by Arabs at the end of the Mandate appear to be part of territories that now came under Jordanian and Egyptian control in the regions of Tulkarm and the Gaza Strip, respectively. Within the Green Line, the young State of Israel now declared most of the citrus lands owned by Arabs "abandoned," as their owners had become refugees. These included refugees who at this stage were living outside the area controlled by Israel, as well as Israel's "internal refugees" who lived within its boundaries.[62] The 1948 "Census of Arab Citrus Groves" discussed in previous chapters of this book, conducted during and after the war, determined that due to the circumstances of the war and the inability of Arab farmers to cultivate their groves, only 35,000 dunams were in good condition. These were handed down now to individual Jewish farmers to cultivate. The rest of the "abandoned" land, about 97,000 dunams that were in poor or even worse condition, was handed over to Jewish-Israeli organizations for their use or converted from agricultural to urban land.[63]

These Jewish-Israeli organizations and entities were entrusted with responsibility for cultivating the "abandoned" groves. They included the kibbutz and moshav movements, the Jewish National Fund, and organizations of private citrus growers, such as the Pardes Syndicate, which before the War of 1948 had maintained strong relationships with leaders of the Palestinian-Arab industry. As seen in the preceding chapter, in the first years after the Nakba a number of leaders in the Jewish-Zionist industry operated, mainly clandestinely, to allow several leaders of the

Palestinian-Arab industry to return to the country and to their properties. Moreover, it is clear from historical sources that at first the leaders of the Israeli industry indeed saw themselves only as caretakers of the "abandoned" groves until such time as their legal owners would return.[64]

However, at the same time this leadership also took part in symbolic as well as practical processes that obliterated all memory of the Palestinian-Arab industry. For example, they participated in the renewed establishment of the Citrus Marketing Board, this time with no slots reserved for Arab owners, and signed contracts to sell the fruit overseas on behalf of all the groves in the country. In early 1959 seven private entrepreneurs, including Yitzhak Rokach, the prime figure in the industry during the Mandate period, established a special company, Mehadrin, charged with planting new groves on "abandoned" land. Minister of Finance Kaplan leased twenty-two thousand dunams of "abandoned" land to the company for a period of forty-nine years for the purpose of planting and cultivating groves. Some leaders of the prewar Jewish industry now became managers of Mehadrin.[65] At the same time, the Custodian of Absentee Property founded a company to cultivate citrus and other groves owned by Arabs. The company was given an Orwellian name, characteristic of the construction of symbolic forgetfulness, "Mata'ey Ha'uma" (Groves of the Nation). Some of its workers were Palestinian Arabs who had remained within the State of Israel and were intimately familiar with the groves that had now allegedly become "abandoned."[66]

Furthermore, while in the first year after the War of 1948 the Hebrew press spoke openly about the existence of a Palestinian-Arab citrus industry, in time any mention of the Arab industry became rare. A search for the word "citrus" in major Zionist-Israeli newspapers (*Davar, Herut, Al-Hamishmar, Ma'ariv, Hatzofe*) shows that by five years after the war any mention of the Arab industry had almost completely disappeared. This is particularly conspicuous in reports by industry leaders, such as Yitzhak Rokach, Yehuda Horin, and Zvi Isaacson, who were among the leaders of the industry in the Mandate period as well and who had good knowledge of the Arab industry. In their reports they either omitted this fact and did not mention it at all or stated that in post-1948 Israel there remained groves of "absentees" that had been "abandoned."[67]

Analysis of the word "abandoned" in these newspapers with regard to groves owned by Arabs shows that in the first year the term "abandoned" in its various forms was still commonly used for groves owned by Palestinian Arabs. However, such usage became rare, until it almost disappeared by around 1954. At the same time, terms expressing clear-cut expropriation of Arab lands and their unequivocal ownership became gradually more common. These terms were usually accompanied by utterances blaming the refugees for "leaving" their property. For example, in a tour of the "abandoned groves," *Davar* claimed that these had been "abandoned" by their owners and therefore the latter had lost all rights to them. Additionally, prominent Labor Movement member Shmuel Dayan (father of the well-known Israeli general and politician Moshe Dayan) blamed the "salary-cheap and disorganized Arab laborer" for "fleeing . . . together with his brethren." Therefore, said Dayan, there is "an urgent need to reclaim for our farms the one hundred and fifty thousand dunams of [Arab] groves destroyed during the war."[68]

A hegemonic literary manifestation of how strongly the term "abandoned" was perceived as a solution to the dissonance between the recognition that seizing Arab property was immoral and the continued practice of this expropriation is evident in Hanoch Bartov's influential book, *Each Had Six Wings*. The book, which was published in 1954 and won much literary and commercial acclaim, describes the life of the Jewish immigrant community formed in several "abandoned" Jerusalem neighborhoods. Bartov was born in Petah Tikva in the early Mandate period and served in the British army during World War II and in the Israeli army in the War of 1948, mostly in Jerusalem. After the war he lived in the German Colony in Jerusalem, in an "abandoned" house he had received from the Custodian of Absentee Property. In addition to his family, many families of Jews, Holocaust survivors as well as Mizrahim who had arrived from Asian and North African countries, resided in this area. His book was lauded as the first important (Jewish) Israeli literary expression of the hardships encountered by Holocaust refugees upon arrival in Israel, and as a sympathetic depiction of the Diaspora and its culture by a native-born Zionist Jew. The opening chapters of the book (aside from the first chapter, which takes place in Europe's camps for Holocaust survivors) provide a vibrant and empathic description of the entry process of the newly arrived to the "abandoned" houses and how they made these their own. However, Bartov, unlike the Holocaust survivors, had firsthand knowledge of the binational reality in the country during the Mandate period. And as one who had fought in the battles that raged throughout Jerusalem, he might have witnessed or learned about the attempts of Jewish and Arab noncombatants to seek a temporary refuge outside the battle zone. Nonetheless, Bartov hardly mentions the previous inhabitants of the "abandoned" Jerusalem neighborhood. Despite the book's strong and sometimes contentious depiction of social life during the mass Jewish migration period of the 1950s, which went counter to the newly founded state's hegemonic metanarrative, the bottom line, as stated by Avner Holtzman in his review of the book, holds Zionist-Israeli ideology accountable.[69]

Another hegemonic and extremely influential literary expression of erasing the very existence of the Palestinian-Arab citrus industry and its hub, Jaffa, is the highly popular children's book written by famous Israeli artist Nahum Guttman, titled *Path of the Orange Peels*.[70] Guttman immigrated to Ottoman Palestine as a child and grew up in Tel Aviv. During the British Mandate Guttman would visit Jaffa frequently and paint its everyday life, from its port and citrus groves to its romantic scenes. In other words, Arab Jaffa and its citrus industry were very familiar to him, and they find prominent expression in his art. However, in *Path of the Orange Peels*, first published in Hebrew in 1958 and republished in several editions since, the storyline and its accompanying illustrations obliterated the reality that Guttman so sympathetically presented in his earlier art. Now, the narrative is the Israeli-Zionist master narrative of military heroism, the centrality of the "first Hebrew city" of Tel Aviv, and the symbolic erasure of the Arabs from the land and its history. It is hard to exaggerate the tremendous impact that Guttman's *Path of the Orange Peels* had on the worldview of generations of Israeli-Jewish children, helping obliterate the Palestinian Arabs from the memory of Israeli-Jewish society.

The educational system as well had a major role in this process of symbolic forgetfulness. As shown by Emil Durkheim and generations of sociologists who followed in his footsteps, the educational system is central in shaping the belief set of new cohorts joining a society. At the same time, transmitting a set of beliefs between generations helps recreate the desired social order.[71]

A review we conducted of textbooks studied at public Jewish elementary schools that served the large majority of Jewish children in Israel's first two decades, as well as of Ministry of Education curricula, literature readers, and several major children's newspapers that were in wide circulation during those formative years of the state—particularly the hegemonic *Davar Li-Yeladim* and *Mishmar Li-Yeladim*—shows that with regard to the groves, their cultivation, fruit, and place in the economy and in Israeli society, there is no mention of or reference to the existence of Arabs or of the Palestinian-Arab citrus industry. Obviously, these textbooks—and the formal and informal Israeli educational system—devote a great deal of attention to the country's past. But it is only the distant past, when Jews lived in the country and maintained their own political and religious institutions. The existence of hundreds of Arab villages, and of the tens of thousands of dunams that housed Palestinian-Arab groves only several years before these books were published, receives no mention. For example, in the book *Zot Moladeti: Sefer Limud Hamoledet Lishnat Halimudim Harevi'it* (This Is My Homeland: A Homeland Studies Textbook for the Fourth Grade, published in 1963), the Sharon region is described as follows:

> The Sharon . . . is the country's most densely populated and fertile region. Travelling the roads, we see flourishing and prospering settlements on both sides: cities, villages, and kibbutzim [plural of kibbutz], as well as many groves, where thousands of agricultural laborers work. The groves are expanding annually and the reputation of the Israeli orange is preceding it in countries overseas.[72]

The text is accompanied by an iconic photograph of a grove planted in technologically modern and organized straight, neat rows.

A similar visual and textual message is conveyed by the *Israel Readers* for elementary school, the major Jewish-Israeli elementary school textbook of the period. The image of joyful healthy "Israeli-born" (Sabra) children wearing shorts and helping pick the citrus fruit recurs in these books. This is also true of older "Israeli-born" laborers, shown wearing work clothes and toiling joyfully. The text that accompanies the illustrations conveys similar messages about the groves and the value of working in them.

Public ceremonies as well served as an important instrument, a vector of memory, for shaping consciousness and memory. A few years after the end of the war in 1948, the city of Rehovot introduced a "Citrus Festival," held in the city for several years in the spring. Even before 1948, Rehovot had been one of the major centers of Jewish citriculture. In its vicinity were Palestinian-Arab villages that, similar to Rehovot, also earned their livelihood from the citrus industry. Rehovot and these villages maintained good work relations and business cooperation, involving cultivating the groves as well as picking, transporting, and marketing the fruit. These places included the villages of Zarnuga, Qubeyba, Na'ana, and Sutriya near Rehovot, as well as the cities of Ramle and Lydda, which constituted, as we have already seen, a Palestinian-Arab citrus hub similar to Rehovot.

During the 1948 War and in its aftermath, the residents of Zarnuga, Qubeyba, Sutriya, and Na'ana became refugees who were not permitted to return to their villages and property. The property and groves were handed over to kibbutz and moshav settlements newly established in the area, or to those that existed prior to 1948, while the villages of Zarnuga and Qubeyba were used to house Jews who arrived in the new state, particularly Mizrahim. In no time at all Qubeyba was renamed Kfar Gvirol and annexed to the municipality of Rehovot. Zarnuga was annexed to Rehovot as well, but the new Rehovot neighborhood surprisingly retained its Palestinian-Arab name. Similar to the characters in Bartov's book, and to Bartov himself, the many testimonies in the Rehovot municipal archives show that the Jewish inhabitants of the villages of Zarnuga and Qubeyba were very much aware of living in "abandoned" property. But this property was not perceived as belonging to the original residents, rather as a mark of the social and ethnic inferiority of the new Jewish immigrants, especially Mizrahi Jews, versus the more veteran Ashkenazi Jews of Rehovot. At the same time, citrus planting around Rehovot was significantly expanded, and mechanized packing plants were established in the city. By several years after the war, Rehovot had become Israel's citrus center. A considerable portion of the fruit was packed there and sent by train to the Haifa Port.

The Citrus Festival reflected the significant role of Rehovot in the industry. School children dressed as citrus trees, and entire "groves" represented by school children marched in parade. The workers and managers of the major packing and marketing companies also took part in the parade. The minister of agriculture went out of his way to participate in the ceremony as the major speaker, while Prime Minister David Ben-Gurion sent his greetings. The entire celebration was reported at length in the Hebrew-language Israeli press. The reality of the Palestinian-Arab villages and citrus groves that had existed in Rehovot and the area only a few years previously was obviously obliterated by this symbolic ceremony.[73]

Another important vector of memory with an impact on collective identity is popular songs. This category as well was used to facilitate symbolic forgetfulness when necessary. In the first years of the state, Hebrew song had an important role in constructing Israeli-Zionist-native culture with regard to the land and the country.[74] Quite a few songs featured groves. These were usually love songs, where fresh oranges, citrus trees, and rainy winter days served as a romantic setting. Poets and songwriters who wrote songs and poems about citrus groves and oranges include prominent figures such as Dalia Ravikovitch, Naomi Shemer, and Hayim Hefer.

One example is the song "Tapuach ha-Zahav" (The Golden Orange), sung by the Gesher Hayarkon Trio, a much admired and hegemonic folk music trio at the height of Statism. The song (first performed in 1965) expresses, in a clearly male-chauvinistic manner, the attraction of a group of Israeli-Jewish orange pickers to a young woman passing by. The autumn rains in the green grove are the song's background. Here is a verse from the song:

We will jump in our boots
In the autumn puddles
Oh, you have such cheeks
Oh, golden orange . . .[75]

Also the song "Im Tirtzi" (If You Would Like) (1963), performed by the Tarnegolim, another popular folk band no less hegemonic than Gesher Hayarkon, is a love song that depicts familiar scenes of the Land of Israel as it was constructed in Zionist-Israeli culture. The grove waiting for its fruit to ripen was the source for this treasure trove of images.

Many of these songs were written by songwriter Hayim Hefer, who arrived in the country in 1936 as a boy. During the 1948 War Hefer was among the founders of the first Israeli army singing bands, the "Chizbatron," a military-civil cultural mix that remained dominant and popular in Israel for many years. Evidently, despite his prior knowledge of life in the country during the Mandate period, Hefer avoided any mention of Palestinian-Arab society and its citrus industry and created a symbolic world in which Arabs had no place. All of Hefer's songs were and still are big hits, showing the level to which Israel's Jewish populace identifies with the state's master commemorative narrative. Another of Hefer's popular songs is "Eyn Kmo Yafo Baleylot" (There Is None Like Jaffa's Nights) (1958). Hefer's song about Jaffa completely erases the city's past. Although this influential song was written a mere ten years after 1948, the city of Jaffa, its port, modern Palestinian life within it, its vibrant commercial relations with neighboring Tel Aviv, and its role as the center of the pre-Nakba Palestinian-Arab citrus industry, are totally absent. Instead, the song portrays with open sympathy, interspersed by conspicuously erotic elements, a multicultural, joyful, criminal world of Jewish immigrant society that settled in "abandoned" Jaffa:

> There is none like Jaffa's nights
> There is none like Jaffa in the world
> When the chicks pass by
> With their blood red lips lifted high
> How they swing
> Wow, that one is a bombshell
> Just call her—she'll jump right up
> As though stung . . .
> Here's Chico the driver
> Thief Moishe the glazier
> Poker Eli the card player
> And one sycophant policeman[76]

A well-known and no less popular song is "Layla Behof Achziv" (Night on Achziv Beach) (1965) by renowned songwriter and poet Naomi Shemer, also performed by the Gesher Hayarkon Trio. Shemer was born in 1930 in Kvutzat (Kibbutz) Kinneret, and her songs quickly became very popular. In no time, Shemer was recognized as a leading cultural figure in Israeli hegemonic culture. "Night on Achziv Beach" is a melancholy love song staged on Achziv's gloomy beach in northern Israel. Similar to Hefer's song describing Jaffa, "Night on Achziv Beach" too completely obliterates the recent Palestinian-Arab past of the village al-Zib, on whose ruins the song takes place:

> The wind, the water, and the darkness
> Remember your last night's steps
> The foam that erased your traces
> Knows that you were here companionless
> As a blind man I follow you
> The wind in the dark kisses the water
> No longer will beckon to me from the beach when you pass
> The white lily in your black hair.[77]

11. A view of al-Zib/Achziv National Park, 1985. Israel National Photo Collection, Ya'acov Sa'ar.

Ambivalence

Concurrent with these methods of erasure and forgetfulness, signs of ambivalence are also evident, as well as the difficulties involved in erasing the recent Palestinian-Arab past. As shown by Eviatar Zerubavel, it is hard to hide the "elephant in the room," despite considerable efforts to do so. That which is repressed repeatedly emerges, despite the repressor's best efforts.[78] In some cases this reflected nostalgia for the rootedness and nativity of the Palestinian Arab, although usually accompanied by a blatantly arrogant tone. This arrogant nostalgia is evident in the popular book *Bag of Lies* (1956), about humor in the time of the Palmach. The duality of the Palmach culture, ranging as it did from the wish to resemble native Arabs to the militaristic violence displayed toward them, is conspicuously present in this collection of humoristic stories. Arabic words and expressions are interspersed throughout the book, as are the Arabic names of some of the main characters and background stories that feature urban and rural Palestinian Arabs.[79]

Ambivalence is also apparent among some kibbutz societies that settled on "abandoned" lands and groves or incorporated them into their pre-1948 space. The cognitive dissonance and the inner conflict are evident in internal kibbutzim deliberations and newsletters. The fact that a kibbutz settled—or expanded to include—a place where only several months earlier there were Palestinian-Arab villages, wheat fields, orchards, and citrus groves, is given voice from time to time.[80] This is particularly evident among kibbutzim belonging to Hashomer Hatza'ir movement, a Zionist-Socialist movement that before 1948 also advocated the idea of an Arab-Jewish binational state once the British Mandate of Palestine was over. For example, in the founding ceremony of a kibbutz that settled on the lands of a former Arab village, the speaker attempted to resolve this internal contradiction:

> We have come to this place. We are not making the desert bloom. We are building our homes on the destroyed homes of Arab laborers. This fact overshadows our joy. This is not what we would have wished for. Our path intersects, along with the many sacrifices made by our own dear members, the destruction and annihilation of the Arab inhabitants. We have not shelved our esteemed ideals. We shall retain them,

nurture them, so that there shall be no more war ... and so that artificial borders and differences shall disappear and true peace and friendship shall exist between all workers whoever they may be.[81]

These soul-searching deliberations, however, were not capable of leading to any real action on behalf of the rights of the original Arab residents of the place. The "civil religion" of Statism and the legal, social, and cultural systems that set its boundaries and maintained its cohesiveness allowed no real deviations. The kibbutz and its residents relegated these unpleasant memories to the backstage of their consciousness and accepted the hegemonic identity and values. Indeed, that same "abandoned" village also had a quite considerable grove on an area of thirty dunams, which for many years served as an important source of income for the kibbutz. At meetings of the kibbutz secretariat, as well as in its newsletters and at various ceremonies, the grove was often mentioned but always with no reference to the fact that it had been planted by the previous inhabitants. Discussions of this issue were strictly financial and expressed the connection with nature and the return to the land. But from time to time that which was repressed emerged.

Here is a story from the kibbutz archives: "One day, in the winter of 1958, the nursery school of a neighboring kibbutz, together with their teacher, decided to hold an educational activity at the abandoned kibbutz grove. On their way back they had the bad luck of encountering a member of our kibbutz, with their pockets and those of the teacher full of illicitly picked oranges. One of the children, probably based on what he had heard from his teacher, said unfearfully: 'We stole oranges from your grove. But it is not yours. The Arabs made it.'"

Since the two neighboring kibbutzim had a history of hostile relations, this story joined the trove of unfriendly incidents. The secretariat of the kibbutz sent a detailed letter of complaint to the neighboring kibbutz with copies to the movement leadership, relating the story. This also shows that, typical of conflicts, here too repressed truths were exposed in times of contention.[82]

Reports in the contemporary press indicate that in 1964 there were more than 300,000 dunams of groves within the Green Line. The high profits of the industry and the fact that it was an important source of foreign currency led to extensive investments and accelerated planting. The large majority of the planting was performed by the government, mainly on the territory of hundreds of moshavim established in the first two decades after 1948. Hence, the 35,000 dunams of "abandoned" Arab-owned groves whose cultivation continued after 1948 (out of the 132,000 Arab-owned dunams), constituted in 1964 only 7 percent of the state's citrus planted land, while the hundreds of moshavim established after 1948 were mostly settled with new arrivals to the young state. This "demographic and physical forgetfulness" did nothing to help preserve memories of the pre-Nakba Palestinian-Arab industry, memories that were to reemerge only at the conclusion of the Israeli identity crisis in the late 1980s and early 1990s.

Notes

Bibliography

Index

Notes

Preface

1. Israel Science Foundation, Grant 681/05. We thank the ISF for its generous and significant support.

2. Karlinsky, *California Dreaming*. Anita Shapira has already put on record the fact that the Zionist citrus industry was not established by the Labor Movement but rather by the Zionist private sector. See Shapira, *Futile Struggle*.

3. Kabha, *Palestinian People*; Gross and Metzer, "Palestine"; Lockman, *Comrades and Enemies*; Jacobson and Naor, *Oriental Neighbors*; Goren, "Change in the Relationships."

Introduction

1. Smooha, "Ethnic Democracy"; Yiftachel, *Ethnocracy*.

2. Karlinsky, "Field of Israel Studies."

3. Vashitz, "Social Transformations"; Gojanski, *Development of Capitalism*; Pappé, *Jewish Arab Relations*; Grinberg, "Transportation Strike"; Lockman, *Comrades and Enemies*; Nimrod, "New Approach"; Bernstein, *Constructing Boundaries*; Bernstein, *Women on the Margins*; Goren, *Cooperation*; Goren, *Rise and Fall*; Klein, *Lives in Common*; Likhovski, *Law and Identity*; Halperin, *Babel in Zion*; Jacobson and Naor, *Oriental Neighbors*.

4. Seikaly, *Haifa*; Seikaly, *Men of Capital*; Cohen, *Year Zero*; Lissak, *History*; Yazbeq, "The Jaffa Orange"; Khalidi, *The Iron Cage*.

5. Zachary Lockman sheds important light on this phenomenon. See Lockman, *Comrades and Enemies*. See also Gross and Metzer, "Palestine"; Assaf, *Arab-Jewish Relations*; Dothan, *Land in the Balance*; Goren, "Change in the Relationships"; Jacobson and Naor, *Oriental Neighbors*.

6. Kabha, *Palestinian People*; see also Owen, "Economic Development."

7. Lockman, *Comrades and Enemies*, 7–9.

8. Wolfe, *Settler Colonialism*; Wolfe, "Elimination of the Native"; Veracini, *Settler Colonialism*; Veracini, "Introducing Settler Colonial Studies"; Elkins and Pedersen, *Settler Colonialism in the Twentieth Century*; O'Brien, *Firsting and Lasting* (we thank Liora Halperin for drawing our attention to this study); Cavanagh and Veracini, *Routledge Handbook*.

9. As is well known, this is the title of the Zionist utopia written by the founder of political Zionism, Theodor Herzl. Herzl, *Old New Land*.

10. See, for example, Shavit, *From Majority to State*; Penslar, *Zionism and Technocracy*; Penslar, "Zionism, Colonialism"; Shafir, *Land, Labor*; Shafir, "Theorizing Zionist Settler Colonialism in Palestine"; Ben-Artzi, *Early Jewish Settlement Patterns*; Aaronsohn, *Rothschild and Early Jewish Colonization*; Bigon and Katz, *Garden Cities and Colonial Planning*; Karlinsky, *California Dreaming*.

11. Choi, "French Algeria"; Porter and Yiftachel, "Urbanizing Settler-Colonial Studies."

12. Obviously, not all growers and practitioners adhered to the national ideology of their respective communities. At the same time, the two sectors maintained separate ecological, economic, and cultural spheres that were based on religious, cultural, lingual, social, and *national* differences. Hence, when we address individuals, we will use the terms "Arab" or "Jew." However, when we address the two sectors as collectives, we will characterize them from time to time according to their national ideology as well.

13. Confino, *The Nation*.

1. The Intertwined Economic, Social, and Ideological Factors, 1850–1919

1. On the relationship of the Palestinian citrus growers and exporters with Arab countries, see *Filastin*, February 19, 1933.

2. Lockman, *Comrades and Enemies*.

3. Saʻid, *Jaffa*, 240–328; Tolkowsky, *Citrus Fruits*, 249–54; Van de Velde quoted in Tolkowsky, 252.

4. One of the many explanations for the name is its connection to the Shamouti family, a family of *bayariya* based in Lydda and Jaffa. However, as of today there is no sound scholarly explanation for the origins of this name.

5. Dickson, "Report on Irrigation."

6. Aaronsohn, *Agricultural and Botanical Explorations*, 25–27.

7. At present, as this book is being written, the local rainy season has become even shorter and more unstable due to the effects of climate change.

8. Gross, "Laying the Foundations"; Gilbar, "Growing Economic Involvement"; Karlinsky, *California Dreaming*, 87–110; Avci, "Jerusalem and Jaffa"; Norris, *Land of Progress*.

9. Gilbar, "Growing Economic Involvement."

10. On Jaffa see Kark, *Jaffa*; Goren, *Rise and Fall*.

11. Von Thünen, *The Isolated State*.

12. See, for example, Cronon, *Nature's Metropolis*. We wish to thank an anonymous reader of this manuscript for referring us to this study.

13. On this see Yazbeq, "The Jaffa Orange."

14. Schwarz, "Jaffa and Its Surroundings."

15. Dickson, "Report on Irrigation"; Weakley, *Report upon the Conditions*, 193–95; Gilbar, "Growing Economic Involvement"; Gerber, "Modernization"; Kark, *Jaffa*; Schölch, *Palestine in Transformation*, 77–117; Glass and Kark, *Sephardi Entrepreneurs*.

16. Karlinsky, *California Dreaming*, 102.

17. Dickson, "Report on Irrigation."

18. Karlinsky, *California Dreaming*, 102.

19. Karlinsky, *California Dreaming*, 102; Dickson, "Report on Irrigation," 2–4.

20. Karlinsky, *California Dreaming*, 101–2; Dickson, "Report on Irrigation," 2–5; Weakley, *Report upon the Conditions*, 193.

21. Dickson, "Report on Irrigation," 2; Karlinsky, *California Dreaming*, 49–50. (Until 1900 both the Templers and a small number of Jews in the Jaffa region owned small groves, but their relative share in the industry was extremely limited.)

22. Pardes, *Protocols*, Aharon Meir Mazie Archives; Karlinsky, *California Dreaming*, 87–110.

23. Karlinsky, *California Dreaming*, 87–110.

24. Karlinsky, *California Dreaming*, 95–97.

25. Gilbar, "Growing Economic Involvement," 191–93.

26. Karlinsky, *California Dreaming*, 87–110.

27. Pardes, *Protocols*, Aharon Meir Mazie Archives.

28. Dickson, "Report on Irrigation"; Aaronsohn and Soskin, "Orange Gardens"; Karlinsky, *California Dreaming*, 87–110.

29. On the changes that occurred in Jaffa in the late Ottoman period see Schölch, *Palestine in Transformation*.

30. Abu al-Jabin, *Stories*, 87–89.

31. A mystical Islamic school that, in addition to the regular precepts, also observes group rituals and maintains an organized and close-knit social and economic community. Jaffa had several tariqas, with the most prominent being the Qadiri tariqa, the Shazli tariqa, and the Tijaniyya tariqa. For more information see Trimingham, *Sufi Orders*.

32. al-Bawwab, *Encyclopedia*, 1144.

33. al-Hudhud, *Alyafawiyya*, 21.

34. An interview by Mustafa Kabha, Qalanswa, January 9, 2001.

35. Haykal, *Days of Youth*, 18.

36. On this see Qalyubi, *Families and Personalities*; al-Bawwab, *Encyclopedia*; interviews by Mustafa Kabha, Jaffa, July 11, 2006, and Jaffa, November 29, 2006.

37. al-Hout, *Leadership*, 309.

38. Diab, *Jaffa*, 117.

39. Diab, *Jaffa*. See chapter 3 for more information about the Citrus Marketing and Control Boards and the joint Arab-Jewish delegations.

40. Qalyubi, *Letter of Love*, 87.

41. Rokach, *Tales*, 169.

42. Qalyubi, *Families and Personalities*, 232.

43. Kabha interview, July 11, 2006.

44. Qalyubi, *Families and Personalities*, 233.

45. Qalyubi, *Families and Personalities*, 61.

46. al-Dajani, *Jaffa*, 189.

47. al-'Aqqad, *Who Is Who?*, 20.

48. al-'Aqqad, *Who Is Who?*.

49. al-Dajani, *Jaffa*, 189.

50. al-Safi, *Lexicon*, 83.

51. Kabha interview, November 29, 2006.

52. Al-Bawwab, *Encyclopedia*, 633.

53. Al-Bawwab, *Encyclopedia*, 205.

54. Al-Bawwab, *Encyclopedia*, 1:637; Kabha interview, November 29, 2006.

55. Nuwayhid, *Men from Palestine*, 222.

56. Nuwayhid, *Men from Palestine*, 224; Kabha interview.

57. Qalyubi, *Families and Personalities*, 205.

58. An interview by Mustafa Kabha, November 2, 2010.

59. al-Aga, *Towns*, 167.

60. Diab, *Jaffa*, 23.

61. Kabha interview, November 2, 2010.

62. An interview by Mustafa Kabha, November 3, 2010.

63. al-Hout, *Leadership*, 885.

64. Qalyubi, *Families and Personalities*, 93.

65. Sharab, Lexicon of Palestinian Families, 321.

66. Sharab, Lexicon of Palestinian Families, 321.

67. Interview by Kabha, Amman, April 12, 2014.

68. Qalyubi, *Families and Personalities*, 280.

69. Abu al-Jabin, *Stories*, 123.

70. Gelber, *Independence versus Nakba*, 137.

71. al-'Awdat, *Illuminaries*, 210.

72. al-Hout, *Leadership*, 884.

73. al-Hout, *Leadership*.

74. Qalyubi, *Families and Personalities*, 286.

75. Abu al-Jabin, *My Story*, 32.

76. Private archive.

77. Private archive.

78. Abu al-Jabin, *Stories*, 86; on the remaining *bayari* houses in the vicinity of Jaffa today and their architecture see Peled, "Well Houses."

79. Abu al-Jabin, *Stories*, 86

80. Private archive.

81. al-Hout, *Leadership*, 883.

82. al-Dabbagh, *Palestine*, 497.

83. For more information about the public career of Khayri Abu al-Jabin see Abu al-Jabin, *My Story*, 81–89.

84. An interview by Mustafa Kabha, August 4, 2007.

85. Qalyubi, *Families and Personalities*, 95.

86. Two interviews by Mustafa Kabha, August 6, 2008.

87. Kabha interviews, August 6, 2008.

88. Qalyubi, *Families and Personalities*, 59.

89. An interview, Tira (the interviewee was originally from the village of Miska), August 2, 2007.

90. Sabri Khalil al-Bana (1937–2003) was born in Jaffa. After 1948 he left to live in exile in Gaza and from there continued to Amman. In the mid-1950s he joined the Syrian al-Ba'th Party and moved to Damascus, and in the late 1960s he joined the Fatah organization and became its representative in Khartoum and Baghdad. In 1974 he quit the organization to found an independent organization that operated in the service of the intelligence agencies of several Arab countries, mainly Libya and Iraq. Several liquidations and assassinations of opposition figures in these countries, as well as of Israeli and Western elements, were ascribed to this organization.

91. An interview by Mustafa Kabha, August 21, 2007.

92. Qalyubi, *Families and Personalities*, 91.

93. Qalyubi, *Families and Personalities*, 92.

94. Al-Bawwab, *Encyclopedia*, 1:623.

95. Al-Bawwab, *Encyclopedia*, 1:624.

96. An interview by Mustafa Kabha, Jaffa, February 3, 2007.

97. al-Dajani, *Lest We Forget*, 155.

98. al-Dajani, *Lest We Forget*, 158.

99. This fund was called "al-Mashru'a al-Insha'i al-'Arabi" and was established by the Arab League at its founding conference held in Alexandria, Egypt, in 1944. The purpose of the fund was to serve as a counterbalance to the Jewish National Fund established by the Zionist organs, particularly with regard to preservation of the lands by Palestinian farmers and their betterment of these lands in a way that would transform them into a profitable source of livelihood and prevent their transfer to the Zionist organs. For more information see Furlonge, *Palestine*.

100. al-Dajani, *Jaffa*, 196.

101. Qalyubi, *Families and Personalities*, 277.

102. al-Dajani, *Lest We Forget*, 156.

103. Qalyubi, *Families and Personalities*, 277.

104. Sharab, Lexicon of Palestinian Families, 33.

105. Qalyubi, *Families and Personalities*, 195.

106. An interview by Mustafa Kabha, August 12, 2008. Al-Bawwab, *Encyclopedia*, 1:623.

107. Qalyubi, *Families and Personalities*, 195.

108. Al-ʿAwdat, *Illuminaries*, 657.

109. Al-ʿAwdat, *Illuminaries*, 658.

110. Diab, *Jaffa*, 75.

111. Qalyubi, *Families and Personalities*, 368.

112. Qalyubi, *Families and Personalities*, 82.

113. al-ʿAwdat, *Illuminaries*, 143.

114. Qalyubi, *Families and Personalities*, 259–60.

115. Goren, *Rise and Fall*.

116. Pardes, *Protocols*.

117. Kolatt, *Ideology*.

118. Kolatt, *Ideology*; Shapira, *Futile Struggle*; Kimmerling, *Zionism and Economy*; Karlinsky, *California Dreaming*.

119. Pardes, *Protocols*; UK National Archives, file FO 3685717.

120. Karlinsky, *California Dreaming*, 87–110.

121. Pardes, *Protocols*; Karlinsky, *California Dreaming*.

122. Budeiri, *The Palestine Communist Party*.

123. Seikaly, *Men of Capital*.

124. Seikaly, *Men of Capital*; Karlinsky, *California Dreaming*.

125. Ben-Bassat, *Petitioning the Sultan*; Doumani, *Rediscovering Palestine*; Tamari, *Mountain against the Sea*; Gribetz, *Defining Neighbors*.

2. The Intertwined Economic, Social, and Ideological Factors, 1919–1948

1. Gilbar, "Growing Economic Involvement."

2. This section is based mainly on Karlinsky, *California Dreaming*, and the sources cited there. For a general macroeconomic picture of Palestine under the British Mandate, including the place of the citrus industry in this picture, we rely on Metzer's groundbreaking study on the economy of the Mandate and of its two national sectors. See Metzer, *Divided Economy*.

3. Central Zionist Archives (hereafter CZA), file S25/7621.

4. CZA, files S25\7620, S25\7621, and S25\7622.

Amos Nadan argued for the separation of the Palestinian-Arab citrus industry from what can be characterized as mainstream Palestinian-Arab noncitrus village agricultural life and economy. However, according to the sources available to us, in the villages where citrus groves were planted, noncitrus crops were cultivated side by side with them. Both types of crops were integral and inseparable parts of the villages' economy and of their economic growth. Thus, we rely on Metzer's data and reasoning in this regard. See Nadan, *Palestinian Peasant Economy*; Metzer, *Divided Economy*, 145–54, 220–25.

5. See also Karlinsky, *California Dreaming*, 111–86.

6. Loewe, "Position of Agriculture"; Barakat, *Observation*, 100.

7. Karlinsky, *California Dreaming*, 111–64; Barakat, *Observation*.

8. Karlinsky, *California Dreaming*. On Palestine's electrical grid and the political implications of its construction see Shamir, *Current Flow*; Meiton, *Electrical Palestine*.

9. CZA, file S25/7621. This is the detailed report written by Ya'akov Lubman Haviv, who gathered information for the Jewish Agency Political Department in its efforts to fend off claims of Arab dispossession from their lands due to Zionist colonization. According to the report, Sheikh Shaker Abu Kishk sold parts of his land to both Jews and Arabs. On the Lubman Haviv report see Karlinsky, *California Dreaming*, 157–60. The quote is from *California Dreaming*, 159.

10. CZA, file S25/7621. Quoted in Karlinsky, *California Dreaming*, 160.

11. Ben Yisrael, "Neighbors' Villages." Quoted in Karlinsky, *California Dreaming*, 164.

12. Anglo-American Committee, *Survey of Palestine*, 337; Israel State Archives (hereafter ISA), files M-18/1461 and M-2/1465; *Al-Hamishmar*, May 8, 1946, 2.

13. ISA, M-18/1461, 18/673.

14. Karlinsky, *California Dreaming*, 49–83; on the development of Palestine's transportation and its infrastructure see Biger, *An Empire in the Holy Land*.

15. Karlinsky, *California Dreaming*, 187–216; on the legal aspects of using the Jaffa oranges' trademark, see Birnhack, "Colonial Trademarks."

16. An interview by Mustafa Kabha, Jaffa, July 11, 2006.

17. Hamed, *Jaffa*, 49–50.

18. On this see, for example, the documents of the Jaffa Orange Syndicate company in CZA, files A323/98 and A323/324. On the Jaffa Orange Syndicate see Karlinsky, *California Dreaming*, 207–16.

19. Hamed, *Jaffa*, 49–50.

20. Gross and Metzer, "Palestine."

21. ISA, files M-18/1461, M-2/1465, M-39/1458, and M-40/1458; *Davar*, July 3, 1943, 6; *Davar*, February 2, 1944, 4; *Haboker*, May 15, 1944, 1; *Davar*, April 18, 1945, 2; Gross and Metzer, "Palestine."

22. Anglo-American Committee, *Survey of Palestine*, 339; ISA, file M-2/1465; *Davar*, January 30, 1945, 3; *Davar*, April 18, 1945; *Ha-Mashkif*, May 5, 1945, 3; *Al-Hamishmar*, May 8, 1946, 2; *Al-Hamishmar*, June 9, 1947, 4.

23. Kabha and Karlinsky, "Lost Orchard."

24. *Davar*, April 18, 1945.

25. See Ben-Bassat and Ginio, *Late Ottoman Palestine*.

26. Gross, "Economic Policy."

27. Anglo-American Committee, *Survey of Palestine*, 387–88.

28. Karlinsky, *California Dreaming*, 181–216; Citrus Fruit Committee protocols: ISA, files M-54/1457 and M-19/1454.

3. A Binational Enclave

1. *Haaretz*, January 16, 1941.

2. *Davar*, January 16, 1941.

3. *Filastin*, January 16, 1941.

4. Based on *Palestine Post*, January 26, 1940; *Palestine Post*, January 30, 1940; *Haboker*, January 16, 1941; notes 1–3 above; CZA, file 323/449 (Yitzhak Rokach's diary). Arab participants in the joint activities and meetings included, among others, Shukri el-Taji from Wadi Hanin, Shaykh Shafiq el Khatib from Qubayba, François Gélat from Jaffa, Shaykh Shaker Abu Kishk from 'Arab Abu Kishk, Radi Nabulsi from Nablus, 'Afif Haj Ibrahim from Tulkarm, and Sa'id Baydas from Shaykh Muwannes. Jewish participants included Zvi Butkowsky, president of the Zionist Farmers' Federation, Baruch Rab from Petah Tikva, 'Oved Eisenberg from Rehovot, Yehuda Pross from Rishon Lezion, Yermiyahu Boxer from Nes Ziona, Yitzhak Levi from Hadar, Yitzhak Mitrani, representing the Zionist Labor citrus growers, Yitzhak Rokach from Tel Aviv, and Yehezkel Goldenberg from Hadera.

5. On this see *al-Wihda*, January 16, 1941, and *al-Difa'*, January 17, 1941.

6. On this see *Filastin*, January 16, 17, 19, 1941.

7. The literature on this topic is voluminous. See for example, Bar-Siman-Tov, *Conflict Resolution*; Bar-Tal and Bennink, "Nature of Reconciliation."

8. This section is based on Kabha and Karlinsky, "From Competition to Bi-Nationalism."

9. Olson, *Collective Action*; Allport, *Prejudice*.

10. Olson, *Collective Action*.

11. Pettigrew and Tropp, "Allport's Intergroup Contact Hypothesis."

12. Allport, *Prejudice*; Pettigrew and Tropp, "Allport's Intergroup Contact Hypothesis."

13. Efforts to ease the national tensions and the level of conflict between Zionist Jews and Palestinian Arabs through various binational and consociational proposals grew abundantly during these years. On these efforts and proposals see Hattis, *The Bi-National Idea*; Peleg and Seliktar, *Emergence*; Heller, *Brit Shalom*; Dothan, *Land in the Balance*; Ben-Porat, "Grounds for Peace"; Fish, "Bi-Nationalist Visions"; Shafir, "Capitalist Binationalism"; Shumsky, *Between Prague and Jerusalem*.

14. Shapira, *Futile Struggle*; Shafir, *Land, Labor*; Lockman, *Comrades and Enemies*; Smith, *Roots of Separatism*.

15. Nets-Zehngut, "Passive Reconciliation"; Hagil'adi, "Rehovot"; Moshe Smilansky addressed this phenomenon in his writings. See Karlinsky, *California Dreaming*, 22–45, 53–64. In his autobiography 'Ezra Danin describes such friendly encounters while

working alongside Arab laborers in Jewish-owned citrus groves. According to his own testimony, the outbreak of the Arab Revolt changed his mind about the relationship between Jews and Arabs. Since then, again by his own testimony, Danin became a central figure in the ethnic cleansing of Palestinians during the Nakba. See Danin, *Zionist*.

16. On the Orange Shows see *Davar*, February 23, 1926, 3; *Davar*, February 15, 27, 28, 1927; *Haaretz*, February 22, 1929; *Filastin*, March 1, 1927, 1; *Filastin*, March 4, 1927, 1; *Filastin*, February 22, 1929, 4; *Filastin*, February 26, 1929, 1. On the noncitrus agricultural exhibitions see Goren, *Rise and Fall*, 76–80. On these exhibitions see also *Filastin*, June 15, 1929, June 18, 1929, June 23, 1926.

17. Karlinsky, *California Dreaming*, 198–203; Goren, *Rise and Fall*, 64–65.

18. Jewish Telegraphic Agency, "Citrus Fruit Trade."

19. Olson, *Collective Action*; the Viteles report is at ISA, file M-2/675.

20. See references in note 19 above.

21. Karlinsky, *California Dreaming*, 167–216.

22. On Walsh see *Haboker*, January 4, 1938, 6; *Palestine Post*, January 3, 1938, 2; *Palestine Post*, October 4, 1945; *Palestine Post*, July 28, 1946, 2.

23. On these first steps toward the establishment of a centralized body for the entire industry, see ISA, files M-36/4318, M-36/58, M-19/1454, M-54/1457, and M-2/47; Yitzhak Rokach's diary in CZA, file A323/435.

24. This description is mainly based on contemporary journalistic reports from the two national communities. See also Lockman, *Comrades and Enemies*; Assaf, *Arab-Jewish Relations*; Dothan, *Land in the Balance*; Goren, "Change in the Relationships."

25. In addition to the references in note 24 above, also see Heller, *Brit Shalom*; Porat, *Blue and Yellow*, 62–63. *Davar*, February 23, 27, 1941; *Haaretz*, May 4, 6, 8, 18, 1941.

26. Gross and Metzer, "Palestine"; Gelber, "Consolidation"; McGarry and O'Leary, *Northern Ireland Conflict*; Tuomela, *Social Ontology*, 242–64.

27. Quotations from Horowitz, *Development*, 175, 237–38; see also 169–246; also, Metzer, *Divided Economy*; and the references in note 26.

28. Lijphart, "Constitutional Design"; Horowitz, "Sources"; Dixon, "Good Friday"; McGarry and O'Leary, *Northern Ireland Conflict*.

29. The following discussion is based on ISA, files M-48/42, M-36/58, M-36/5063, M-36/4318, M-2/675, and M-4/1462; UK National Archives, file CO/852/317/1; *al-Difa'*, January 15, 1940, and January 18, 1940.

30. The following discussion is based on *Filastin*, January 11, 15, 16, 17, 1940; *Filastin*, December 1, 1940, December 5, 1940, December 14, 1941, December 15, 1941, December 16, 1941; *al-Difa'*, January 17, 1940, January 18, 1940; *Palestine Post*, January 26, 1940, January 30, 1940, January 14, 1941, January 16, 1941; *Davar*, January 17, 1940; *Hatzofe*, January 17, 1940; *Haboker*, January 8, 1940. This is only a partial list. The contemporary newspapers covered this joint organization extensively.

31. See the references in notes 29–30 above.

32. Lev Grinberg analyzed the short-lived 1931 Arab-Jewish drivers' strike accord-ing to the class-solidarity perspective. See Grinberg, "Transportation Strike." Our under-standing is that the citrus industry presents a different reality.

33. ISA, file M-15/1461.

34. *Davar*, September 24, 1940.

35. *Davar*, September 24, 1940; *Hatzofe*, September 24, 1940.

36. *Filastin*, September 18, 1940.

37. On this see *al-Difa'*, September 24, 1940; *Filastin*, September 26, 1940.

38. Rokach diary, CZA, file A323.

39. *Filastin*, September 27, 1940.

40. "Citrus Control Bill, 1940," *Palestine Gazette*, 1032, July 25, 1940.

41. ISA, file M-4/5117.

42. ISA, file M-39/1458.

43. ISA, files M-39/1458 and M-2/1465; UK National Archives, files CO/442/2 and CO/442/5–6.

44. See previous chapters.

45. *Al-Difa'*, April 7, 1944.

46. *Haboker*, March 23, 1944, and August 23, 1944.

47. Williams and Jesse, "Resolving Nationalist Conflicts."

4. Nakba

1. Rokach diary, CZA, file A323.

2. Rokach diary, July 2, 1945; January 25, 1946.

3. On the joint delegations see *Al-Hamishmar*, July 29, 1945, 4; *Palestine Post*, July 30, 1945, 3; *Haboker*, August 14, 1946, 1; *Haboker*, November 6, 1946, 4; *Haboker*, June 15, 1947, 4; *Davar*, August 13, 1947, 3. Rokach diary, CZA, file A323; ISA, file M-31/5118.

4. Gélat's letter, December 13, 1947, ISA, file M-31/5118.

5. Oz, *Tale of Love and Darkness*, 185–86.

6. Karp, "Legal Council"; Alsberg, "Emergency Committee"; Fine, *Birth of a State*.

7. ISA, files GL-5/45515 (Greenbaum memorandum) and G-13/110 (Pines report).

8. S. Yizhar Archives, the National Library of Israel; Danin, *Zionist*.

9. Yizhar, *Letters of Yehiam Weitz*, 249–50.

10. ISA, file M-31/5118.

11. Guy Ben-Porat, who studied the impact of Northern Ireland and Israeli busi-ness communities on the peace processes in their respective countries, astutely concluded that "their empowerment enabled them to exert political influence but fell short of hege-mony that would enable them to set the wider political agenda. The impact of both busi-ness communities, for different reasons, was therefore limited." See Ben-Porat, "Between Power and Hegemony," 325.

12. On this process, where during periods of intensifying conflict members of the dissenting societies tend to play down shared identities with members of the other society in favor of rallying around primordial intraethnic or intranational elements, see Kaufmann, "Possible and Impossible Solutions"; Petersen, *Understanding Ethnic Violence.*

13. Rokach's diary, CZA, file A325.

14. CZA, file A325/259. See letter to Moshe Sharet.

15. Letter from Moshe Sharet as cited in note 14.

16. See the detailed discussion in Arnon Golan's important book on the fate of the Palestinian-Arab property after the Nakba: Golan, *Wartime Spatial Changes.* See also Fischbach, *Records of Dispossession.*

5. Memory and Forgetfulness

1. Zerubavel, *Recovered Roots*; Rousso, *Vichy Syndrome*; Confino, "Collective Memory"; Confino, *The Nation*; Slyomovics, *Object of Memory*; Bardenstein, "Threads of Memory"; Bardenstein, "Trees, Forests"; Sorek, *Palestinian Commemoration.*

2. Ram, "Ways of Forgetting."

3. See the courageous testimony of the renowned Israeli writer, S. Yizhar, about the ethnic cleansing of a Palestinian village, published immediately after the war: Yizhar, *Khirbet Khizeh.* In his well-known autobiography, originally published in Hebrew in 1979, Yitzhak Rabin not only testified that Ben-Gurion gave the orders to expel the thousands of Palestinian civilians who inhabited Lydda and Ramle in July 1948, but also discussed the emotional difficulties experienced by the soldiers who carried out these orders. It seems that this cognitive dissonance between Zionist and Israeli ideals and the reality of the Nakba was on Rabin's mind as well. Nevertheless, Rabin does not mention that anyone disobeyed Ben-Gurion's orders. As it is well known, this section of Rabin's memoirs was censored from the Hebrew-language version of the book. So far, it is available only in the 1996 English-language edition of the memoirs. See *The Rabin Memoirs*, Appendix A. See also the testimonies of Israeli soldiers and commanders about the planned and systematic ethnic cleansing of villages and towns in Galilee even before May 15, 1948, as well as new revelations about the notorious Lydda expulsion, brought by the Israeli columnist Ari Shavit in his book *My Promised Land*, 99–132. In his autobiography, published in 2014, the influential Israeli sociologist Moshe Lissak testified that as a Palmach soldier in 1948 he took part in the "cleansing" of several Arab villages near Safed before May 15, 1948. Lissak also testified that he was part of the infamous expulsion of Arabs from Lydda, during which children, old people, and pregnant women were forced to march toward the lines of the Trans-Jordanian's forces in the burning heat of Palestine's summer without sufficient water. Many died along this march. In contrast to Yizhar, Rabin, Ari Shavit's interviewees, and even Shavit himself, who all show some signs of regret or soul searching, Lissak coldheartedly declares that he "did not hear voices that opposed

[the expulsion] or expressed reservations" about it. Lissak, *Future That Never Occurred*, 86, 74–88. See also Morris, *The Birth*; Ram, "Ways of Forgetting"; Ben-Ze'ev and Lomsky-Feder, "Canonical Generation"; Ben-Ze'ev, *Remembering Palestine*; Confino, "Miracles and Snow"; Confino, "Warm Sand"; Shapira, "Hirbet Hizah"; Kadman, *Erased from Space*; Sabbagh-Khoury, "Memory for Forgetfulness."

4. Olick, Vinitzky-Seroussi, and Levy, *Collective Memory Reader*; Schwartz, "The Social Context"; Zerubavel, *Recovered Roots*; Confino, "Collective Memory"; Confino, *The Nation*; Handelman, *Nationalism and the Israeli State*.

5. Halbwachs, *On Collective Memory*. See also Coser's illuminating introduction.

6. Zerubavel, *Recovered Roots*; Slyomovics, *Object of Memory*; Confino, "Collective Memory." Pierre Nora presents a more sophisticated perspective on the relationships between history and memory than Halbwachs', but nonetheless laments the decline of memory and of *milieu de mémoire*. Nora, *General Introduction*, 1–20.

7. Rousso, *Vichy Syndrome*.

8. Olick, Vinitzky-Seroussi, and Levy, *Collective Memory Reader*, 36–39.

9. Slyomovics, *Object of Memory*; Bardenstein, "Threads of Memory"; Bardenstein, "Trees, Forests"; LeVine, *Overthrowing Geography*; Ankori, *Palestinian Art*; Tamari, *Mountain against the Sea*; Hanafi, "Haifa and Its Refugees"; Masalha, *The Palestine Nakba*; Kabha, *Palestinian People*; Peled, *Noura's Dream*; DeYoung, "Disguises of the Mind"; Ben-Ze'ev, "Living Together Separately"; Litvak, "Introduction"; Litvak, "Constructing a National Past"; O'Brien, *Firsting and Lasting*; Sorek, *Palestinian Commemoration*.

10. Rousso, *Vichy Syndrome*; Zerubavel, *Elephant in the Room*; Ram, "Ways of Forgetting." See also Ben-Ze'ev and Lomsky-Feder, "Canonical Generation"; Ben-Ze'ev, Ginio, and Winter, *Shadows of War*; Winter, "Thinking about Silence"; Zerubavel, "Social Sound."

11. Jabra, *The Ship*, 17.

12. Schwartz, "Social Context"; Kabha, *Palestinian People*.

13. Darraj, "Citrus Fruit."

14. Bardenstein, "Threads of Memory"; Bardenstein, "Trees, Forests"; Slyomovics, *Object of Memory*; Ankori, *Palestinian Art*; LeVine, *Overthrowing Geography*; Tamari, *Mountain against the Sea*; Masalha, *The Palestine Nakba*; Davis, Palestinian Village Histories.

15. On Mansour see Ankori, *Palestinian Art*.

16. https://ar-ar.facebook.com/che.rami.rain/ . . . /53864195619702.

17. al-Bahiri, *Thirsty Rivers*, 47.

18. al-Jawahiri, *My Memories*, 427–29.

19. Husayn, *Poetry*.

20. Husayn, *Poetry*.

21. Husayn, *Poetry*.

22. al-Bayati, *Collected Works*.

23. Bseiso, *Palestinian Notebooks.*

24. Habibi, *Book of Letters.*

25. Darwish, *Leaves*, 62.

26. Darwish, *Leaves*, 70.

27. Darwish, *Lover*, 81.

28. Darwish, *End of the Night*, 221.

29. Darwish, *Birds Dead*, 259.

30. Darwish, *Do Not Be Sorry*, 126.

31. Mahamid, "The Ten Commandments."

32. Boym, *The Future of Nostalgia.* These two aspects of nostalgia were also identified by Carol Bardenstein in her study of Palestinian and Israeli memories of trees, forests, oranges, and cacti fruit. See Bardenstein, "Threads of Memory"; Bardenstein, "Trees, Forests."

33. al-'Irani, *Together*, 18–37.

34. Sharabi, *Images from the Past*, 98.

35. Darraj, "Citrus Fruit."

36. Darraj, "Citrus Fruit."

37. Kanafani, *Land of the Sad Oranges*, 74–75.

38. Jabra, *The Ship*, 51.

39. Hamed, *Jaffa*, 21.

40. Hamed, *Jaffa*, 32.

41. Hamed, *Jaffa*, 36.

42. Fayyad, *Wadi al-Hawarath*, 59.

43. Fayyad, *Wadi al-Hawarath*, 42.

44. On the Palestinian press during the Mandate period and its treatment of these elements see Kabha, *Palestinian Press.*

45. Abu al-Rub, "I, the Bullets."

46. Khalidi, *All That Remains.*

47. Stamatopoulou-Robbins, *Palestine Online*; See also Habib, "Transnational Transformation"; Ben-David, "Palestinian Diaspora on the Web"; Aouragh, *Palestine Online.*

48. https://www.facebook.com/pg/multaqabeitdajan/events; see also Tamari and Hammami, "Virtual Returns to Jaffa."

49. *Al-Hamishmar*, July 11, 1947, 3.

50. http://www.palestineremembered.com/Jaffa/al-Shaykh-Muwannis/index.html# Pictures (photos from 1946).

51. http://www.palestineremembered.com/Jaffa/Abu-Kishk/Picture103593.html.

52. Confino, *The Nation.*

53. Doumani, "Palestine Versus"; Conversation between Beshara Doumani, Issam Nassar, and Salim Tamari, accessed December 10, 2017, Vimeo video, 55:47, https://vimeo.com/127736799.

54. Zerubavel, *Recovered Roots*, 6; Kabha, *Palestinian People*.

55. Ram, "Ways of Forgetting."

56. Central Bureau of Statistics, *Population*; Central Bureau of Statistics, "Immigrations."

57. Kabha, *Palestinian People*; Bäuml, *Blue and White*.

58. Morris, *The Birth*; Golan, *Wartime Spatial Changes*; Shai, "Fate of Abandoned"; Benvenisti, *Sacred Landscape*; Benvenisti, *The Dream of the White Sabra*.

59. Kadman, *Erased from Space*; Sabbagh-Khoury, "Memory for Forgetfulness"; Sharon, "Lakhish"; Sharon, *A Homeland Is Conquered*.

60. Ram, "Ways of Forgetting"; Freud, *Ego and Mechanisms*; Winter, "Thinking about Silence"; Zerubavel, "Social Sound"; Zerubavel, *Elephant in the Room*. Omer Bartov, an Israeli-born leading scholar of the German Army in World War II, has turned his scholarly attention in recent years to the physical and consciousness erased past of World War II Europe, and Israel/Palestine. See Bartov, *Erased*; Bartov, *Israel/Palestine*.

61. Ram, "Ways of Forgetting." See also Benvenisti, *Sacred Landscape*.

62. *Hatzofe*, June 10, 1952; *Herut*, July 12, 1952.

63. *Herut*, July 12, 1952; Golan, *Wartime Spatial Changes*, 246–49.

64. CZA, file A/323.

65. *Davar*, March 20, 1953; Supreme Court verdict on the matter of "Mehadrin," June 5, 2014, http://www.psakdin.co.il/Court.

66. *Al-Hamishmar*, January 18, 1953; *Herut*, January 18, 1953; ISA, file C-2424/12.

67. The analysis is based on the Historical Jewish Press website, http://web.nli.org.il/sites/JPress/Hebrew/Pages/default.aspx; Yehuda Horin, *Davar*, June 14, 1957; Zvi Isaacson, *Herut*, March 25, 1955; *Davar*, March 20, 1953.

68. Here too the analysis is based on the Historical Jewish Press website; Shmuel Dayan is quoted from *Davar*, November 18, 1951; on the accusations against the refugees see, for example, "Tour of Abandoned Groves," *Davar*, January 22, 1952.

69. Bartov, *Each Had Six Wings*, and Avner Holtzman's essay on pp. 273–88.

70. Guttman, *Path of the Orange Peels*.

71. Handelman, *Nationalism and the Israeli State*.

72. Shaked, *This Is My Homeland*, 121–22; on Israeli newspapers for children see Shikhmanter, *Paper Friend*.

73. Municipal Archives, Rehovot; Binyamin, "Present Absentees."

74. Regev and Seroussi, *Popular Music*.

75. Hayim Hefer, "Tapuach ha-Zahav." © Author and ACUM.

76. Hayim Hefer, "Eyn Kmo Yafo Baleylot." © Author and ACUM.

77. Naomi Shemer, "Layla Behof Achziv." © Author and ACUM. This is a verbal, not artistic, translation of the song. On the popular song genre see, in addition to the book by Regev and Seroussi cited in note 74, Shahar, "Army Bands."

78. Zerubavel, *Elephant in the Room*.

79. Ben-Amotz and Hefer, *Bag of Lies*.

80. Kadman, *Erased from Space*; Sabbagh-Khoury, "Memory for Forgetfulness"; Kibbutz #1 Archives.

81. Kibbutz #2 Archives.

82. Kibbutz #2 Archives.

Bibliography

Archives

Aharon Meir Mazie Archives
Central Zionist Archives, Jerusalem
Haganah Historical Archives, Tel Aviv
Israel State Archives, Jerusalem
Kibbutz #1 Archives
Kibbutz #2 Archives
Municipal Archives, Rehovot
The National Archives, United Kingdom
Private archive
S. Yizhar Archives, The National Library of Israel, Jerusalem

Newspapers

Davar	*Ha-Mashkif*
al-Difaʻ	*Hatzofe*
Filastin	*Herut*
Haaretz	*Palestine Gazette*
Haboker	*Palestine Post*
Al-Hamishmar	*al-Wihda*

Books and Periodicals

Aaronsohn, Aaron. *Agricultural and Botanical Explorations in Palestine*. Washington, DC: Government Printing Office, 1910.
Aaronsohn, Aaron, and Selig Soskin, "Die Orangengaerten von Jaffa" [The Orange Gardens of Jaffa]. *Der Tropenpflanzer* 4 (1902): 341–61.
Aaronsohn, Ran. *Rothschild and Early Jewish Colonization in Palestine*. Lanham, MD: Rowman & Littlefield, 2000.

Abu al-Jabin, Khayri. *Hikayat 'an Yafa* [Stories about Jaffa]. Amman: dar al-Shuruq, 2008.

————. *Qissat Hayati fi Filastin wa'al Kuwait* [My Story of My Life in Palestine and Kuwait]. Kuwait: dar al-Shuruq, 2012.

Abu al-Rub, Bassam. "Ana al-Rasas al-Burtuqal wa al-Zakira" [I Am the Bullets, the Oranges, and Memory]. Fateh Syria website, posted November 15, 2015.

Aga, Nabil Khaled al-. *Mada'in Filastin* [The Towns of Palestine]. Beirut: Al-Mu'assasa al-'Arabiyya lildirasat wa al-Nashr, 1993.

Allport, Gordon. *The Nature of Prejudice*. Reading, MA: Addison-Wesley, 1979.

Alsberg, Paul. "The 'Emergency Committee' (Va'adat Hamatzav), October 1947–May 1948: Preparing for Statehood." *Studies in Zionism* 10, no. 1 (1989): 49–64.

Anglo-American Committee of Inquiry on Jewish Problems in Palestine and Europe. *A Survey of Palestine, Prepared in December 1945 and January 1946 for the Information of the Anglo-American Committee of Inquiry*. Palestine: Printed by the Government Printer, 1946.

Ankori, Gannit. *Palestinian Art*. London: Reaktion, 2006.

Aouragh, Miriyam. *Palestine Online: Transnationalism, the Internet and the Construction of Identity*. New York: I.B. Tauris, 2012.

'Aqqad, Ahmad Khalil al-. *Man huwa? Rijalat Filastin* [Who Is Who? Persons from Palestine]. Damascus: Matba'at Yafa, 1964.

Assaf, Michael. Hayahasim Beyn 'Aravim Veyehudim Be'eretz Yisra'l, 1860–1948 [Arab-Jewish Relations in Palestine, 1860–1948]. Tel Aviv: Tarbut Vehinuch, 1970.

Avci, Yasemin. "Jerusalem and Jaffa in the Late Ottoman Period: The Concession-Hunting Struggle for Public Works Projects." In *Late Ottoman Palestine: The Period of Young Turk Rule*, edited by Yuval Ben-Bassat and Eyal Ginio, 81–102. London: I.B. Tauris, 2011.

'Awdat, Ya'qub al-. *Min A'lam al-Fikr wa'al Adab fi Filastin* [Among the Illuminaries in Culture and Thought in Palestine]. Amman: Wakalat al-Tawzi'a al-Urduniyya, 1987.

Bahiri, Hasan al-. *al-Anhar al-Tham'a* [Thirsty Rivers]. Damascus: Dar al-Haya, 1982.

Barakat, Galib Z. "Observation of the Development of the Citrus Industry in Palestine" (paper submitted as a requirement for BBA degree, American Univ. of Beirut, May 9, 1949).

Bardenstein, Carol. "Threads of Memory and Discourses of Rootedness: Of Trees, Oranges and the Prickly-Pear Cactus in Israel/Palestine." *Edebiyât* 8 (1998): 1–36.

———. "Trees, Forests, and the Shaping of Palestinian and Israeli Collective Memory." In *Acts of Memory: Cultural Recall in the Present*, edited by Mieke Bal, Jonathan Crewe, and Leo Spitzer, 148–67. Lebanon, NH: Univ. Press of New England, 1999.

Bar-On, Dan. *The Others Within Us: Constructing Jewish-Israeli Identity*. Translated by Noel Canin. Cambridge: Cambridge Univ. Press, 2008.

Bar-Siman-Tov, Yaacov, ed. *From Conflict Resolution to Reconciliation*. New York: Oxford Univ. Press, 2004.

Bar-Tal, Daniel. *Intractable Conflicts: Socio-psychological Foundations and Dynamics*. New York: Cambridge Univ. Press, 2013.

Bar-Tal, Daniel, and Gemma Bennink. "The Nature of Reconciliation as an Outcome and as a Process." In *From Conflict Resolution to Reconciliation*, edited by Yaacov Bar-Siman-Tov, 11–38. New York: Oxford Univ. Press, 2004.

Bartov, Hanoch. *Shesh Knafayim Le'ehad* [Each Had Six Wings]. Tel Aviv: Hakibbutz Hameuchad, 2014.

Bartov, Omer. *Erased: Vanishing Traces of Jewish Galicia in Present-Day Ukraine*. Princeton, NJ: Princeton University Press, 2015.

———, ed. *Israel/Palestine: Lands and Peoples*. New York: Berghahn Books, 2021.

Bäuml, Yair. *Tzel Kahol Lavan: Mediniyut Hamimsad Hayisre'eli Ufe'ulotav Beqerev Ha'ezrahim Ha'aravim—Hashanim Hame'atzvot: 1958–1968* [Blue and White Shadow: The Israeli Establishment's Policy and Actions among Its Arab Citizens—The Formative Years: 1958–1968]. Haifa: Pardes, 2007.

Bawwab, 'Ali al-. *Mawsu'at Yafa al-Jamila* [Encyclopedia of Lovely Jaffa], vols. 1 and 2. Amman: Al-Mu'assasa al-'Arabiyya lildirasat wa al-Nashr, 2003.

Bayati, 'Abd al-Wahhab al-. *Diwan* [Collected Works]. Beirut: Dar al-'Awda, 1972.

Ben-Amotz, Dahn, and Haim Hefer, eds. *Yalkut Hakzavim* [Bag of Lies]. Tel Aviv: Hakibbutz Hameuchad, 1956.

Ben-Artzi, Yossi. *Early Jewish Settlement Patterns in Palestine, 1882–1914*. Jerusalem: Magnes Press, 1997.

Ben-Bassat, Yuval. *Petitioning the Sultan: Protests and Justice in Late Ottoman Palestine, 1865–1908*. London: I.B. Tauris, 2013.

Ben-Bassat, Yuval, and Eyal Ginio, eds. *Late Ottoman Palestine: The Period of Young Turk Rule*. London: I.B. Tauris, 2011.

Ben-David, Anat. "The Palestinian Diaspora on the Web: Between De-Territorialization and Re-Territorialization." *Social Science Information* 51, no. 4 (2012): 459–74.

Ben-Porat, Guy. "Between Power and Hegemony: Business Communities in Peace Processes." *Review of International Studies* 31, no. 2 (2005): 325–48.

———. "Grounds for Peace: Territoriality and Conflict Resolution." *Geopolitics* 10, no. 1 (Spring 2005): 147–66.

Benvenisti, Meron. *Halom ha-Tzabar ha-Lavan: Otobiographia shel Hitpakhut* [The Dream of the White Sabra]. Jerusalem: Keter, 2012.

———. Sacred Landscape: The Buried History of the Holy Land since 1948. Berkeley: Univ. of California Press, 2000.

Ben Yisrael (Smilansky, Ze'ev). "Bi-Kfarei Shekhenenu." [In Our Neighbors' Villages]. *Bustenai* 6, nos. 15–16 (1934): 16–17, 25–27.

Ben-Ze'ev, Efrat. "Living Together Separately: Arab-Palestinian Places Through Jewish-Israeli Eyes." In *Toward an Anthropology of Nation Building and Un-building in Israel*, edited and with an introduction by Fran Markowitz, Stephen Sharot, and Moshe Shokeid, 3–26. Lincoln: Univ. of Nebraska Press, 2015.

———. *Remembering Palestine in 1948: Beyond National Narratives*. New York: Cambridge Univ. Press, 2011.

Ben-Ze'ev, Efrat, and Edna Lomsky-Feder. "The Canonical Generation: Trapped between Personal and National Memories." *Sociology* 43, no. 6 (2009): 1047–65.

Ben-Ze'ev, Efrat, Ruth Ginio, and Jay Winter, eds. *Shadows of War: A Social History of Silence in the Twentieth Century*. Cambridge: Cambridge Univ. Press, 2010.

Bernstein, Deborah. *Constructing Boundaries: Jewish and Arab Workers in Mandatory Palestine*. Albany: State Univ. of New York Press, 2000.

———. *Women on the Margins: Gender and Nationalism in Mandate Tel Aviv*. Jerusalem: Yad Itzhak Ben Zvi, 2008.

Biger, Gideon. *An Empire in the Holy Land: Historical Geography of the British Administration in Palestine, 1917–1929*. New York: St. Martin's Press, 1994.

Bigon, Liora, and Yossi Katz, eds. *Garden Cities and Colonial Planning: Transnationality and Urban Ideas in Africa and Palestine*. Manchester: Manchester Univ. Press, 2014.

Binyamin, Shlomit. "Nochehim Nifqadim: Hamiqre shel Qubeyba / Kfar Gvirol" [Present Absentees: The Case of Qubeyba / Kfar Gvirol]. *Teoria Uvikoret* 29 (Autumn 2006): 81–102.

Birnhack, Michael. "Colonial Trademarks: Law and Nationality in Mandate Palestine, 1922–1948." *Law & Social Inquiry*, 2020, 1–34.

Boym, Svetlana. *The Future of Nostalgia*. New York: Basic Books, 2001.

Brinkerhoff, Jennifer. *Digital Diasporas: Identity and Transnational Engagement*. Cambridge: Cambridge Univ. Press, 2009.

Bseiso, Muʿin. *Dafater Filistiniyya* [Palestinian Notebooks]. Beirut, Dar al-Farabi, 2014.

Budeiri, Musa. *The Palestine Communist Party, 1919–1948: Arab and Jew in the Struggle for Internationalism*. London: Ithaca Press, 1979.

Cavanagh, Edward, and Lorenzo Veracini, eds. *The Routledge Handbook of the History of Settler Colonialism*. New York: Routledge, 2016.

Central Bureau of Statistics (Israel). "Immigrations (1), by Period of Immigration and Last Continent of Residence." *Statistical Abstract of Israel 2009* 60: 234–35.

———. *Population—Statistical Abstract of Israel 2020*. https://www.cbs.gov.il/he/publications/doclib/2020/2.shnatonpopulation/st02_01.pdf.

Choi, Sung. "French Algeria, 1830–1962." In *The Routledge Handbook of the History of Settler Colonialism*, edited by Edward Cavanagh and Lorenzo Veracini, 201–15. New York: Routledge, 2017.

Cohen, Hillel. *Year Zero of the Arab-Israeli Conflict 1929*. Translated by Haim Watzman. Waltham, MA: Brandeis Univ. Press, 2015.

Confino, Alon. "Collective Memory and Cultural History: Problems of Methods." *American Historical Review* 102, no. 5 (December 1997): 1386–1403.

———. "Miracles and Snow in Palestine and Israel: Tantura, a History of 1948." *Israel Studies* 17, no. 2 (Summer 2012): 25–61.

———. *The Nation as a Local Metaphor: Wurttemberg, Imperial Germany, and National Memory, 1871–1918*. Chapel Hill: Univ. of North Carolina Press, 1997.

———. "The Warm Sand of the Coast of Tantura: History and Memory in Israel after 1948." *History & Memory* 27, no. 1 (Spring/Summer 2015): 43–82.

Cronon, William. *Nature's Metropolis: Chicago and the Great West*. New York: W. W. Norton, 1991.

Dabbagh, Mustafa Murad al-. *Biladuna Filastin* [Palestine Is Our Country], vol 4. Beirut: Mu'assat al-Dirasat al-Filistiniyya, 1972.

Dajani, Ahmad Zaki al-. *Madinatuna Yafa Wathawrat 1936* [Our City of Jaffa and the Revolt of 1936]. Cairo: Huquq al-Taba'a Mahfuz'e lel-mu'alef, 1989.

Dajani, Sa'ad Yusuf al-. *Ki la nansa Yafa* [Lest We Forget Jaffa]. Amman, 1991.

Danin, 'Ezra. *Tsiyoni be-khol Tenai*. [Zionist at All Costs]. Jerusalem: Kidum, 1987.

Darraj, Faysal. "Burtuqal Kanafani, Zaytun Darwish, wa-'Enab al-Manasra" [The Citrus Fruit of Kanafani, the Olives of Darwish and the Grapes of al-Manasra]. *al-Mawqef*, April 18, 2014. http://almawqef.com/spip.php?article 9446&lang=ar.

Darwish, Mahmud. *Aakhir al-Layl* [The End of the Night]. Acre: Dar al-Jalil, 1967.

———. *al-'Asafir Tamut fi al-Jalil* [The Birds Dead in the Galilee]. Beirut: Dar al-Aadab, 1970.

———. 'Asheq min Filastin [A Lover from Palestine]. Nazareth: Matba'at al-Hakeem, 1966.

———. *Awraq al-Zaytun* [The Leaves of the Olive Tree]. Haifa: Matba'at al-Etihad al-Ta'awuniyya, 1964.

———. *La Ta'tazer 'Amma Fa'alat* [Do Not Be Sorry for What You Have Done]. Beirut: Dar al-Rayyis, 2004.

Davis, Rochelle. *Palestinian Village Histories: Geographies of the Displaced*. Stanford, CA: Stanford University Press, 2010.

DeYoung, Terri. "The Disguises of the Mind: Recent Palestinian Memoirs." *Review of Middle East Studies* 51, no. 1 (2017): 5–21.

Diab, Imtiyaz, ed. *Yafa 'Itr Medina* [Jaffa: The Fragrance of a City]. Nazareth: Markaz Yafa Lilabhath, 1991.

Dickson, John. "Report on Irrigation and Orange Growing at Jaffa." *Diplomatic and Consular Reports*. Miscellaneous Series No. 300. London: UK Foreign Office, 1893.

Dixon, Paul. "Why the Good Friday Agreement in Northern Ireland Is Not Consociational." *Political Quarterly* 76, no. 3 (2005): 357–67.

Dothan, Shmuel. *A Land in the Balance: The Struggle for Palestine, 1918–1948*. Tel Aviv: MOD Books, 1993.

———. *Pulmus ha-Khaluka bi-Tekufat ha-Mandat* [Partition of Eretz-Israel in Mandatory Period]. Jerusalem: Yad Izhak Ben-Zvi, 1979.

Doumani, Beshara. "Palestine versus the Palestinians? The Iron Laws and Ironies of a People Denied." *Journal of Palestine Studies* 36, no. 4 (2007): 49–64.

———. *Rediscovering Palestine: Merchants and Peasants in Jabal Nablus, 1700–1900*. Berkeley: Univ. of California Press, 1995.

Elkins, Caroline, and Susan Pedersen, eds. *Settler Colonialism in the Twentieth Century: Projects, Practices, Legacies*. London: Routledge, 2005.

Fayyad, Tawfiq. *Wadi al-Hawarath*. Beirut: Dar al-'Awda, 1994.

Fine, Jonathan. *Kakh Nolda: Hakamat Ma'arekhet ha-Mimshal be-Israel, 1947–1951* [The Birth of a State: The Establishment of the Israeli Governmental System, 1947–1951]. Jerusalem: Carmel, 2009.

Fischbach, Michael. *Records of Dispossession: Palestinian Refugee Property and the Arab-Israeli Conflict*. New York: Columbia Univ. Press, 2003.

Fish, Rachel. "Bi-Nationalist Visions for the Construction and Dissolution of the State of Israel." *Israel Studies* 19, no. 2 (2014): 15–34.

Freud, Anna. *The Ego and the Mechanisms of Defense*. New York: International Universities Press, 1950.

Furlonge, Geoffrey W. *Palestine Is My Country: The Story of Musa Alami*. New York: Praeger, 1969.

Gelber, Yoav. "Hitgabshut haYishuv ha-Yehudi be-Eretz Yisrael, 1936–1947" [The Consolidation of the Jewish Community in the Land of Israel, 1936–1947]. In *Toldot ha-Yishuv ha-Yehudi be-Eretz Yisrael Meaz ha-'Aliyah ha-Rishona* [History of the Jewish Community in the Land of Israel since the First 'Aliya], edited by Moshe Lissak, 2:303–463. Jerusalem: Ha'aqademyah Hale'umit Hayisre'elit Lemada'im: Mosad Bialik, 1989–2009.

———. *Komemiyut ve-Nakbah: Yiśra'el, ha-Falastinim u-medinot 'Arav, 1948.* [Independence versus Nakba: Israel, the Palestinians, and the Arab States, 1948]. Or Yehuda: Dvir, 2004.

———. *Palestine, 1948: War, Escape and the Emergence of the Palestinian Refugee Problem*. Brighton: Sussex Academic Press, 2001.

Gerber, Haim. "Modernization in Nineteenth-Century Palestine: The Role of Foreign Trade." *Middle Eastern Studies* 18, no. 3 (1982): 250–64.

Gilbar, Gad. "The Growing Economic Involvement of Palestine with the West, 1865–1914." In *Palestine in the Late Ottoman Period: Political, Social and Economic Transformation*, edited by David Kushner, 188–210. Jerusalem: Yad Izhak Ben-Zvi, 1986.

Glass, Joseph B., and Ruth Kark. *Sephardi Entrepreneurs in Eretz Israel: The Amzalak Family, 1816–1918*. Jerusalem: Magnes Press, 1991.

Gojanski, Tamar. *Hitpathut Hakapitalizm Bepalestina* [The Development of Capitalism in Palestine]. Haifa: Mif'alim Universita'iyim Lehotsa'ah Le'or, 1986.

Golan, Arnon. "Hahityashvut Ba'asor Harishon" [Settlement during the First Decade]. In *He'asor Harishon, 1948–1958* [The First Decade, 1948–1958], edited by Hanna Yablonka and Zvi Zameret, 83–102. Jerusalem: Yad Ben-Zvi, 1997.

————. *Shinuy merhavi—Totza'at milhama* [Wartime Spatial Changes]. Sede-Boker: Ben-Gurion Research Institute, 2001.

Golani, Motti. *Palestine between Politics and Terror, 1945–1947. Waltham, MA: Brandeis Univ. Press, 2013.*

Goren, Tamir. *Geut va-Shefel: Hitpathuta ha-'Ironit shel Yafo u-Mekomah ba-'Imut ha-Yehudi-'Aravi be-Eretz Yisrael, 1917–1947* [Rise and Fall: The Urban Development of Jaffa and Its Place in Jewish-Arab Strife in Palestine 1917–1947]. Jerusalem: Yad Itzhak Ben Zvi, 2016.

————. "Mifneh be-Yakhasay 'Aravim ve-Yehudim be-Yafo uv-Tel Aviv bi-Shnot Melkhemet ha-'Olam ha-Rishona" [Change in the Relationships between Jews and Arabs in Jaffa and Tel Aviv during World War Two]. *Iyunim Bitkumat Israel* 28 (2017): 169–96.

————. *Shituf be-Tzel 'Imut: 'Aravim vi-Yehudim ba-Shiltom ha-Mekomi be-Heifa bi-Tkufat ha-Mandat ha-Briti* [Cooperation in the Shadow of Confrontation: Arabs and Jews in Local Government in Haifa during the British Mandate]. Ramat Gan: Bar Ilan, 2008.

Gribetz, Jonathan Marc. *Defining Neighbors: Religion, Race, and the Early Zionist-Arab Encounter.* Princeton, NJ: Princeton Univ. Press, 2014.

Grinberg, Lev. "A Historical Slip of the Tongue, or What Can the Arab-Jewish Transportation Strike Teach Us about the Israeli-Palestinian Conflict?" *International Journal of Middle East Studies* 35, no. 3 (2003): 371–91.

Gross, Nachum. "The Economic Policy of the Mandatory Government in Palestine." *Research in Economic History* 9 (1984): 143–85.

————. "Hanahat Hayesodot" [Laying the Foundations]. In *Bankai Le'uma Behitpathuta: Toldot Bank Le'umi Leyisra'el* [Banker for a Renewed Nation: The History of Bank Leumi Le'Israel], edited by Nadav Halevi, 7–110. Ramat Gan: Massada, 1977.

Gross, Nachum, and Jacob Metzer. "Palestine in World War Two: Some Economic Aspects." In *The Sinews of War,* edited by Geofrey T. Mills and Hugh Rockoff, 59–82. Iowa City: Univ. of Iowa Press, 1993.

Gurevich, Dov, and Aharon Gerz. *Ha-Hityashvut ha-'Ivrit be-Eretz Yisrael* [Jewish Agricultural Settlement in Palestine]. Jerusalem: The Jewish Agency, Department of Statistics, 1938.

Guttman, Nahum. *Path of the Orange Peels: Adventures in the Early Days of Tel Aviv.* Translated by Nelly Segal. New York: Dodd, Mead, 1979.

Habib, Jasmin. "Transnational Transformation: Cyberactivism and the Palestinian Right of Return." In *Renegotiating Community: Interdisciplinary Perspectives,*

Global Contexts, edited by Diana Brydon and William D. Coleman, 183–201. Vancouver: UBC Press, 2008.

Habibi, Emil, ed. *Kitab al-Ras'il* [The Book of Letters]. Haifa: Dar Arabesk, 1989.

Hagil'adi, Nimrod. "'Adayin Anu Mamshikhim be-Khayenu ha-Regilim': ha-Hitargenut ha-Ezrakhit ba-Moshava Rehovot bi-Tekufat Milkhemet ha-'Atzmaut" ["'We Still Continue with Our Regular Daily Life': Civil Society in the Moshava Rehovot during the War of Independence"]. In *Citizens at War*, edited by Meir Hazan and Mordechai Bar-On, 9–43. Jerusalem: Yad Yitzhak Ben-Zvi, 2006.

Halamish, Aviva. *Kibbutz, Utopia and Politics: The Life and Times of Meir Yaari, 1897–1987*. Translated from the Hebrew by Lenn Schramm. Brighton, MA: Academic Studies Press, 2017.

Halbwachs, Maurice. *On Collective Memory*. Edited, translated, and with an introduction by Lewis A. Coser. Chicago: Univ. of Chicago Press, 1992.

Halperin, Liora. *Babel in Zion: Jews, Nationalism, and Language Diversity in Palestine, 1920–1948*. New Haven, CT: Yale Univ. Press, 2015.

Hamed, Anwar. *Yafa Tu'id Qahwat al-Sabah* [Jaffa Prepares the Morning Coffee]. Beirut: Al-Mu'assasa al-'Arabiyya lildirasat wa al-Nashr, 2012.

Hanafi, Sari. "Haifa and Its Refugees: The Remembered, the Forgotten and the Repressed." *Kyoto Bulletin of Islamic Area Studies* 3, no. 1 (July 2009): 176–91.

Handelman, Don. *Nationalism and the Israeli State: Bureaucratic Logic in Public Events*. Oxford: Berg, 2004.

Hattis, Susan Lee. *The Bi-National Idea in Palestine during Mandatory Times*. Tel Aviv: Shikmona, 1970.

Haykal, Yusuf. *Ayyam al-Siba* [The Days of Youth]. Amman: Dar al-Jalil, 1988.

Heller, Joseph. *Mi-"Berit Shalom" le-"Ikhud": Yehuda Lev Magnes veha-Maavak li-Medina Duleumit* [From "Brit Shalom" to "Ichud": Judah Leib Magnes and the Struggle for a Binational State in Palestine.] Jerusalem: Magnes, 2003.

Herzl, Theodor. *Old New Land: Altneuland*. Translated from the German by Lotta Levensohn. New York: Markus Wiener and the Herzl Press, 1987.

Horowitz, David. *Hakalkalah Ha'eretz Yisra'elit Behitpathuta: Bilivyat Tavla'ot Vediagramot* [The Development of the Palestinian Economy: With Tables and Diagrams]. Tel Aviv: Dvir, 1948.

Horowitz, Donald. "Explaining the Northern Ireland Agreement: The Sources of an Unlikely Constitutional Consensus." *British Journal of Political Science* 32, no. 2 (2002): 193–220.

Hout, Bayan Nuwayhid al-. *al-Qiyadat wa-al Mu'assasat al-Siyasiyya fi Filastin, 1917–1948* [The Leadership and Institutions in Palestine, 1917–1948]. 'Akka: Dar al-Aswar, 1986.

Hudhud, Rawda al-Farkh al-. *Alyafawiyya* [A Woman from Jaffa]. 2nd ed. Amman: Muderiyyt al-Thaqafa, 2014.

Husayn, Rashed. *al-A'mal al-Shi'riyya* [The Complete Works of Poetry]. Taybeh: Markaz Ihya' al-Turath, 1990.

'Irani, Mahmud Sayef al-Din al-. *Ma' al-Nas* [Together with the People]. Amman: Dar al-Nashr wa al-Tawzee', 1956.

'Issa, Malik Hana. *al-Juzhur al-Yafiyya* [The Jaffa Roots]. Jerusalem: Matba'at al-sharq al-Ta'awuniyya, 1993.

Jabra, Jabra Ibrahim. *Al-Safina* [The Ship]. 5th ed. Beirut: Al-Hayaa al-'Amma liqusur al-Thaqafa, 2008.

Jacobson, Abigail, and Moshe Naor. *Oriental Neighbors: Middle Eastern Jews and Arabs in British Mandate Palestine.* Waltham, MA: Brandeis Univ. Press, 2016.

Jawahiri, Muhammad Mahdi al-. *Dhikraiati* [My Memories]. Beirut: Ar al-Rafidayn, 1997.

Jewish Telegraphic Agency. "The Citrus Fruit Trade in Palestine: Growers Protest against Proposed Government Levy." Accessed December 18, 2016. http://www.jta.org/1932/02/25/archive/the-citrus-fruit-trade-in-palestine-growers-protest-against-proposed-government-levy.

Kabha, Mustafa. *The Palestinian People: Seeking Sovereignty and State.* Boulder, CO: Lynne Rienner, 2014.

———. *The Palestinian Press as Shaper of Public Opinion: Writing up a Storm.* London: Vallentine Mitchell, 2007.

Kabha, Mustafa, and Nahum Karlinsky. "Ha-Pardes ha-Ne'elam: Ha-Pardesanut ha-'Aravit 'ad Shenat 1948" [The Lost Orchard: The Palestinian-Arab Citrus Industry up to the Nakba]. *Zemanim* 129 (Winter 2015): 94–109.

———. "mi-Taharut le-Duleumiyut: ha-Pardesanut ha-'Aravit-Falastinit veha-Yehudit-Zionit bi-Tekufat ha-Mandat" [From Competition to Bi-Nationalism: The Palestinian-Arab and Jewish-Zionist Citrus Industries during the Mandate Period]. *Israel* 27–28 (2021): 137–64.

Kabha, Mustafa, and Nimr Sirhan. *Mu'jem al-Qada wa'al Thuwwar wa'al Mutataww'in* [Lexicon of the Commanders and Fighters and Volunteers in 1936–1939 Revolt in Palestine]. Kufr Qara': Dar al-Huda, 2009.

Kadman, Noga. *Erased from Space and Consciousness: Israel and the Depopulated Palestinian Villages of 1948.* Bloomington: Indiana Univ. Press, 2015.

Kanafani, Ghassan. *Ard al-Burtuqal al-Hazin* [Land of the Sad Oranges]. 4th ed. Beirut: Mu'ssasat al-Abhath al-'Arabiyya, 1987.

Kark, Ruth. *Jaffa: A City in Evolution, 1799–1917.* Jerusalem: Yad Izhak Ben-Zvi, 1990.

Karlinsky, Nahum. *California Dreaming: Ideology, Society and Technology in the Citrus Industry of Palestine, 1890–1939.* Albany: State Univ. of New York Press, 2005.

———. "Hirhurim 'Al Tzmihat Limudei Medinat Yisrael" [Paradigm Shift: The Emergence of the Field of Israel Studies]. In *Am ve-Olam: A Tribute to Israel Bartal,* edited by Dmitry Shumsky, Jonathan Meir, and Gershon David Hundert, 271–300. Jerusalem: Zalman Shazar Center, 2019.

———. "Li-Shlilat ha-Musag 'Arim Me'oravot" ["Mixed" or Multiethnic Cities? Revisiting the "Mixed" Cities Paradigm in Israeli Historiography]. In *Sugiyot Nivharot be-Heker Toldot ha-Mizrah ha-Tikhon ha-Moderni* [Studies in the History of the Modern Middle East], edited by Mustafa Kabha, 73–101. Ra'anana: Open Univ. of Israel Press, 2020.

Karp, Yehudit. "Ha-Mo'etza Hamishpatit: Reshit 'Alilot Hakika" [The Legal Council: The Beginnings of Legislation Plots]. In *Sefer Uri Yadin,* edited by Aharon Barak and Tanah Shapnits, 2:209–55. Jerusalem: Bursi, 1990.

Kaufmann, Chaim. "Possible and Impossible Solutions to Ethnic Civil Wars." *International Security* 20, no. 4 (Spring 1996): 136–75.

Khalidi, Rashid. *The Iron Cage: The Story of the Palestinian Struggle for Statehood.* Boston: Beacon Press, 2007.

Khalidi, Walid, ed. *All That Remains: The Palestinian Villages Occupied and Depopulated by Israel in 1948.* Washington, DC: Institute for Palestine Studies, 1992.

Kimmerling, Baruch. *The Invention and Decline of Israeliness: State, Society, and the Military.* Berkeley: Univ. of California Press, 2001.

———. *Zionism and Economy.* Cambridge, MA: Schenkman, 1983.

Kimmerling, Baruch, and Joel Migdal. *The Palestinian People: A History.* Cambridge, MA: Harvard Univ. Press, 2003.

Klein, Menachem. *Lives in Common: Arabs and Jews in Jerusalem, Jaffa and Hebron.* Translated by Haim Watzman. London: Hurst, 2014.

Kolatt, Israel. "Ideologia u-Metziut bi-Tenuat ha-'Avoda be-Eretz Yisrael, 1905–1919" [Ideology and the Impact of Realities upon the Jewish Labor Movement in Palestine, 1905–1919]. PhD diss., Hebrew Univ. of Jerusalem, 1964.

LeVine, Mark. *Overthrowing Geography: Jaffa, Tel Aviv, and the Struggle for Palestine, 1880–1948.* Berkeley: Univ. of California Press, 2005.

Liebman, Charles, and Eliezer Don-Yehiya. *Civil Religion in Israel: Traditional Judaism and Political Culture in the Jewish State.* Berkeley: Univ. of California Press, 1983.

Lijphart, Arend. "Constitutional Design for Divided Societies." *Journal of Democracy* 15, no. 2 (2004): 96–109.

Likhovski, Assaf. *Law and Identity in Mandate Palestine.* Chapel Hill, NC: Univ. of North Carolina Press, 2006.

Lissak, Moshe. *He-'Atid Shelo Hayah* [Future That Never Occurred: Autobiographical Notes]. Jerusalem: Carmel, 2014.

———, ed. *Toldot ha-Yishuv ha-Yehudi be-Eretz Yisrael Meaz ha-'Aliyah ha-Rishona* [History of the Jewish Community in the Land of Israel since the First 'Aliya]. Jerusalem: Ha'aqademyah Hale'umit Hayisre'elit Lemada'im: Mosad Bialik, 1989–2009.

Litvak, Meir. "Constructing a National Past: The Palestinian Case." In *Palestinian Collective Memory and National Identity*, edited by Meir Litvak, 97–133. New York: Palgrave Macmillan, 2009.

———. "Introduction: Collective Memory and the Palestinian Experience." In *Palestinian Collective Memory and National Identity*, edited by Meir Litvak, 1–26. New York: Palgrave Macmillan, 2009.

Lockman, Zachary. *Comrades and Enemies: Arab and Jewish Workers in Palestine, 1906–1948.* Berkeley: Univ. of California Press, 1996.

Loewe, L. "The Position of Agriculture in Palestine." *Palnews: Economic Annual of Palestine* 5 (1939).

Mahamid, Ziyad. "Wasaya al-Burtuqal al-'Ashar" [The Ten Commandments of Jaffa's Oranges]. Al-Hiwar al-Mutamaddin, posted July 17, 2010.

Masalha, Nur. *The Palestine Nakba: Decolonising History, Narrating the Subaltern, Reclaiming Memory.* London: Zed Books, 2012.

McGarry, John, and Brendan O'Leary. *The Northern Ireland Conflict: Consociational Engagements.* Oxford: Oxford Univ. Press, 2004.

Meiton, Fredrik. *Electrical Palestine: Capital and Technology from Empire to Nation.* Oakland: Univ. of California Press, 2019.

Metzer, Jacob. *The Divided Economy of Mandatory Palestine.* Cambridge: Cambridge Univ. Press, 1998.

Metzer, Jacob, and Oded Kaplan. *Meshek Yehudi u-Meshek 'Aravi be-Eretz Yisrael: Totzar, Ta'asuka u-Tzmiha bi-Tekufat ha-Mandat* [The Jewish and Arab Economies in Mandatory Palestine: Product, Employment and Growth]. Jerusalem: Maurice Falk Institute for Economic Research in Israel, 1990.

Morris, Benny. *The Birth of the Palestinian Refugee Problem Revisited*. Cambridge: Cambridge Univ. Press, 2004.

Nadan, Amos. *The Palestinian Peasant Economy under the Mandate: A Story of Colonial Bungling*. Cambridge, MA: Harvard Univ. Press, 2006.

Nathan, Robert R., Oscar Gass, and Daniel Creamer. *Palestine: Problem and Promise; An Economic Study*. Washington, DC: Public Affairs Press, 1946.

Nets-Zehngut, Rafi. "Passive Reconciliation in the Context of the Israeli-Palestinian Conflict." In *The Failure of the Middle East Peace Process? A Comparative Analysis of Peace Implementation in Israel/Palestine, Northern Ireland and South Africa*, edited by Guy Ben-Porat, 178–94. New York: Palgrave Macmillan, 2008.

Nimrod, Yoram. "'Ma'aseikha Yekarvum': Yahasei Yehudim-'Aravim be-Fo'alo ha-Tziburi she Zvi Botkowsky" [A New Approach to Jewish-Arab Relations: The Economic Initiative of Zvi Botkowsky]. *Zion* 1 (1992): 429–50.

Nora, Pierre. *Realms of Memory: Rethinking the French Past. Volume 1: Conflicts and Divisions*. Edited and with a foreword by Lawrence D. Kritzman. Translated by Arthur Goldhammer. New York: Columbia Univ. Press, 1996.

Norris, Jacob. *Land of Progress: Palestine in the Age of Colonial Development, 1905–1948*. Oxford: Oxford Univ. Press, 2013.

Nuwayhid, 'Ajaj. *Rijal min Filastin* [Men from Palestine]. Beirut: Manshurat Filastin, 1981.

O'Brien, Jean M. *Firsting and Lasting: Writing Indians Out of Existence in New England (Indigenous Americas)*. Minneapolis: Univ. of Minnesota Press, 2010.

Olick, Jeffrey K., Vered Vinitzky-Seroussi, and Daniel Levy, eds. *The Collective Memory Reader*. New York: Oxford Univ. Press, 2011.

Olson, Mancur. *The Logic of Collective Action: Public Goods and the Theory of Groups*. New York: Schocken, 1965.

Owen, Roger. "Economic Development in Mandatory Palestine: 1918–1948." In *The Palestinian Economy: Studies in Development under Prolonged Occupation*, edited by George T. Abed, 13–35. London: Routledge, 1988.

Oz, Amos. *A Tale of Love and Darkness*. Translated from the Hebrew by Nicholas de Lange. Orlando, FL: Harcourt, 2004.

Pappé, Ilan, ed. *'Aravim ve-Yehudim bi-Tekufat ha-Mandat: Mabat hadash 'al ha-Mehkar ha-Histori* [Jewish Arab Relations in Mandatory Palestine]. Giv'at Havivah: Hamakhon Leheker Hashalom, 1995.

Pardes Cooperative. *Protocols 1901–1910*. Aharon Meir Mazie Archives.

Peled, Kobi. "Batei ha-Be'er shel Yafo." [Well Houses: The Disappearing Palaces of Jaffa]. *Zmanim* 103 (2008): 38–45.

———. *Ḥalomah shel Nurah: dyoḳan hisṭori shel sheveṭ Bedu'i* [Noura's Dream: A Historical Portrait of a Bedouin Tribe]. Tel Aviv: Yediot Aharonot, 2015.

Peleg, Ilan, and Ofira Seliktar, eds. *The Emergence of Binational Israel: The Second Republic in the Making.* Boulder, CO: Westview Press, 1989.

Penslar, Derek J. *Zionism and Technocracy: The Engineering of Jewish Settlement in Palestine, 1870–1918.* Bloomington: Indiana Univ. Press, 1991.

———. "Zionism, Colonialism, and Postcolonialism." *Journal of Israeli History* 20, nos. 2–3 (2001): 84–98.

Petersen, Roger. *Understanding Ethnic Violence: Fear, Hatred, and Resentment in Twentieth-Century Eastern Europe.* Cambridge: Cambridge Univ. Press, 2002.

Pettigrew, Thomas F., and Linda R. Tropp. "Allport's Intergroup Contact Hypothesis: Its History and Influence." In *On the Nature of Prejudice: Fifty Years after Allport,* edited by John F. Dovidio, Peter Glick, and Laurie A. Rudman, 262–77. Malden, MA: Blackwell, 2005.

Porat, Dina. *The Blue and the Yellow Stars of David: The Zionist Leadership in Palestine and the Holocaust, 1939–1945.* Cambridge, MA: Harvard Univ. Press, 1990.

Porter, Libby, and Oren Yiftachel. "Urbanizing Settler-Colonial Studies: Introduction to the Special Issue." *Settler Colonial Studies* 9, no. 2 (2019): 177–86.

Qabbani, Nizar. *al-A'mal al-Shi'riyya al-Kamila* [The Complete Poetical Works]. Beirut: Manshurat Nizar Qabbani, 1993.

Qalyubi, Taher. '*Ailat Washakhsiyyat min Yafa Waqada'iha* [Families and Personalities from Jaffa and Its Subdistrict]. Amman: Al-Mu'assasa al-'Arabiyya lildirasat wa al-Nashr, 2006.

———. *Risalat 'ishq ila Yafa* [A Letter of Love to Jaffa]. Amman: Al-Mu'assasa al-'Arabiyya lildirasat wa al-Nashr, 2002.

Rabin, Yitzhak. *The Rabin Memoirs.* Translated by Dov Goldstein. Berkeley: Univ. of California Press, 1996.

Ram, Uri. "Ways of Forgetting: Israel and the Obliterated Memory of the Palestinian Nakba." *Journal of Historical Sociology* 22, no. 3 (2009): 366–95.

Regev, Motti, and Edwin Seroussi. *Popular Music and National Culture in Israel.* Berkeley: Univ. of California Press, 2004.

Rokach, Isaac. *Pardesim Mesaprim* [Tales of the Jaffa Orange Groves]. Ramat Gan: Masada, 1970.

Rousso, Henry. *The Vichy Syndrome: History and Memory in France since 1944*. Cambridge, MA: Harvard Univ. Press, 1991.

Safi, ʿAbd al-Rida al-. *Iftekhar al-Farkh, Muʿjam Abna Yafa* [Lexicon for the Sons of Jaffa]. Amman: dar al-Shuruq, 1998.

Saʿid, Hassan Ibrahem. *Yafo: Minhal, Hevrah ve-Kalkala, 1799–1831, ʿAl Pi Sijjil ha-Mahkama shel haʾIr* [Jaffa: Administration, Society and Economy, 1799–1831—According to the City Sijil of the Mahkama]. PhD diss., Bar Ilan Univ., 1995.

Schölch, Alexander. *Palestine in Transformation, 1856–1882: Studies in Social, Economic, and Political Development*. Translated by William C. Young and Michael C. Gerrity. Washington, DC: Institute for Palestine Studies, 1993.

Schwartz, Barry. "The Social Context of Commemoration: A Study in Collective Memory." *Social Forces* 61, no. 2 (December 1982): 374–402.

Schwartz, Gottfried. "Jafa und Umgebung" [Jaffa and Its Surroundings]. *Zeitschrift des Deutschen Palaestina-Vereins* 3 (1880): 44–50.

Seikaly, May. *Haifa: Transformation of a Palestinian Arab Society 1918–1939*. London: I.B. Tauris, 1995.

Seikaly, Sherene. *Men of Capital: Scarcity and Economy in Mandate Palestine*. Stanford, CA: Stanford Univ. Press, 2016.

Shafir, Gershon. "Capitalist Binationalism in Mandatory Palestine." *International Journal of Middle East Studies* 43, no. 4 (2011): 611–33.

———. *Land, Labor, and the Origins of the Israeli-Palestinian Conflict, 1882–1914*. Cambridge: Cambridge Univ. Press, 1989.

———. "Theorizing Zionist Settler Colonialism in Palestine." In *The Routledge Handbook of the History of Settler Colonialism*, edited by Edward Cavanagh and Lorenzo Veracini, 339–52. New York: Routledge, 2016.

Shahar, Natan. "Halahaqot Hatzvaʾiyot Veshireyhen" [The Army Bands and Their Songs]. In *Heʿasor Harishon, 1948–1958* [The First Decade, 1948–1958], edited by Hanna Yablonka and Zvi Zameret, 299–318. Jerusalem: Yad Ben-Zvi, 1997.

Shai, Aron. "Goral hakfarim haʿarviyim hanetushim bemedinat yisraʾel ʿerev milhemet sheshet hayamim veʾahareyha" [The Fate of Abandoned Arab Villages in Israel on the Eve of the Six Day War and Its Immediate Aftermath]. *Cathedra* 105 (2002): 151–70.

Shaked, S. *Zot Moladeti: Sefer Limud Hamoledet Lishnat Halimudim Hareviʿit* [This Is My Homeland: A Homeland Studies Textbook for the Fourth Grade]. Tel Aviv: Niv, 1963.

Shamir, Ronen. *Current Flow: The Electrification of Palestine*. Stanford, CA: Stanford Univ. Press, 2013.

Shapira, Anita. *Ben-Gurion: Father of Modern Israel*. New Haven, CT: Yale Univ. Press, 2014.

———. *Ha-Maavak ha-Nikhzav: ʿAvoda ʿIvrit, 1929–1939* [Futile Struggle: The Jewish Labor Controversy, 1929–1939]. Tel Aviv: Hakibbutz Hameuchad, 1977.

———. "Hirbet Hizah: Between Remembrance and Forgetting." *Jewish Social Studies*, n.s. 7, no. 1 (2000): 1–62.

Sharab, Muhammad Hasan. *Muʿjam al-ʿAshaʾir al-Filistiniyya* [Lexicon of Palestinian Families]. ʿAmman: Al-Ahliyya li al-Nashir, 2002.

Sharabi, Hisham. *Suwar min al-Madhi* [Images from the Past]. Nazareth: Dar Nilson, 1994.

Sharon, Smadar. *"Kakh Kovshim Moledet": Tikhnun ve-Yishuv Hevel Lakhish bi-Shnot ha-Hamishsim* ["And Thus a Homeland Is Conquered": Planning and Settlement in the 1950s Lakhish Region]. Haifa: Pardes, 2017.

———. "Yivu ve-Tirgum shel Model ha-Hityashvut ha-Koloniali ha-Italki le-Hevel Lakhish" [Importation and Translation of the Italian Settler Colonial Model to the Lakhish Region]. In *Ha-Tziyonut veha-Imperiyot* [Zionism and Empires], edited by Yehuda Shenhav, 301–26. Tel Aviv: Van Leer Institute Press and Hakibbutz Hameuchad, 2015.

Shavit, Ari. *My Promised Land: The Triumph and Tragedy of Israel*. New York: Spiegel & Grau, 2013.

Shavit, Yaacov, *Merov Limedinah: ha-Tenuʾah ha-Revizionistit, ha-Tokhnit ha-Hityashvutit veha-Raʾayon ha-Khevrati, 1925–1935* [From Majority to State: The Revisionist Movement, the Colonization Plan and the Social Ideal, 1925–1935]. Tel Aviv: Hadar, 1977.

Shikhmanter, Rima. *Haver me-Niyar: ʿItonut Yeladim Yisreʾelit be-ʿAsor ha-Rishon la-Medina* [Paper Friend: Israeli Juvenile Newspapers during the First Decade of the State]. Jerusalem: Yad Izhak Ben-Zvi, 2014.

Shumsky, Dimitry. *Ben Prag li-Yerushalayim: Ziyonut Prag ve-Raʾayon ha-Medinah ha-Du-Leumit be-Erez-Yisrael* [Between Prague and Jerusalem: The Idea of a Binational State in Palestine]. Yerushalayim: Makho Leo Baeck and Merkaz Zalman Shazar, 2010.

Sirhan, Nimr, and Mustafa Kabha. ʿAbd al-Rahim al-Haj Muhammad, al-Qaʾid al-ʿAm Lithawrat 1936–1939 [ʿAbd al-Rahim al-Haj Muhammad, the General

Commander of the Arab Revolt of 1936–1939]. Ramallah: Silsalat Dirasat al-Tarikh al-Shafwi Lifilastin, 2000.

Slyomovics, Susan. *The Object of Memory: Arab and Jew Narrate the Palestinian Village.* Philadelphia: Univ. of Pennsylvania Press, 1998.

Smith, Barbara. *The Roots of Separatism in Palestine: British Economic Policy, 1920–1929.* Syracuse: Syracuse Univ. Press, 1993.

Smooha, Sammy. "Ethnic Democracy: Israel as an Archetype." *Israel Studies* 2, no. 2 (1997): 198–241.

Sorek, Tamir. *Palestinian Commemoration in Israel: Calendars, Monuments, and Martyrs.* Stanford, CA: Stanford Univ. Press, 2015.

Stamatopoulou-Robbins, Sophia Chloe. *Palestine Online: An Emerging Virtual Homeland?* Oxford: Refugee Studies Centre, 2005.

Supplement to Survey of Palestine: Notes Compiled for the Information of the United Nations Special Committee on Palestine. Jerusalem: Government Printer, 1947.

Tamari, Salim. *Mountain against the Sea: Essays on Palestinian Society and Culture.* Berkeley: Univ. of California Press, 2009.

Tamari, Salim, and Rema Hammami. "Virtual Returns to Jaffa." *Journal of Palestine Studies* 27, no. 4 (1998): 65–79.

Teveth, Shabtai. *Ben-Gurion and the Palestinian Arabs: From Peace to War.* Oxford: Oxford Univ. Press, 1985.

——. *Ben-Gurion: The Burning Ground, 1886–1948.* Boston: Houghton Mifflin, 1987.

Tolkowsky, Shmuel. *Pri 'Etz Hadar: Toldotav Betarbut He'amim, Besifrut, Be'omanut Ufolklor, Miyemey Qedem Ve'ad Yameynu* [Citrus Fruits: Their Origin and History throughout the World]. Jerusalem: Bialik Institute, 1966.

Trimingham, J. Spencer. *The Sufi Orders in Islam.* New York: Oxford Univ. Press, 1998.

Tuomela, Raimo. *Social Ontology: Collective Intentionality and Group Agents.* New York: Oxford Univ. Press, 2013.

Vashitz, Joseph. "Temurot Hevratiyot ba-Yeshuv ha'Aravi shel Haifa bi-Tekufat ha-Mandat ha-Briti: Soharim ve-Yazamim Aherim" [Social Transformations in Haifa's Arab Society: Merchants and Other Entrepreneurs]. In *Kalkala ve-Hevra bi-Yemei ha-Mandat, 1918–1948* [Economy and Society in Mandatory Palestine, 1918–1948], edited by Avi Bareli and Nahum Karlinsky, 393–438. Sede Boquer: Ben-Gurion Research Institute, 2003.

Veracini, Lorenzo. "Introducing Settler Colonial Studies." *Settler Colonial Studies* 1, no. 1 (2011): 1–12.

———. *Settler Colonialism: A Theoretical Overview.* Basingstoke, UK: Palgrave Macmillan, 2010.

Von Thünen, Johann Heinrich. *The Isolated State.* Translated by Carla M. Wartenberg. Edited by Peter Hall. Oxford: Pergamon, 1966.

Waxman, Dov. *The Pursuit of Peace and the Crisis of Israeli Identity: Defending/Defining the Nation.* New York: Palgrave Macmillan, 2006.

Weakley, Ernest. *Report upon the Conditions and Prospects of British Trade in Syria Presented to Both Houses of Parliament by Command of Her Majesty.* London: HMSO, 1911.

Williams, Kristen P., and Neal G. Jesse. "Resolving Nationalist Conflicts: Promoting Overlapping Identities and Pooling Sovereignty; The 1998 Northern Irish Peace Agreement." *Political Psychology* 22, no. 3 (2001): 571–99.

Winter, Jay. "Thinking about Silence." In *Shadows of War: A Social History of Silence in the Twentieth Century,* edited by Efrat Ben-Ze'ev, Ruth Ginio, and Jay Winter, 3–31. Cambridge: Cambridge Univ. Press, 2010.

Wolfe, Patrick. "Settler Colonialism and the Elimination of the Native." *Journal of Genocide Research* 8, no. 4 (2006): 387–409.

———. *Settler Colonialism and the Transformation of Anthropology.* London: Cassell, 1999.

Yazbeq, Mahmoud. "Burtuqal Yafa wa-Athruhu fi al-Thaghyirat al-Ijtima'iyya wa-al Iqtasadiyya fi Madinat Yafa wa-Muhitiha fi al-Qarn al-Tasa' 'Asar" [The Jaffa Orange in the Social and Economic Developments in the City of Jaffa]. In *al-Zira'ah fi Bilad al-Sham* [Agriculture in Greater Syria], edited by Muhamad 'Adnan al-Bakhit and Husayn Mahmoud al-Qahuti, 3:419–35. Amman: Markez al-Watha'iq wa al-Makhtutat fi Bilad al-Sham, 2014.

Yiftachel, Oren. *Ethnocracy: Land and Identity Politics in Israel/Palestine.* Philadelphia: Univ. of Pennsylvania Press, 2006.

Yizhar, S. *Khirbet Khizeh.* Translated by Nicholas de Lange and Yaacob Dweck. Jerusalem: Ibis Editions, 2008.

———, ed. *Michteve Yehi'am Weitz* [The Letters of Yehiam Weitz]. Tel Aviv: 'Am 'Oved, 1966.

Young, James. *The Texture of Memory: Holocaust Memorials and Meaning.* New Haven: Yale Univ. Press, 1993.

Zerubavel, Eviatar. *Elephant in the Room: Silence and Denial in Everyday Life.* New York: Oxford Univ. Press, 2006.

————. "The Social Sound of Silence: Toward a Sociology of Denial." In *Shadows of War: A Social History of Silence in the Twentieth Century*, edited by Efrat Ben-Ze'ev, Ruth Ginio, and Jay Winter, 32–44. Cambridge: Cambridge Univ. Press, 2010.

Zerubavel, Yael. *Recovered Roots: Collective Memory and the Making of Israeli National Tradition*. Chicago: Univ. of Chicago Press, 1995.

Index

Page numbers appearing in italics refer to illustrations.

Mustafa Kabha is full professor of history, philosophy, and Judaic studies and the head of Middle Eastern studies at the Open University of Israel. He is also the head of the Palestinian Center for Heritage and Memory in Nazareth. He is the author of *The Palestinian People: Seeking Sovereignty and State* (Lynne Rienner, 2013).

Nahum Karlinsky is a senior lecturer at the Ben-Gurion Research Institute, Ben-Gurion University of the Negev, Israel. Since 2008 Karlinsky has been a visiting associate professor at the Department of Political Science at the Massachusetts Institute of Technology. Since 2012 he has also been a visiting associate professor at Boston University's Center for Jewish Studies. He is the author of *California Dreaming: Ideology, Society, and Technology in the Citrus Industry of Palestine, 1890–1939* (SUNY Press, 2005).